T0300243

ROUTLEDGE LIBRARY EDITIONS:
ACCOUNTING

Volume 54

DEVELOPING CONTROL CONCEPTS IN THE 20TH CENTURY

DEVELOPING CONTROL CONCEPTS IN THE 20TH CENTURY

LEE D. PARKER

Routledge
Taylor & Francis Group

LONDON AND NEW YORK

First published in 1986

This edition first published in 2014
by Routledge
2 Park Square, Milton Park, Abingdon, Oxon, OX14 4RN

and by Routledge
711 Third Avenue, New York, NY 10017

Routledge is an imprint of the Taylor & Francis Group, an informa business

British Library Cataloguing in Publication Data
A catalogue record for this book is available from the British Library

ISBN: 978-0-415-53081-1 (Set)
eISBN: 978-1-315-88628-2 (Set)
ISBN: 978-0-415-71803-5 (Volume 54)
eISBN: 978-1-315-87095-3 (Volume 54)

Publisher's Note
The publisher has gone to great lengths to ensure the quality of this book but points out that some imperfections in the original copies may be apparent.

Disclaimer
The publisher has made every effort to trace copyright holders and would welcome correspondence from those they have been unable to trace.

DEVELOPING CONTROL CONCEPTS IN THE 20TH CENTURY

Lee D. Parker

Garland Publishing, Inc.
New York and London
1986

For a complete list of Garland's publications in accounting,
please see the final pages of this volume.

Library of Congress Cataloging-in-Publication Data

Parker, Lee David.
Developing control concepts in the 20th century.

(Accounting thought and practice through the years)
Bibliography: p.
1. Managerial accounting.   2. Industrial management.
3. Controllership.   4. Management literature.   I. Title.
II. Series.
HF5635.P28   1986   658.1'51   86-15023
ISBN 0-8240-7854-3 (alk. paper)

Design by Bonnie Goldsmith

The volumes in this series are printed on acid-free, 250-year-life paper.

Printed in the United States of America

DEVELOPING CONTROL CONCEPTS IN THE 20TH CENTURY

by

Professor Lee D Parker

School of Social and Industrial Administration
Griffith University
Nathan, Brisbane, Queensland
Australia

To Susanne, Karen, Jay and Rhys
for always brightening the testing days

CONTENTS

TABLES

FIGURES

SUMMARY

This text is a revised version of the author's PhD thesis. It presents a shortened version of the original study with significant reduction in explanatory footnotes, source referencing, control model diagrams, and text length. The original thesis (419 pp.) can be consulted in the Donald Cochrane Library at Monash University, Melbourne. The conceptual development of control in the literature of both the management and accounting disciplines is examined for the period 1900 to 1979 inclusive. In order to portray the development of control concepts over time, they are assembled into groups relating to the schools of thought from which they emanated and a model of control is constructed to represent each group of concepts and their hypothesised inter-relationships. An attempt is later made to construct a framework representing the control models and their interrelationships.

Having traced the development of control models in both management and accounting streams of literature, a comparative analysis of historical development in the two streams is undertaken. A management-model framework is constructed and compared with the lack of a justifiable accounting-model framework. The 80 year period of the study is then reviewed to assess whether any particular control model gained ascendancy in each stream of literature.

Comparisons of timing of model development between the two streams of literature reveal a pronounced lag of accounting development behind that of the management literature. This is argued in part to be a product of an accounting preoccupation with control tools, its neglect of conceptual aspects of control, an absence of management accounting-oriented professional or public body practice standards, and the recency of conceptual and theoretical research and teaching in academic accounting education. The time-lag, and the consistent emergence of accounting control concepts identical to their management predecessors, are proferred as evidence of the derivative nature of accounting models. Although apparently derived from management concepts and models, the accounting models for the most part appear only to offer an imperfect reflection of management models of control.

ACKNOWLEDGEMENTS

The number of people to whom I am indebted is too great to
adequately recognise here. Patient supervisors of the original study at
Monash University were Professor Graham Peirson (accounting) and
Dr Michael Knowles (administrative studies), with important guidance also
being provided by Dr Keith Trace (economic history). Ms Toni Borrett
faithfully typed original drafts and manuscript.

In the production of this revised text, I wish to acknowledge the
comments and encouragement of thesis examiners Professors Thomas Johnson
(University of Washington) and Anthony Hopwood (London School of
Economics). The editor of this series, Professor Richard Brief (New York
University) has given invaluable advice on revision of the text, with
further advice and encouragement being given by Professor Gary Previts
(Case Western Reserve University) and Emeritus Professor Louis Goldberg
(Melbourne University). I am also grateful for comments received from
seminar participants at the Universities of Melbourne, New South Wales,
Adelaide, Case Western Reserve, Ohio State and Leeds, at Mid-Atlantic and
Ohio region AAA conferences, and at the 4th International Congress of
Accounting Historians in Pisa. Ms Olwen Schubert of Griffith University
efficiently typed and Ms Susanne Parker proof read the manuscript for
this revised text.

Finally my deepest gratitude must be reserved for my own family who
have always given me their unconditional support and encouragement.

CHAPTER 1

INTRODUCTION

Control has traditionally been a focus of attention for practitioners and researchers in the management and accounting disciplines. Together with planning it has often been treated as an indispensible requirement for effective organisational functioning. While the subject of control has consistently attracted interest and discussion over many years, its conceptual nature does not appear to have been particularly well understood. This general lack of understanding has been reflected in the apparent failure of many writers to appreciate the variety of control concepts which they utilise (possibly unconsciously) from time to time, the schools of thought from which such concepts emanated and the historical development of such concepts. All too often the conceptual nature of control has been accorded little more than a brief and trite definitional statement.

The basic theme which underpins this study is a concern to reach an understanding of the conceptual characteristics which have been attributed to the term 'control' as it has been used in the literature of the management and accounting disciplines in the 20th century.[1] Such an understanding would not only be valuable in itself but also would allow researchers to make a better judgment about the appropriateness of control strategies, measures and effects which they may seek to design or observe.

This text examines the progression of conceptual ideas concerning the nature of control[2] in both the management literature and the accounting literature during the 1900-1979 period. To that end concepts developed during this period have been studied with several purposes in view. Within each of the two streams of literature[3] an attempt has been made to identify key concepts of control in the context of schools of thought from which they appear to have developed. The possible relationships between such concepts have been considered and models of control (COM)[4] which embody them have then been constructed. Further, investigations have been conducted in order to suggest likely socio-economic variables which may have created conditions conducive to the appearance of such models of control. Over time these models have been examined for significant changes in their conceptual content and structure.

The above historical analysis has been carried out in order to compare the paths of control concept development taken by each stream of literature with a view to determining whether they developed in isolation from each other, whether one stream predated another in timing of control model appearance, and whether either stream produced an array of various separate models and concepts or some framework of interconnected models. Where differences in control model development between the two streams of literture have become apparent, their intrinsic nature has been explored and identification of likely contributing factors has been attempted.

THE PATTERN OF ANALYSIS

The text is divided into three major parts. Part I is concerned with the conceptual development of control in the period 1900 to 1959. Similarly Part II is concerned with the conceptual development of control in the period 1960 to 1979. These include analyses of the progressive development of schools of thought and their control concepts in each literature stream. Control models are constructed as representations of groups of control concepts and elements of the socio-economic scenario underpinning their development are examined. Part III incorporates a detailed comparative analysis of the conceptual content of model development and its timing in both the control-related literature of management and accounting.

Part I begins with an analysis in Chapter 2 of the scientific management foundations of management thought on control. The control-related writings of Frederick Taylor and Henri Fayol are combined to form a classical management COM. Social, economic and personal factors which influenced the resulting model are considered and continued support for its component concepts in the management literature of the 1920s to the

1950s are reviewed. In Chapter 3 the significance of Mary Parker Follett's contribution to the management literature on control is assessed and two major new developments in conceptual management thought on control appearing before the 1960s are examined. On this basis a structural COM and a behavioural COM are both constructed and socio-economic factors which influenced these models are considered. Chapter 4 investigates the conceptual development of control in the accounting literature from 1900 to 1959. This results in the construction of the classical accounting COM. Factors which appear to have influenced its replication of the classical management COM are then discussed.

In Part II, Chapter 5 explores the further development of conceptual approaches to control in the management literature of the 1960s and 1970s. Critiques of the classical model are reviewed, revised models of structural and behavioural control are constructed, and the appearance of a systems COM is constructed. Once again socio-economic factors underpinning these observed conceptual developments during the 1960-1979 period are discussed. Chapter 6 examines further developments in the accounting literature's conceptual approach to control in the 1960s and 1970s. The persistence of the classical model is considered as well as the failure of any serious structural approach to appear. The emergence of a behavioural accounting approach to control is discussed and a representative COM is constructed. The beginnings of a systems approach to control is also reviewed and a partial COM constructed.

In Part III the foregoing parallel analyses are brought into sharper focus and the analysis of historical development is extended. In Chapter 7 a conceptual study of the overall correspondence between management and accounting models of control is undertaken. The conceptual components of the classical, structural, behavioural, and systems control models are compared betweeen the two streams of literature. A framework of management models of control is constructed to reflect model interrelationships and this is contrasted with the lack of a justifiable accounting model framework. As at the close of the 1970s the 80 year period is reviewed to determine whether any particular control model or models dominated the literature of each stream. Chapter 8 contains an analysis of the relative timing of management and accounting model development with respect to publication dates of the literature sample used as the basis for this study. The extent of any accounting time-lags behind management developments is investigated and their implications considered. Factors which may have contributed to accounting time-lags are explored and evidence relating to their possible influence is tested. The final arguments are concluded and summarised in Chapter 9.

LITERATURE SELECTION AND CLASSIFICATION

Published journal articles, papers, and books have been chosen as the best available evidence for the purposes of examining the conceptual development of control. Discussions of contributions to control concepts appearing in this study for the most part utilise primary sources of literature on control. In attempting to portray conceptual history as faithfully as possible the analysis reflects both normative and positive contributions to the literature on control. No attempt is made to discriminate between these two types of contribution since the focus of this study is upon the conceptual characteristics ascribed to control by management and accounting writers rather than whether the route they took was positive, normative or a mixture of the two.

The literature which forms the basis for this study has been published predominantly in the USA and the UK. The collection of the literature has been facilitated by the use of bibliographic indexes identifying control-related publications in the English language. Hence publications appearing in languages other than English have been excluded from the sample of literature collected. Furthermore no attempt is made to undertake any form of international comparisons between publication sources. Rather literature published in the USA and UK is treated in combination as representing the predominant source of management and accounting thought on control in the 20th century.[5]

This study has been confined to an examination of literature on control in the management and accounting fields of knowledge. Approaches to control which may have appeared in such fields as philosophy,

political science, economics, operations research or engineering fall
outside its scope. The classification of publications as falling within
either the literature of management or accounting proved at times to be a
complex question. Some accounting journals contained papers by
management writers on management aspects of control while some management
publications contained accounting contributions, for instance, on
budgetary control. Indeed in admittedly a minority of cases, a writer
can be found to have written at different times on management aspects of
control and then on accounting aspects of control. Accordingly the
decision was made to classify publications as being in the management or
accounting streams by reference to their content. Where the subject
matter of a publication was considered to be predominantly management-
oriented, referring for instance to management theories, planning and
control strategies, management functions, organisation structure,
employee characteristics etc, that publication was classified as being
part of the management literature. Where the subject matter of a
publication was considered to be predominantly accounting-oriented,
referring for instance to cost control, budgeting, financial standards,
management accounting, financial accounting controls etc., that
publication was classified as being part of the accounting literature.
While this method admitted to the classification a degree of
subjectivity, it avoided the above-mentioned problem of journals and
authors presenting both management and accounting discussions of control
on some occasions. It also avoided the problems of authors of
unidentified professional category as in Lewis, Parker and Sutcliffe
[1984]. Accordingly some degree of subjectivity has been allowed in
order to maintain the relevance of the classification for the purposes of
this study.

The search for control literature in the management and accounting
streams was predominantly conducted using the following bibliographic
reference tools:

London Bibliography of the Social Sciences
Index of Economic Journals
Library of Congress Catalog - Books: Subjects
Business Periodicals Index

Public Affairs Information Service Index

The Subject Index to Periodicals

Social Sciences Citation Index

Commerce Clearing House Accounting Articles

The London Bibliography of the Social Sciences was searched up to 1950 utilising Volumes 1 to 9. The Index of Economic Journals of the American Economic Association was searched from its first year of coverage, 1886, to 1959 utilising Volumes I to V. The Library of Congress Catalog was searched from 1950-59 utilising 1950-54 Volumes 1-20 (A-2) and 1955-59 Volumes 1-22 (A-2). The Business Periodicals Index was searched from 1958-1979 utilising Volumes 1-22. The Accountants Index was searched from 1920 to 1979. The Public Affairs Information Service Index was searched from 1915 to 1979. The Subject Index to Periodicals was searched from 1915 to 1962. The Commerce Clearing House Accounting Articles Index was searched from 1963 to 1981. In addition, use was also made of the Social Sciences Citation Index, Monash University Library subject and author indexes and the Australian Society of Accountants Library indexes. The approximate periods referenced by the combination of these indexes are shown in Table 1.1.

The extent of periodic coverage by indexes shown in Table 1.1 allowed for relative equality of opportunity to identify control-related material in the literature of management and accounting throughout the 1900-1979 period. This resulted in the collection of a basic sample for analysis of 341 publications in total as shown in Table 8.1. The bibliography attached to this study references in excess of 500 publications in the course of investigating control-related material, underlying socio-economic factors, personal biographies etc.

Index	Pre-1900	1900 -09	1910 -19	1920 -29	1930 -39	1940 -49	1950 -59	1960 -69	1970 -79
London Bibliography of Social Sciences	x	x	x	x	x	x			
Index of Economic Journals	x	x	x	x	x	x	x		
Library of Congress Catalog							x		
Business Periodicals Index								x	x
Accountants Index				x	x	x	x	x	x
Public Affairs Information Service			x	x	x	x	x	x	x
Subject Index to Periodicals			x	x	x	x	x	x	
Commerce Clearning House Accounting Articles Index								x	x
Number of Indexes Referenced Per Period	2	2	4	5	5	5	5	5	4

Table 1.1

Periods Covered by Bibliographic Indexes

Referenced for this Study

MODELLING METHODOLOGY

The control-related literature in the management and accounting disciplines have been examined in order to determine the major schools of thought represented. From writing influenced by each school of thought,[6] control concepts which appeared to attract a reasonable level of support amongst writers have been identified. The analysis of each concept's ascribed characteristics has been carried out to the degree required to justify its inclusion in a particular COM. Once a series of control concepts are identified as having emerged under the influence of a particular school of thought, a COM is constructed. This model represents the control concepts and the hypothesised relationships between them. In this way the study constructs models of control representative of conceptual developments between 1900 and 1979. In Chapter 7, management models of control[7] are assembled into a framework that represents the control models and their interrelationships as suggested by the literature from which they were generated.

In order to identify control concepts and construct control models, a degree of generalisation in classifying authors' writings has been necessary. This is the almost inevitable consequence of a study which extracts the essence of a particular school of thought on control for the purpose of distilling concepts to which groups of writers have contributed. The objective of concept classification and model construction has thus on occasion required the bypassing of some nuances of a particuar author's conceptual contribution.

In relation to text structure, it should be noted that each chapter and its component sections is focussed upon developing models of control and their constituent concepts. Accordingly, within major periods being studied, from time to time the discussion of constituent concepts or issues within a model may be ordered in a logical conceptual order or linkage which however, causes some publications to be referred to without regard to strict chronological sequence. This has been the almost inevitable results of gathering contributions to a particular concept or issue that have occurred over a relatively wide span of time. Some chronology at this 'micro' level has been sacrificed in order to preserve the logical order of treatment of issues and concepts within each model.

It must also be pointed out that the task of tracing the conceptual development of control in the literature of management and accounting has necessitated the repetition of certain models and their constituent concepts. This has been the unavoidable consequence of the accounting literature being found to have largely duplicated conceptual developments in the management literature. The classicial management model constructed in Chapter 2 is found to reappear in the accounting literature up to the end of the 1950s, so that the classical model is reconstructed from an accounting literature base in Chapter 4. Evidence of the classical model's reiteration in the accounting literature of the 1960s and 1970s is produced in Chapter 6 as an indicator of its continued predominance in accounting thought on control. The behavioural and systems control models constructed from the management literature analysed in Chapter 5, reappear (albeit with fewer constituent concepts) in the accounting literature analysed in Chapter 6. This apparent duplication becomes an important topic of discussion in Chapters 7, 8 and 9.

PERIOD SELECTION

The period selected for study in this thesis was the whole of the 20th century up to the close of the most recently concluded decade at the time of writing the text. This resulted in the period 1900-1979 inclusive being selected for study.

Chapters in Parts I and II of the thesis have been so grouped to cover the periods 1900-1959 and 1960-1979.[8] The purpose of this form of presentation has been to protray the historical development of control-related literature in a more easily digestible form and to better facilitate the highlighting of major changes in direction occurring at various points of time in each stream of literature. The two periods were selected on the following basis. Preliminary scrutiny of the sample of literature collected revealed that both management and accounting publications on control had proliferated in volume after 1960, that the accounting literature appeared to have remained largely oriented towards classical management until the close of the 1950s, and that on a first inspection both streams of literature appeared to have spawned a greater variety of conceptual approaches to control in the years afer 1960 than in the decades before. These two periods facilitated clarity of analysis without biasing analytical results. As will become evident in Chapters 7 and 8, the comparative analysis of COM development focusses upon the periods relating to each model's own appearance and development, and transcends the artificiality of the preceding section structure.

HISTORICAL METHODOLOGY EMPLOYED

The historical methodology employed in this study has involved a number of constituent strategies. A chronological analysis of the management and accounting literatures on control has been undertaken, with models of control being constructed through cumulative analysis in which predecessors' work has been examined together with subsequent literature to determine whether the predecessors' work was built upon and advanced. In addition, attempts have been made to determine the role which particular individuals or schools of thought played in generating new or revised approaches to the conceptualisation of control. Comparative analysis has also been applied by the comparison of developmental paths taken by management and accounting streams of literature on control. By comparing the timing of development of models in each stream implications for the precedence of management models have been derived [Committee on Historiography, 1954; Clark, 1972].

An attempt has also been made to outline a scenario of factors which may plausibly have influenced the development of control models identified in this study. In attempting to gain a deeper understanding of the models outlined, the socio-economic context within which they were set has been examined as well as biographical details of major contributors in a limited number of cases. Biographical analysis, where relevant, has been undertaken to identify any personal characteristics or other personal factors which may have contributed to control models as well as to assist in estimating the real extent of a writer's influence upon a model relative to that of his or her socio-economic environment [Committee on Historiography, 1954; Clark, 1967].

A major thrust of the review of socio-economic factors at various points in the thesis and of the investigation of factors contributing to the accounting lag in Chapter 8, has been a concern to identify some of the variables which may have provided conditions conducive to the emergence of various models of control and to their relative timing. Thus an interrelated examination of model development trends and likely conditioning factors is presented in this thesis. Models will be viewed in general in the light of a multiplicity of potentially conditioning factors where the likelihood of their influence can be rationally and reasonably argued. Such arguments identify variables which may possibly provide developmental explanations for model appearance and timing while of necessity being couched in general terms. The results of such historical analysis must of necessity be tentative, approximate and less than certain. Problems of underlying assumptions, value judgments and the assigning of weights to factors reduce arguments to a balancing of probabilities [Committee on Historiography, 1954; Carr, 1964; Clark, 1967; Barzun and Graff, 1970; McClelland, 1975].

While evidence for a relationship between a set of socio-economic factors and the emergence of a COM may appear to be particularly strong, it cannot be assumed to be inevitable. When discussing potentially conditioning factors influencing model development, the term 'probably' must be used because it is not possible to assert that the factors identified constitute the complete population of factors which may have led to a model's emergence. While probability is not dealt with in a mathematical sense, it is pursued through a process of critical judgment [Carr, 1964; McClelland, 1975].

NOTES

1. To the close of the 1970s.

2. Observation of control practice lies outside the scope of this study except where such observations have been cited by writers whose work falls within the literature sample utilised for the purposes of this thesis.

3. Management and Accounting.

4. The acronym 'COM', representing 'control model', will be employed throughout this text.

5. A notable exception in this regard is the writing of Frenchman, Henri Fayol.

6. Consistent with the 'content' orientation of literature classification (into management and accounting streams) adopted in this thesis, some authors (admittedly a minority) have been recognised as contributing to control concepts characteristic of more than one school of thought.

7. Arguments are mounted as to the lack of justification for the construction of a similar accounting model framework.

8. Part I covers 1900-1959 inclusive. Part II covers 1960-1979 inclusive.

PART ONE

MANAGEMENT AND ACCOUNTING APPROACHES TO CONTROL: 1900 - 1959

CHAPTER 2
THE FORMATION OF THE CLASSICAL MANAGEMENT MODEL OF CONTROL

The foundation for the development of a management theory of control this century was laid by the scientific management school. Since this period was a watershed for the conceptual development of control in management and accounting literature, some appreciation of prevailing socio-economic conditions at the time will serve as a background scenario to the subsequent analysis of control concepts.

The number of scientific management writers who concerned themselves with the inherent nature of the concept which they were utilising was small indeed. While some such as Metcalfe[1], Taylor[2] [1916, 1947] and Fayol[3] [1949] did pause to consider this question, others such as Gilbreth and Gantt [George, 1968] restricted their concerns more completely to time and motion study, remuneration plans, performance measures and so on. From among the scientific management advocates, it is Taylor and Fayol who must be credited as being the main sources of the school's specification of control [Urwick and Brech, 1951], whereas the control concepts used by their contemporaries were invariably dealt with by implication only. Indeed, Taylor and Fayol became the focal point and key catalysts in continued efforts to develop a scientific approach to organisational management, even well beyond their own lifetimes. They worked in different continents from opposite ends of the organisational hierarchy, and yet their ideas interlocked and formed a basis for management thought for decades to come.

This chapter identifies the control concepts to be found in each author's work and assembles them into a Taylor COM and a Fayol COM. The genesis and nature of these two models is then explored through a review of each author's personal background and his socio-economic environment. The observed similarities between Taylor and Fayol, their backgrounds, and their models of control, facilitate the combining of these two models to form a composite classical management COM. The component concepts of the classical model are identified and evidence of their reiteration over subsequent decades is then considered.

THE TAYLOR MODEL OF CONTROL

While Taylor did not devote a specific passage of writing to the nature of the control concepts which he embraced, their nature becomes evident from a study of his work and philosophy in general. His views on control were coloured by and oriented towards his desire to induce employees on the shop floor to work harder and more quickly [Taylor, 1916, 1947a].[4]

A Moral Foundation

Taylor's view of control was bedded in his moral stance. He called for a revolution in the mental attitude of management and workers where both parties ceased quarrelling over the division of productive gains and devoted themselves to increasing total productive gains. This mental revolution was to extend to employees' attitudes to work, to each other and to management [Taylor, 1947b]. Furthermore Taylor regarded workers as being naturally lazy and 'systematic soldiering' (deliberate slackness) on the job as a universal 'evil' being 'suffered' by both workers and employers. Thus he saw output restriction as a case of 'mere robbery'. The resolution of this evil lay in control and he sought to enshrine this moral conviction in principles which he saw as being as stable and permanent as religious principles [Taylor, 1947b; Haber, 1964].

Taylor's fight against moral evil in industry was in some respects a 'fight' in the true sense of the word. He admitted that his introduction of scientific management at both Bethlehem Steel Company and Midvale Steel Company had encountered worker resistance and had engendered considerable acrimony between himself and workers involved [Taylor, 1916, 1947b]. In his own words Taylor fought them and was branded a tyrant as a result.

Total Control of the Individual

Taylor sought complete control of every aspect of a worker's job, from method of execution to final results [Taylor, 1916, 1947b] through the adoption of his system of management in its entirety. Prescription and enforcement of working method and speed were its critical components and was levelled at the individual rather than at any group or category of employees. For instance:

> "It is of the utmost importance in starting to make a change that the energies of the management should be centred upon one single workman ... ."
>
> [Taylor, 1947b:192]

The method of maintaining control over individual performance involved the giving of orders and expectation of worker obedience. As each man was converted to Taylor's system of working, another individual was to be selected for training and so on until the whole shop was converted to his minutely specified and total control. This was amply demonstrated by his often quoted example of the retraining of the Dutch worker, Schmidt, in pig iron handling [Taylor, 1916, 1947a]. The individual worker was subject to detailed control of his physical working actions, his pace of work, his rest periods and his output. No aspect of his working day fell outside the scope of Taylor's total control.

Control Enforcement by Legalised Controls

> "It is only through *enforced* adoption of the best implements and working conditions, and *enforced* co-operation that this faster work can be assured. And the duty of enforcing the adoption of standards and of enforcing this co-operation rests with *management* alone."
>
> (emphasis in original)
>
> [Taylor, 1916:83]

On the basis of this type of statement it is arguable that Taylor advocated an autocratic[5] concept of control that emphasised the need for direction and close supervision. Any reference to co-operation in reality implied a considerable degree of compulsion accompanied by close monitoring of means and results. Control through enforced worker co-operation was to be secured through the 'carrot' of differential piece rates and the ultimate 'stick' of dismissal. Indeed while the 'carrot' was limited essentially to an increase in pay, the potential 'sticks' were several [Taylor, 1916, 1947a], including fines, lowering wages, laying off, and dismissal. The extent of the severity of discipline built into Taylor's notion of control enforcement was a matter of some dispute at the time. Hoxie [1961:95][6] observed that organised labour had criticised the severity of Taylor-style discipline whereas Taylor had claimed his sytem of control to be democratic. While Taylor argued that scientific management was a substitute for close supervision and threats and punishments, Hoxie had found that supervision in these shops was more intensive, workers were constantly reminded of their degree of incurred demerit, and punitive disciplinary devices multiplied

Within Taylor's concept of control, what was the trigger mechanism for sanctions to be applied? The answer lay in another facet of his control concept. Sanctions were activated when 'controls' were breached. As primary scientific controls Taylor set standards for work pace and output. Further controls in the form of speed of work were written on job instruction cards for each worker, then shop reports, time cards, expense sheets, cost sheets, pay sheets, etc, proliferated [Taylor, 1916, 1947a].

Taylor's concentration upon the mechanistic approach to control became most clearly manifest in his preoccupation with the design of 'controls'[7] as the best path to control. This approach was founded in his firm belief that methods of product engineering could be equally applied to man management. He did not consider the possible complications incurred by people being less behaviourally predictable than objects because he treated workers as completely rational beings who made simple calculations of costs and benefits of his system to them and made their choices with no personal feelings about the system of control itself [Taylor, 1916, 1947a]. Thus for him, people could be expected to be just as rational and predictable in their activities as machines.

Taylor did not escape criticism of this mechanistic emphasis on controls (during or after his own lifetime). Hoxie [1916] severely criticised him for treating people as simply another factor of production like machinery and supplies and treating their control as a mere question of setting tasks and making rates. Later, writers such as Shields [1928] also recognised the argument that Taylor's procedure for instance, of time study, was scientifically, sociologically and psychologically unsound.[8]

The ultimate expression of Taylor's commitment to control enforcement through controls was his attempt to legalise through conversion of all traditional craft and factory knowledge into clearly defined laws, rules and principles [Taylor, 1916, 1947b]. When enshrined as laws, in Taylor's view, his controls then became uncontestable and unchanging. Thus for Taylor, control was to be enforced by sanctions that themselves were triggered by mechanistic and legalised controls.

Information-Based Control by Exception

Taylor's approach relied particularly upon the collection and recording of information about all factory workings, right down to the individual worker's knowledge of his craft and its associated skills including such quantitative information as working methods, timing of operations, pace of production etc [Taylor 1947a,b].

Information became both the source of Taylor's legalised controls and the means for comparing actual worker performance against those controls to determine whether 'carrot' or 'stick' sanctions should be triggered. Through the assignment of daily tasks to workers:

"The success of a good workman or the failure of a
poor one is thereby daily and prominently called to
the attention of the management."

[Taylor, 1947a:701]

The recording of daily failure, he felt, would be too much for the
average worker to bear and would therefore stimulate him to greater
effort. This became enshrined in his exception principle [Taylor, 1947a]
by which management received condensed, summarised reports of operating
results in which significant variations of actual performance from
controls (e.g. standards) only were highlighted. As a result, sanctions
would be triggered for the enforcement of control.

Authority-Based Control

Once a worker had been socialised into Taylor's system, his
obedience to direction was critical to Taylor's authority-based concept
of control. Failure to carry out work directions, according to Taylor's
view of control, constituted "direct disobedience of a single,
staightforward order" [Taylor, 1947a:192]. Ultimately, continued
disobedience incurred the sanction of dismissal [Taylor, 1947b].

The authority-based concept came in for considerable criticism, even
in Taylor's own time. Hoxie [1916] saw scientific management as falling
short of its utopian dream, and instead reverting to industrial
autocracy, intensifying managerial dictation and discipline. This also
constituted the basic union view of Taylor's control concept and indeed
his complete management system [Hoxie, 1916; Shields, 1928].

Taylor pursued a policy of 'divide and rule'. All judgment,
planning and thinking were removed from the worker and transferred to the
planning department, and ultimately to higher levels of management. Even
preparatory work for each task was transferred from workmen to
management. Furthermore, Taylor tried to divide work gangs by
dismantling their group methods of working and superivising workers as
individuals [Taylor, 1916, 1947a]. Taylor also believed that workers

were to be manipulated as children. He saw adults simply as grown up children who could do their best "only under pressure of a task of comparatively short duration" [Taylor, 1947a:69]. This served as his rationale for rigid standardisation of working methods and replacing worker judgment with laws, rules, formulae etc. In Taylor's view a workman handling pig iron was "too stupid properly to train himself" [Taylor, 1916:63], and he therefore expected workers, like children, to do as they were told [Taylor, 1916, 1947a].[9] Such restriction of worker liberty did not appear to trouble Taylor in the least [Dutton, 1953; Haber, 1964] although such removal of worker autonomy came in for criticism. The Special House Committee investigating the Taylor system expressed doubts that the worker could protect himself against unscrupulous employers and arbitrary decisions of management. Indeed they compared the worker's situation to one of the lamb lying down with the lion and to one of the slave and master relationship [Hoxie, 1916; Taylor, 1947b].

A Summary View

The foregoing analysis of the concepts of control reflected in Taylor's writing and testimony facilitates the construction of a Taylor COM as represented in Figure 2.1. This model depicts hypothesised relationships between control concepts identified above. The focal point is the concept of individual control since Taylor focussed his writing upon the control of the individual. The outer circle represents the concept of total control and encompasses all of the other control concepts, since Taylor sought total control over the individual at work. This total control was to be expedited by the following control concepts. Control of the individual was to be achieved by exception control (operating through the agency of information-based control), by enforced control (operating through the agency of legalised 'controls' based controls), and by authority-based control. In addition, the concepts of authority-based, exception and enforced control were all interrelated. Exception control required enforcement control to make it an effective influence upon individual activity, yet enforcement control

could not proceed unless exception control provided the appropriate
trigger and directions for the enforcement operation. Both exception and
enforcement control were related to authority-based control since Taylor
envisaged them as being exercised within the context of an authoritarian
management style.

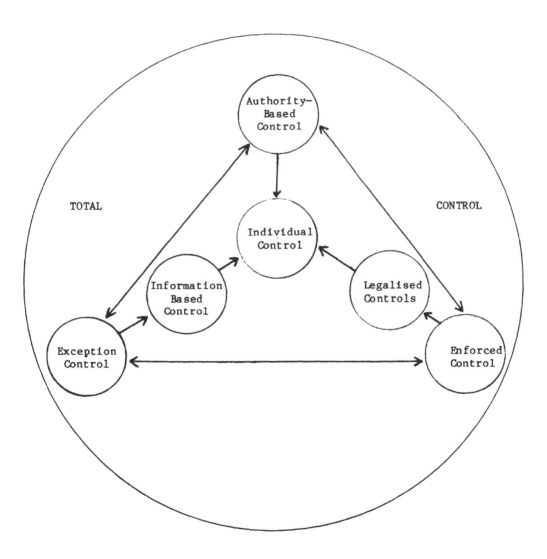

Figure 2.1: The Taylor Model of Control

FREDERICK TAYLOR'S AMERICA

In 1850 the American economy was largely founded upon primary production, with over 60% of the labour force engaged in agriculture. This proportion steadily fell over the next sixty or more years with a simultaneous rise in the proportion of labour engaged in manufacturing, mining and building. During the same period the United States had become the world's leading industrial nation, accounting for almost 36% of the world's manufacturing output by 1910 [Bagwell and Mingay, 1970].

The growing complexity of industrial corporations stimulated management's receptivity to the ideas of scientific management which also appeared to offer solutions to the human limitations of workers compared to the increasing efficiency of machines [Aitken, 1960; George, 1972]. Taylor's ideas represented the dominant synthesis of the scientific management drive for harder and faster work and reflected his working experience in the American steel industry [Urwick and Brech, 1951].

In Pursuit of Economy

While the beginning of the 1890s still saw a large number of relatively small firms making up the American steel industry, towards the end of that decade a large number of horizontal (as well as vertical) mergers were taking place. Consistent with the general American trend towards corporate mergers, product standardisation and mass production techniques in chemicals, shipping, clothing and footwear, steel also pursued economies of scale. A concern for economy in the steel industry was also prompted by a sharp decline in steel prices in the late 1870s with depressed market conditions pertaining right through the 1890s. The growth in demand occurred mainly west of the Mississippi, leaving many steel districts in Pennsylvania at a disadvantage [Temin, 1964; Bagwell and Mingay, 1970; Robertson, 1973].

Cut-throat competition fostered adaptation, absorption and the elimination of the inefficient. Cost consciousness was seen as a prerequisite for survival, so that improved, lower cost methods of production were continually sought and exact cost information (particuarly labour) was demanded. Continuous attempts were made to multiply labour's productivity and to reduce labour cost to the lowest level possible. Long hours, low wages, poor working conditions and anti-unionism were all products of this relentless drive for economy, as was the elimination of workers, increasing operational speed, close supervision and the scientific management approach to work organisation. Steelmakers' success in economising with respect to labour costs was such that their labour costs shrank by almost one third in the twenty years after 1890 [Brody, 1965, 1970; Hogan, 1971; Warren, 1973].

Taylor's COM reflected a number of basic attitudes and conditions in the American steel industry of his day. Like the steelmakers, he saw labour as a key cost item to be reduced while at the same time extracting increased productivity if at all possible. Mechanisation and the rational, cost-minimising attitude of employers fostered Taylor's tendency to treat the control of personnel in a mechanical, engineering fashion as in his preoccupation with 'controls'. Facing intense competition, steelmakers demanded and relied upon exact information concerning operational performance. From this background emerged Taylor's interest in information-based control. His authority-based and legalistic approaches to control also reflected the general management style of the American steel industry of his day.

The Labour-Technology Interface

The increasing scale of American industrial operations gave particular impetus to improvements in labour efficiency through mechanisation combined with scientific management methods. Industrialists adopted mechanical methods of materials handling and transport, production scheduling, standardisation of products and operations in the Taylor style, as well as the general substitution of power for human muscle. Similarly, during Taylor's period of employment and consultancy in the years around 1880–1915, steelmakers sought increased productivity at reduced cost through increased mechanisation, tighter control of operations and improved efficiency [Soule, 1964; Robertson, 1973; Hendricksen, 1978].

New scooping machinery, car dumpers, trestle systems, better hoisting equipment and bigger barrows eliminated the jobs of many labourers so that untrained men could be used to replace any striking workers. While steelworkers had formerly "been the manipulators of raw materials and molten metal", they became the "tenders of machines". Little more was required of many workers than to carry out instructions given to them without recourse to their own judgment. Mechanisation appeared to break the pay-productivity link, productivity gains acted to reduce labour costs rather than to raise wage rates, long hours permitted the industry to hold down its wage rates, and the wage differential between skilled and unskilled workers diminished to a significant degree. This all combined to create an 'every-man-for-himself' attitude in the workforce and limited the desire to work together or organise [Brody, 1965, 1970; Hogan, 1971]. Such an environment was conducive to Taylor's concept of total control over the individual, particularly as top management actively encouraged competition between individuals at all levels of the firm.

Mass production of goods had permitted standardisation of design and production methods and requirements for inputs (materials and labour) of uniform quality. This made the use of mechanistic controls and performance standards more feasible than in earlier times. Taylor's use of sanctions in enforcing adherence to those controls can also be partly attributed to his socio-economic environment. Even before Taylor's system the advance of organisational size, complexity and technology, had prompted businessmen's interest in incentive-payments systems. This constituted a crude response to their perceived problems of managing a large labour force [Aitken, 1960]. Thus while Taylor departed from the piece-rate system, his differential pay system still constituted a 'carrot' sanction for conformity to controls. Similarly, in Taylor's day, conditions of mass unemployment and plentiful availability of unskilled immigrant labour had provided management (and Taylor) with easy recourse to the ultimate sanction of dismissal.

Labour and Unionism

Growing markets and industrial production combined with a labour shortage in America meant that industrialists faced costlier wage bills than their European counterparts. The American labour shortage was being filled not only by its own population growth but by the influx of European immigrants. Immigrants' experience in America however, did not always match their expectations, with many falling prey to unemployment and poverty, particularly in the financial crashes of 1873, 1893, and 1907. In large industrial cities many lived in overcrowded slum tenements and suffered poor diet, poor sanitation and disease [Bagwell and Mingay, 1970].

In factory towns labourers became imprisoned by their choice of location, with employment possibilities outside the factory being severely restricted. Many were at the mercy of employers who did not feel socially responsible for their employees. The European migrant was often ignorant, untrained, virtually penniless and unable to speak the English language. In this predicament he was left to battle for any chance to earn a wage, no matter how small. Thus many took jobs, regardless of working conditions [Allen, 1952]. In the steel industry skill no longer conferred job security and competitiveness between workers intensified. Unskilled labour was considered by management to be a 'floating labour supply'. Other than at peak periods of production, employment was uncertain. Managers drove workers relentlessly, with the piece-rate system, competition between workers and pressure for production all speeding up work [Brody, 1965, 1970].

Immigrant labourers also accepted jobs in the mills at low wages in order to acquire sufficient capital to return to Europe and establish themselves. They had generally left their families in Europe, lived in crowded boarding houses, undertook long hours of work (some up to 84 hours per week) that was often dangerous and exhausting, saving as much as half of their wage. Poles, Croats, Serbs, Slovaks, Hungarians and Italians filled bottom ranks in the steel industry and constituted nearly two thirds of the labour force in a typical large steel plant by 1910.

Their regard for their plight as being temporary, their belief that low wages were still better than their earning potential at home and their wish to do little more than work and save, suited employers' labour policies [Brody, 1965, 1970; Hogan, 1971] and Taylor's approach to control.

Such a situation could not be exploited by the union movement. While unionism had not been widespread in the steel industry between 1880 and 1890, the reduced need for skilled labour that came with increasing mechanisation also made companies less dependent on unions as a bargaining agent. Further, the objective of minimising labour costs left little room, in the steelmakers' view, for collective bargaining. The years after 1891 saw the progressive decline in influence of the Amalgamated Association of Iron and Steel Workers of North America and after unsuccessful strikes and punitive corporate strategies, 1910 saw the effective collapse of unionism in the steel industry with a reorganisation in 1919 still meeting with little success. Mechanisation had undermined the source of craft-union power while the fighting capacity of steel firms had grown as their size increased. Firms employed close supervision, blacklists of union members and detectives to counteract union influence which they saw to be incompatible with lower labour costs [Brody, 1965; Hogan, 1971]. Thus "by 1910 the steel industry was effectively unorganised from the ore to the finished product" [Brody, 1970:77].

Thus for a significant part of his working life, Taylor's system was not introduced in a plant where a strongly organised union presence existed. Even where a union did exist, workers either left the union or left their jobs when the Taylor system was introduced [Aitken, 1960]. With growing unemployment, plentiful unskilled labour was available to replace them at cheaper wage rates. Management's authority remained uncontested. This situation allowed Taylor's authority-based concept of control to go relatively unchallenged. Indeed, the rise of a man through ambition and entrepreneurship to the top of a great corporate empire was a socially approved phenomenon. In this atmosphere of social approbation his right of authority and command was hardly likely to be questioned.

The American Business Psyche

It has been said that the migrant population, trying to 'make good' helped even more to promote the ambitious, industrious and adaptable character of Americans that has been so often noted by social commentators and foreign laymen alike. Furthermore it has been claimed that Americans' geographic and occupational mobility and their great belief in progress formed the basis for the great value that they placed upon the 'virtues' of self-help and self-reliance [Bagwell and Mingay, 1970]. This attitude was also embraced by Taylor. Unions, for instance, simply did not fit into Taylor's ethical framework because they tried to bargain for a standard wage for all workers of a particular classification, regardless of their individual contribution to productivity. To Taylor, this meant that the most efficient were penalised to support the inefficient and lazy. This was unethical – a moral sin [Aitken, 1960]. However it is arguable that to a considerable degree, Taylor's beliefs merely reflected the contemporary social focus upon individuality and led him to pursue the control of each workman as an individual.

The Taylor model, in this setting, can also be seen as a response to the new value which society had settled upon – efficiency. This term appeared as the rejuvenated form of exhortations to duty, as the embodiment of personal morality in society and as a means in society of exercising control as a surrogate for morality. Its advocates were to be found in politics, churches, educational institutions, reformists' and businessmen's organisations and even penetrated the American home [Haber, 1964; Wren, 1979]. This social preoccupation with efficiency therefore reinforced businessmen's ethic of competition and profit. Thus the Taylor COM comfortably mirrored the social and business ethos of the day. On the other hand it reflected a social complacency which obscured underlying problems of unemployment, poverty and social dislocation. From 1900 onwards, however, a change in social attitudes began. Roosevelt had moved to rejuvenate the moral standards of the business world. People began to investigate the world about them in a new inquiring mood [Allen, 1952; Aitken, 1960; Bagwell and Mingay, 1970].

For Taylor however, the belief in 'self-help' and 'making good', still held sway.

A Man of His Time

In part then, Taylor's concepts of control reflected socio-economic influences of his day. He was very much an individualist in a society that valued individualism and self sufficiency. He sought efficiency and economy in an industrial climate governed by the pursuit of economy and increased productivity. He advocated an autocratic style of management in an industry accustomed to it. He sought standardisation of tools and operating methods in the midst of the move to mass production and standardisation of products and many other aspects of industry. He manipulated labour as a mechanical variable in an industry accustomed to such a view.

THE PSYCHOLOGICAL INPUT

The Taylor COM was also very much a product of his own psychological makeup. His extant behaviour patterns revealed attitudes and cognitions formed since childhood, and these can be linked as a contributory source of explanation for the rationale behind his COM. Before considering the development of these characteristics, a brief review of his life's major works sets the following analysis in some perspective. After a dramatic change in direction from University entrance to factory apprenticeship, Taylor had later taken a labourer's job amid a scarcity of available employment, had risen through the ranks at a 'meteoric' pace,[10] changed firms for a management position, set up his own consulting practice, was hired to solve a major corporation's (Bethlehem Steel) problems, eventually encountered management animosity and retired from working life [Wren, 1979]. At the age of 45 years he had given up full-time attempts to implement his system of scientific management and devoted himself to promoting it by speaking and writing.[11]

Taylor is said to have been an aggressive and self-confident individual who lived an ascetic life (he neither drank nor smoked) and who was greatly concerned with the development of character and self-control. He had a strong Quaker background which left its puritanical mark upon him. His technical skills were considerable but his ability and patience in human relations were not as great [Urwick, 1956a; Aitken, 1960; Wren, 1979].

The Influence of Taylor's Childhood

Frederick Winslow Taylor was born into the family of Franklin Taylor and Emily Annette Winslow. Franklin was of Quaker descent, while Emily was of Puritan descent.[12] The Puritans were noted for their bold spirit of enquiry, for their independence and for their insistence upon obedience to the law as they saw it. This old-fashioned zeal for righteousness was inherited by Taylor and applied by him to his work in industry. It is in this sense that he was said to have inherited "a *whale* of a New England Conscience" [Copley, Vol I, 1923:23-43]. This particular view of the world would appear to have contributed something to the concepts of enforced control, legalised controls and authority-based control in the Taylor COM.

Taylor's mother, Emily, had a particularly strong influence upon him. She pursued Puritan and Quaker ideals in her system of child-training and has been portrayed as a rigid disciplinarian. Of the Taylor household, it was observed that "It was work, and drill, and discipline" [Copley, Vol I, 1923:52]. Emily encouraged open competition between children, associated tact with hypocrisy, ruled her household with attention even to the regularising of servants' duties:

> "... and when, after two years, the mistress of the household one day found a receptacle that had not been filled, the important thing with her was not that all the receptacles had been kept filled for two years, but that on this day there had been a lapse."

[Copley, Vol I, 1923:53]

Her approach to child rearing regarded a child's nature as being depraved, willful and intensely selfish. To correct this, the child should submit to the will of the parents, with obstinacy being severely punished [Kakar, 1970].

Taylor's control focussed upon the individual, just as his mother's discipline focussed upon each child. Taylor saw the individual worker as still a child to be subject to authority-based control, just as he himself had been. Just as open competition had been fostered between children, so it should be allowed between workers in a gang. Just as Emily ignored a servant's years of good performance in condemning a single omission, so Taylor built his concept of control by exception, focussing on substandard performance. As the child had been punished for disobedience, so worker contravention of controls should be punished by sanctions in the Taylor model. Elements of his mother's training are at least to some extent reflected in component concepts of Taylor's model of control such as authoritarian, individual, exception and enforced control.

To his friends Taylor appeared to be at times a 'crank' who sought to confine even a game of rounders to strict rules, exact formulae, and precise court measurements:

> "It seemed to some of us also that Fred was a trifle over-severe in his insistence upon the strictest possible observance of all the rules of the game — whatever it might be that we happened to be playing."
>
> [Copley, Vol I, 1923:56]

At the age of twelve years, he constructed a spartan harness of straps and wooden points to combat insomnia. Later he experimented with his legs on cross-country walks to discover the step which allowed greatest total distance with least output of energy and before going to a dance he would systematically list attractive and unattractive girls with the intention of dividing his time equally between them [Copley, Vol I, 1923; Kakar, 1970].

Kakar [1970] cites such examples of Taylor's behaviour patterns as being reactions to a child's sense of badness and unworthiness intensified by a mother's discipline and shaming for undesired behaviour. The result can be the development of an excessively sensitive conscience (Taylor's "*whale* of a New England conscience") which can cause an obsession with repetitive attempts to gain minute control over one's environment. It can become manifest in adult life in attempts to govern activities by the letter rather than by the spirit. Thus Taylor may have indeed arrived at his concept of enforced control through legalised controls, via this route. Such a pre-occupation with gaining control of every minute aspect of his own environment may also have prompted Taylor's concept of total control. As Kakar [1970:25] puts it:

> "For Fred, then, this severe outer control was not enough, or rather it inspired an even harsher inner control."

Just as childhood friends had seen him as somewhat of a crank, so did some working associates and subordinates (for instance, at Midvale). The following conversation between Taylor and a former associate of Midvale days is indicative:

> "'Oh', said Mr Harrah, 'I am doing fine. I am making a lot of money. And do you know what I am going to do when I have made a few more millions? I am going to build the finest insane asylum this world has ever known and you, Taylor, are going to have there an entire floor'."

> [Copley, Vol I, 1923:120]

A Question of Authority

Just as Taylor had been subject to an authoritarian regime at home, he expounded his preference for authority-based control at work. In Taylor's reported words:

> "'Most men, if they ever learn it, learn it by having
> it pounded into them.'"

[Copley, Vol I, 1923:131]

What had been required of him, Taylor came to require of others. He
believed in each organisation having a directing head who steered it to a
common purpose by issuing orders which all sections were required to
obey. Thus, Taylor advocated and admired the notion of a 'corporate
captain':

> "'Through all times and in all ages the great personal
> leaders of men have had rare gifts which command at
> the same time *the admiration, the love, respect,* and
> *the fear of those under him.*'
>
> 'The great captains of industry were usually
> physically large and powerful ... ready at any minute
> to damn up and down hill the men who needed it, or to
> lay violent hands on any workmen who defied them, and
> throw them over the fence, ...'"

(emphasis in original)

– from Taylor's 1903 Harvard Lectures

[Copley, Vol I, 1923:152]

This also reflected the presence of great entrepreneurial leaders of the
steel industry in which Taylor worked [Schroeder, 1953]. Steelmaking at
that time was said to be a "merciless game in the hands of strong men"
[Brody, 1970:2].

Similarly Taylor often acted imperiously himself. He was said to be
"quick on the trigger", acting on the principle that "he who is not with
me is against me" and frequently made his order absolute [Copley, Vol 1,
1923:174-176]. Yet Taylor also talked of co-operation with the
workers. As Kakar [1970] points out, Taylor attempted to resolve this
contradiction by arguing that under scientific management co-operation
meant eliminating the arbitrariness from authority rather than scrapping
authority-based relationships altogether. Yet while he claimed to have
friendly relations with workers Taylor had to admit the truth behind many
reports of worker animosity towards him and his authority-based

control. The Taylor model of control therefore included the concept of authority-based control because he was an authoritarian personality himself, both by breeding and self-admitted attitude. Yet in one sense he was anti-authoritarian.

Control: Taylor's Life Focus

It is now possible to see the Taylor COM as having its roots both in the American socio-economic environment of the period and in Taylor's own character. Virtually all of the conceptual components of his model have been traced back to these two areas of influence. Of course these two sources are themselves related to a degree. For instance, Taylor's upbringing in part reflected some of the social beliefs of his day. Still it might be argued that for the development of the Taylor COM his own character was the initiating influence while the socio-economic environment acted as the permissive influence. Such factors as unemployment, a belief in individualism and a social approval of enterprise and efficiency, allowed Taylor's personal approaches to control to develop relatively unhindered, at least for a period.

Taylor wanted *total* control of the workplace. As a manager he wanted to control even the minutest aspect of workers' operations. In summary, he took this view because to him, control was central to living itself. Copley [Vol I, 1923:84] argued:

> "Back of all this intellection of his can be seen the grand aim of *control*. The importance he placed on control cannot be exaggerated."

(emphasis in original)

The manifest issue which Taylor addressed was that of increasing total output, but in fact the latent issue which he addressed was that of *control* [Copley, Vol I, 1923; Kakar, 1970].

THE FAYOL MODEL OF CONTROL

In 1916, the year after Taylor's death, Fayol, the managing director of a French mining firm, published his now famous, "Administration Industrielle et Generale - Prevoyance, Organisation, Commandement, Co-ordination Controle", in the *Bulletin de la Societé de l'Industrie Minérale*.[13]   He attempted to develop a teachable theory of general management via a comprehensive set of fourteen principles. This theory was intended to demonstrate the benefits of adopting a scientific approach to the management of large organisations and represented the first attempt to outline a general theory of administration. Henri Fayol [1949] developed his theory of administration by a process of induction through which he attempted to analyse scientifically the reasons for the success of his own past experience in terms of general principles [Collis, 1949].   His ultimate aim was, by treating work as a technical process, to formulate specific principles which could then be taught to management and workers alike [Urwick and Brech, 1951].

Control Defined

Fayol constructed a definition of control which has endured in the management literature to the present day:

> "In an undertaking, control consists in verifying whether everything occurs in conformity with the plan adopted, the instructions issued and the principles established. It has for object to point out weaknesses and errors in order to rectify them and prevent recurrence. It operates on everything, things, people, actions."

[Fayol, 1949:107]

While many subsequent writers chose to focus their attention upon the above definition, Fayol also recognised that control was related to other concepts and principles which he had developed. The resulting COM becomes rather more comprehensive than the basic definition and incorporates a number of interrelated principles. A detailed overview is

provided in Figure 2.2 and will be used as a reference point for the
following discussion.

Control and Authority

The principles of authority and responsibility were linked to
control. Fayol [1949:21] defined authority as "the right to give orders
and the power to extract obedience" and responsibility was its corollary,
enforced by sanctions. This is represented in Figure 2.2 by (A-M) and
$(A-C_s)$. Good management was held to require the "application of sanction
to acts of authority" [Fayol, 1949:21]. Fayol's inclusion of the idea of
monitoring and enforcing standards through sanctions in his COM,
therefore, appears to have been a logical product of his view of
authority and responsibility.

Control and Discipline

Fayol [1949:22] defined discipline as "obedience, application,
energy, behaviour and outward marks of respect observed in accordance
with the standing agreements between the firm and its employees". This
view is symptomatic of the authoritarian and paternalistic approach to
organisational management adopted by both Taylor and Fayol and the
classical management school that followed. Indeed Fayol argued that it
was generally accepted that discipline was absolutely essential for the
smooth running of business, and was to be secured through good superiors,
clean and fair agreements and judiciously applied sanctions. Figure 2.2
represents this as $(D-C_s)$.

Again sanctions recur as a key elment in the principle of
discipline, just as they did in those of control and authority. In the
context of discipline, sanctions such as remonstrances, warnings, fines,
suspensions, demotion and dismissal were suggested for the prevention or
minimisation of offences against discipline. It is interesting at this
point to note that while Fayol earlier defined sanctions in terms of both

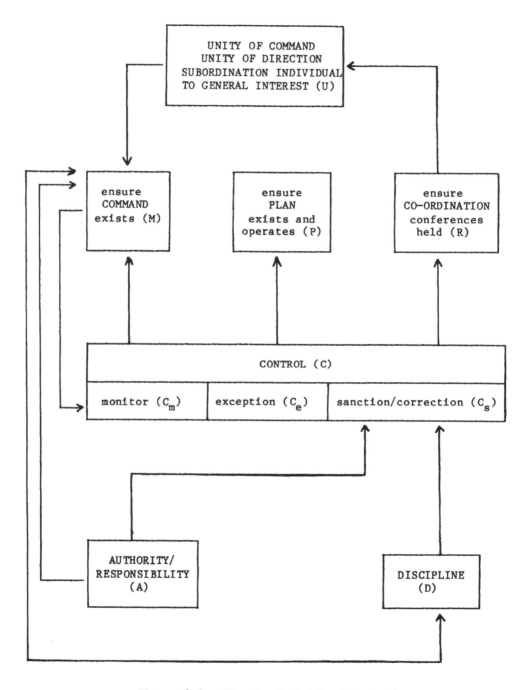

Figure 2.2: The Fayol Model of Control

rewards and penalties, in the context of discipline he only specified a range of penalties.

Control and Command

Fayol also linked discipline and command when he stated that "In the matter of influence upon discipline, agreements must be set side by side with command" [Fayol, 1949:23]. Figure 2.2 represents this as (D-M). Command was also linked to authority and responsibility by Fayol's opening definitional statement:

> "The organisation, having been formed, must be set going and this is the mission of command. This mission is spread over the different heads of the concern, each in charge of and responsible for his particular unit."
>
> [Fayol, 1949:97]

Again this appears in Figure 2.2 as (A-M).

The object of command, consistent with Fayol's scientific management approach was to secure the optimal return from all employees. Not only was command indirectly related to control via authority-responsibility and discipline (M-A-C and M-D-C in Figure 2.2), but Fayol directly related command to control by describing one of the duties of command as being the conduct of periodic audits of the organisation "in connection with the drawing up of the annual plan"[14] [Fayol, 1949:101]. Figure 2.2 shows this relationship as ($M-C_m-P$).

Control and Unity of Command-Direction-Interest

Unity of direction and effort were also laid down as prerequisites for effective command. It was argued that an identifiable relationship existed between control and a group of principles known as Unity of Command, Unity of Direction and Subordination of Individual Interest to General Interest.[15] Unity of Command stated that each employee should receive orders from only one superior and that if this were violated, authority, discipline, order and stability would all be undermined. The principle of Unity of Direction stated that a group of activities having the same objective should have one head and one plan. This was held to be a prerequisite condition for unity of action, co-ordination of strength and focussing of effort. Subordination of Individual Interest to General Interest held that in a business, the interest of employees, as individuals or groups, should not prevail over the interests of the organisation. The means for effecting this principle were by superiors' example, by fair agreements and by constant supervision. The relationship between control and the conglomerate of the above three principles was derived via command. It appears in Figure 2.2 as (U-M-C). Fayol saw them as prerequisites to command which in turn, as explained earlier, influenced his concept of control.

Control and Co-Ordination

Essentially Fayol defined co-ordination as the harmonising of all activities for an organisation in order to facilitate its successful operation. He argued that the consequences of any action (e.g. technical or commercial) affected all functions of the business. Accordingly, Fayol saw the characteristics of a well co-ordinated organisation as comprising each department working in harmony with the rest, subsections of the department being informed about their share in the command task and about their role in assisting each other in a reciprocal manner, and the working schedule of departments being constantly attuned to circumstances. He stressed that the object of this co-ordination effort was to:

1. Establish harmony between parts of the material and social organism.

2. Maintain equilbrium between forces at play in the organisation.

3.   Ensure unity of direction and focussing of efforts.

4.   Produce collaboration on the part of different department
       heads called upon to pursue a common aim.

[Fayol, 1949:106-107]

It becomes clear that in Fayol's conception of control the principle
of co-ordination was really a prerequisite to the attainment of unity of
command-direction-interest.   Unity of command-direction-interest was in
turn a precondition for effective command which in itself affected
control through its duty of monitoring activities by periodic audits of
the organisation.   Figure 2.2 represents this chain of relationships as
$(R-U-M-C_m)$.

In fact, there is a complete circularity of relationships here.
Fayol saw one objective of control as ensuring co-ordination which was a
prerequisite for unity of command-direction-interest which in turn was a
prerequisite for effective command which in turn activated control! Thus
in Figure 2.2 (C-R-U-M-C). The circularity did not end there. Command
activated control which itself had as one of its objectives, ensuring
that command existed! Again this appears in Figure 2.2 as (M-C-M).

The Human Factor Discounted

True to his scientific management orientation Fayol paid little
attention to the human factor in his COM. He paid greater attention to
structural factors and mainly dealt with employees in terms of their
technical characteristics.   This initiated the tendency in classical
management writing to treat the human factor in a mechanistic fashion or
to define it out of a problem or issue completely.

Fayol must, however, be acknowledged as having recognised the
possible dysfunctional effects of what he called 'irresponsible' and
'hostile' control [Fayol, 1949:109].   His concern was that the
irresponsible exercising of control might 'infiltrate' management

practices with disruptive consequences for organisational operations, while departments might be left relatively defenceless against what they saw to be the exercising by higher management of control that was hostile to them. To avoid any tendency of control to encroach upon operations in which it had no legitimate interest, Fayol recommended precise definition of powers of control and the limiting of its scope at the beginning of organisational operations.

The Substance Reviewed

From the COM constructed from Fayol's writings, it is clear that to him control permeated activities throughout the whole organisation. Indeed the model emerges as an almost circular network in which control is an initiator and end product of a whole series of interlocking principles. When discussing administration of State affairs Fayol [1937:102-103] argued that to prepare operations was to 'plan' and 'organise', to see that they were carried out was to 'command' and 'co-ordinate' and to watch results was to 'control'. In examining results he argued that control compared, discussed, criticised, stimulated planning, strengthened organisation, increased the efficiency of command and facilitated co-ordination. This serves to further justify the interpretation of his COM as a network of interrelated concepts.

The COM that can therefore be constructed on the basis of Fayol's writing exhibits a circularity of relationships. Whether Fayol himself recognised this is difficult to establish given that his writings provide no hint of his summarising such interconnections. Such circularity of relationships should not be automatically interpreted as a weakness of the Fayol model, since it could be construed as a reflection of the complexities of actual organisational life. The breadth of dimensions comprising the network constituting the Fayol COM, however, appear to have been almost overlooked by his classical management followers of later decades, who restricted their interpretations to the repetition of his basic definition stated earlier.

Control, for Fayol, included the tasks of monitoring performance, identifying exceptions and correcting them. This control was founded upon authority to act and responsibility for those actions as well as the maintenance of discipline. Operating from this foundation, control facilitated planning, co-ordination and command. The relationship with command was the most complex of these three. Control and command were viewed as directly interdependent but control also facilitated command indirectly through the agency of co-ordination and unity of command-direction-interest. Indeed Fayol also saw command as being facilitated by discipline and authority/responsibility.

FRANCE IN THE TIME OF HENRI FAYOL

Fayol developed his 'Theory of Administration' from 58 years' experience in the one mining and metallurgical organisation from 1860 to 1918. It is from this period that his ideas on control were also formulated.

The Pace of Industrial Development

The moderate pace of industrial and economic development in France from the 1850s onwards stands in quite marked contrast to the experience of the USA in that period. French industrial development during 1830-1870, underwent a period of rapid, but highly diversified industrial growth. However the pace of growth began to slacken after 1860 and entered a relatively stagnant phase till nearly the end of the 19th century. Even a basic change in technology, from water-steam power pre-1870, to electricity, internal combustion and heavy oil engines did not appear to significantly affect French industrialists in the 19th century or even until 1914 [Palmade, 1961; Hohenberg, 1968; Caron, 1979]. When the pace of industrial development post-1896 did accelerate, "it still retained characteristic French *mesure*" [Hohenberg, 1968:118]. In the whole period of 1860-1914 there were no sizeable industrial booms or movements into new industries through market or technological changes in

France.   Indeed, industrial growth differed quite markedly between
sectors, with iron and steel numbering among the most active industries
[Hohenberg, 1968; Caron, 1979].   French management's caution and short
time horizon was in part a conditioned response to a shortage of raw
materials, high cost factors and limited markets.   They found themselves
at a disadvantage in comparison with an industrial leader like Britain
[Kemp, 1972].

Fayol's Organisation in Geographic Perspective

Fayol was appointed Engineer of the Commentry pits of the S.A.
Commentry-Fourchambault in 1860 and after further promotions, in 1880 he
was appointed managing director of Commentry-Fourchambault (later to
become Commentry-Fourchambault-Decazeville).   At that time the
organisation was nearly bankrupt, but by the time of his final retirement
as chief executive in 1918, its financial position is said to have become
'impregnable'.   Fayol attributed his practical success to the application
of simple principles which constituted his 'Theory of Administration'
[Urwick, 1956a] but both his success and his principles also appear to
reflect French steel industry conditions.

Commentry, where Fayol began his career, was situated a little over
200 kilometres north-west of Lyon and Decazeville, whose mines and works
his organisation absorbed in 1892, was situated approximately 270
kilometres south-west of Lyon.   Thus Fayol's organisation and his
management experience can be placed as having been in central and south-
central France.

Until the close of the 1850s and early 1860s, leading steel
producers were to be found in Lorraine and Alsace (north-east France),
Anzin and Denain (northern France), Fraisans (eastern France), near
St Etienne (south-east of central France) and at Commentry and
Fourchambault (central France).   Commentry-Fourchambault by the close of
the 1850s, however, was entering a period of decline from its prominence
of earlier days.   General changes of industrial location meant that a

large part of French steelmaking after 1860 gradually shifted away from central France to the north and north-east. The decline of steel making in central France continued to the close of the 19th century [Palmade, 1961; Clapham, 1966]. After 1878, the development of a process allowing phosphoric ore to be used, increased the importance of metalmaking in Lorraine. In many locations organisations pursued vertical integration as mines, blast furnaces, steelworks and rolling mills were absorbed into one organisation through either amalgamation, joint partnerships, or holding companies and subsidiaries. Ties were formed between the east of France and central or northern locations. The east was the main location for pig iron production while central and northern organisations concentrated upon finished or specialised products [Palmade, 1961].

Fayol's organisation reflected these basic trends. His organisation was of long-established reputation, operated in central France and suffered failing fortunes at the time of the general decline of the region, but survived and purchased or absorbed not only the Bressac mines and the mines and works of Decazeville but also purchased the Joudreville mines in the eastern French coalfield. Thus Commentry-Fourchambault pursued a policy of integration and the forming of links with east France.

The Mining and Metallurgical Industries

During the first half of the 19th century the iron and steel industry, while being archaic in some respects, achieved satisfactory increases in productivity through the intensive exploitation of French ores which, however, showed signs of exhaustion by 1860. Fuel was also a problem to French industrialists. Even when fresh sources were discovered (e.g. in the north of France), they were often difficult and expensive to extract and did not tend to yield top quality coal. Imports of coal grew and French coal production steadily decelerated. Compared to the larger coal reserves of England and Germany, France was in a poor position. The accompanying high price of French coal, imported and home produced, caused higher French steel prices and placed French steelmakers at a disadvantage in international markets [Friedlaender and Oser, 1953; Clapham, 1966; Caron, 1979].

Nevertheless steelmaking continued in France and gained renewed impetus from processes for making steel from the phosphorous-bearing cast iron of Lorraine enabling medium-sized factories to produce high quality output. The post-1890 recovery of the French steel industry was further aided by the integrated structuring of plants, concentration of control in large organisations increasingly drawing on capital market funds, and a shifting of the base of French industrial activity towards heavy industry. By the eve of World War I the French iron and steel industry technically ranked among the best in Europe [Kemp, 1972; Caron, 1979].

During World War I, however, the northern and eastern areas of France were enemy-occupied or in the front-line war zone, so that valuable industrial capacity was lost. This gave fresh impetus to the iron and steel industry in southern regions and encouraged more rapid technological and managerial development as attempts were made to replace losses in the north [Kemp, 1972].

While French industrialists experienced difficulties in competing in international markets, their problems were not resolved by the home market (in contrast to the Americans). Population in France continued to grow at a slow rate for most of the 19th century so that the home market grew only slowly [Kemp, 1972]. Yet French heavy industry was confined to this home market. The high price of French coal mentioned earlier meant that on international markets French steel was 9 francs per ton dearer than Belgian steel, 14 francs per ton dearer than German steel and 21 francs per ton dearer than British steel. Even in the home market consumers limited their use of French steel because of its high price [Friedlaender and Oser, 1953]. French industrial prices had in fact stagnated from the mid-1840s to the mid-1860s and then fell during the remainder of the 19th century. The rate of industrial growth and new products, some high profit margins and techniques for improving labour efficiency became available. New profit peaks for the iron and steel industry were reached by 1914, at the onset of World War I [Caron, 1979].

Again, it is evident that the reported rise in the fortunes of Fayol's organisation coincided with the general trend in the fortunes of the metallurgical industry. When he took over control of the reputedly ailing organisation, the industry as a whole was experiencing difficulties due to uncompetitive coal prices, a stagnant home market, falling prices and profits and a concentration of mining and metallurgy activities in Northern France. His organisation's later growth was consistent with a tendency to vertically integrate in the industry. While it is said that Fayol retired in 1918 leaving the company in an 'impregnable' position, it must be remembered that the industry as a whole had experienced an upturn since around 1905, and that the War had restored the central and south central French mining and metallurgical industry's importance due to the loss of northern regions to enemy occupation and front-line battles.

The State of Management and Labour

Conservatism was the hallmark of French management from the mid-19th century to World War I [Friedlaender and Oser, 1953]. This reflected the management 'class' of that period. So-called 'self made men' and family firms were prominent among French industry of the 19th century. Firms were closely identified with owners and the succeeding generations of the proprietary family. With family influence and seniority often playing a greater role in manager selection than skill or aptitude, French industrial management remained conservative and hostile to outside influences and resources which it tended to regard as a threat to family control of the organisation. Bankruptcy and takeover were much feared by the family management and only aggravated the conservative nature of management decisions. Indeed young graduates of engineering schools were said to find difficulty in gaining positions in such firms and many consequently turned away from industry, to its own technological and financial disadvantage [Palmade, 1961; Hohenberg, 1968].

While old dynasties did survive technological change and changes in regional activity, boards of directors began to replace the old individual 'ironmaster'. This began to widen the gap between workers and management as personal master-servant relationships disappeared. Nevertheless there often remained a 'director-general' in charge of firm operations and this appointment required technical skill, commercial ability and human management skills [Palmade, 1961]. This was the role that Fayol came to fulfill at Commentry-Fourchambault.

As to the state and role of labour in industry, France had plentiful unskilled rural labour. Some workers joined industry for a few years before returning to their inheritance, or worked in industry while maintaining their share in village or property. Indeed the 19th century factory not only used a great deal of labour but often employed organising methods used under the domestic system, though by the end of the 19th century capital was gradually being substituted for labour [Kemp, 1972; Caron, 1979].

After 1860 the government moved towards a system of greater industrial freedom and the taking of industrial action became no longer a crime. Trade unions were tolerated after 1871 but with their short histories, remained small, only loosely associated and poor [Clapham, 1966].

Thus Taylor and Fayol shared a similar experience of working with largely unskilled labour, and neither appeared to have risked encountering significantly organised unionism until the advent of the 20th century, although it is not recorded that Fayol faced union opposition as Taylor did after 1900.

An Atypical Executive?

Management historians such as Urwick have implied that Fayol was a somewhat unusual manager, extraordinarily successful in his day. While he was a young educated engineer who gained a place in industry and later became a man of talent and perception, the above analysis of French industry and the French economy during Fayol's lifetime would suggest that like Taylor he was an exceptional figure but that also like Taylor, he reflected the beliefs and the fortunes of his day. Both Fayol's success at Commentry-Fourchambault and his COM, while being in part a product of his own abilities, stemmed also from the changes in fortune of the mining and metallurgy industry as a whole.

The French steel industry's predicament in international markets and the restricted demand for its output at home would certainly have predisposed managers such as Fayol to emphasise the need to control or restrict costs, to stress discipline in exacting conformity to plans and to concentrate upon technological aspects of operations (rather than human). His working in a time when family companies employed rural labour often using domestic styles of organisation would be in accord with a paternalistic, authoritarian approach to management in general and control in particular. His overseeing of a large scale integrated 'combine' would certainly have prompted his interest in control-associated principles such as authority, command, co-ordination and discipline, especially in relation to a geographically diverse operation such as Commentry-Fourchambault-Decazeville. Futhermore, Fayol's definition of control reflects, at least in part, a conservative French managerial and social stance which in turn may have provided further impetus to his concern with maintaining authority, command and disciplinary-based control concepts.

Fayol's lack of interest in the human parameters of control could also in part, be attributed to the economic necessity for French management to concentrate upon cost restriction and technological improvements in industrial and mining operations. The human aspect of managing resources may well have seemed of no great importance to organisations struggling to survive in a highly competitive international market and in a depressed home market.

A PERSONAL APPROACH

A further influence upon Fayol's COM was his own personal background and character. Henri Fayol was born into a middle class French family in

1841 and was educated at the Lycée at Lyons and then at the National
School of Mines at St Etienne. He trained as a mining engineer, joined
the Commentry-Fourchambault Company, a coal mining and iron foundry
combine, in 1869 and remained with that company until his retirement in
1918. He had been the youngest student at the School of Mines and
graduated as an engineer at the age of 19 years. He rose rapidly through
management positions in his company, from engineer to manager of the
Commentry pits at the age of 25 years, to manager of a group of coal
mines at the age of 31 years, to managing director of Commentry-
Fourchambault in 1888 (at the age of 47). He remained as chief executive
of the company until his retirement. During his lifetime he was awarded
a number of prizes and honours, and though his work was intially
overshadowed by the promotion of Taylorism in France it achieved
increasing recognition in the later years of his life [Urwick, 1956a;
Brodie, 1967; Wren, 1979].

Building on Engineering

Like Taylor, Fayol's background was firmly based in the field of
engineering and this clearly influenced his writing on administration,
done later in his life. Here again is a strong similarity between Taylor
and Fayol. As Urwick and Brech [1951:40] put it, "both men were
scientists before they were managers". First and foremost, Fayol was a
mining engineer [Brodie, 1967]. From the engineering science standpoint
then, Fayol, just as Taylor had done, used his observations of industrial
activity around him in a methodological pursuit of engineering and
management principles. These were subsequently to be elevated to the
status of laws and enshrined as general truths or dicta designed to apply
in all commercial, industrial and public administration situations.

Beyond Industry

Just as Taylor had sought control over employees' work activities
with a view to influencing their morals, attitudes and living patterns

outside work, Fayol saw his management principles, including control, as
being applicable beyond the boundaries of industry to include government
and civil service organisations. Indeed, Fayol saw his principles as
useful for all walks of life and all forms of human organisation
[Merrill, 1960].

As if to demonstrate his breadth of view, Fayol [1949], in his
General and Industrial Management, even discussed the subjects of health,
marriage, primary and post-primary school education, the place of the
home and the place of the State. Thus he was not only concerned about
raising standards of management practice in industry but wished to spread
the knowledge of recommended 'good' practice to other sectors of the
economy and to society in general. Hence he even advocated the teaching
of administration in schools [Brodie, 1967].

Proselytising

With this breadth of vision with regard to the possible application
of his management principles, Fayol, in his later years, set about the
task of promoting them in industry and society at large. Once again this
proselytising at the latter stage of life was common to both Taylor and
Fayol.

Fayol's promotion of his ideas was not done as completely or for as
long a period as those of Taylor. Unlike Taylor, Fayol had retired at a
ripe old age. He did not publish his now famous "Administration
Industrielle et Generale' until 1916 in the *Bulletin de la Societé de
l'Industrie Minérale* and it did not appear in book form in English until
1929. Hence for a time his ideas took a 'back seat' to those of Taylor
[George, 1972]. Unfortunately, Fayol did not complete his work and added
no further publication to the management field [Brech, 1953].

After his retirement in 1918, however, Fayol did set up a Centre of
Administrative Studies to advance 'Fayolism', though shortly before his
death in 1925 this group merged with a French 'Taylorism' group to form

the Comite National de l'Organisation Francaise [Wren, 1979]. Yet after Fayol's death the publication of his book in English promoted his ideas so that even French executives saw him as a man of experience who spoke their language and recognised their problems [George, 1972]. Possibly the apparent neatness of his package of principles added to his influence over management thinking in subsequent decades.

The Man Himself

Unlike Taylor, little is known about Fayol, the man, in terms of personality, lifestyle and personal correspondence. An observer of his demeanour in the last year of his life [Urwick, 1956a] reported that he was still upright, smiling and possessing a penetrating and direct glance. Furthermore he was said to have a natural air of authority, kindness and youthfulness of spirit which made him interested in everything. George [1972] has argued that while Fayol, like Taylor, was a philosopher, he did not have the almost religious zeal which Taylor exhibited in promoting his philosophy.

Some interesting comparisons can be drawn between the life patterns of Henri Fayol and Frederick Taylor. They were both born of 'well-to-do' parents, and both were educated and worked as engineers. Taylor began work on the factory floor as a labourer, while Fayol entered the managerial class directly. Both worked their way up the organisational hierarchy quite quickly, though Taylor worked for several organisations while Fayol remained with one for the duration of his working life. Taylor died at a relatively young age amid considerable public attention and controversy while Fayol died at a very old age and avoided any controversy. After being eclipsed for a time Fayol's ideas gained prominence in management thinking after his death [Wren, 1979].

- 51 -

His Basic Philosophy

Two aspects of Fayol's philosophy deserve particular note. While Taylor sought to improve the work (and management) of the worker, Fayol sought to improve the operation of managers [Urwick and Brech, 1951]. In a sense, even though he struggled to identify with the workers, Taylor pursued a notion of management that was 'other-directed' whereas Fayol pursued a notion of management that was rather more 'self-directed'. Fayol's work assumed importance moreover, because it was a first attempt at a systematic analysis of the process of management and because it advocated that (the discipline of) management could and should be taught [Brech, 1953]. Indeed Merrill [1960] has described Fayol as the Francis Bacon of management literature. Nevertheless, while Fayol's general approach was oriented towards the work of managers it still arrived at a similar authority-based model of control to Taylor. Indeed, Hodgkinson [1978] has argued that Fayol's work was consistent with the more general theory of bureaucracy later developed by Max Weber.

Fayol's was a COM that was derived from observations of his management work and of managers around him. His scientific-engineering training appears to have conditioned his approach to control in terms of a predisposition to formulate static principles as its fundamental components. His interest in applying his theories beyond industry probably encouraged his specification of these control-related principles (and of control itself) in fairly general terms. The lesser degree of promotion of his work which he undertook, in comparison with Taylor, probably helped him avoid controversy, but also gave him less reason to defend or amplify his principles and views in more specific terms. The 'neatness' of his seemingly all-inclusive control package probably encouraged its later acceptance by managers seeking simple, pragmatic tools for their work. Finally, while the Fayol COM framework may at first sight appear to have been arrived at deductively, it would seem that it was in fact based on his own management experience which also clearly reflected the socio-economic influences of his time.

THE SCENARIO FOR A CLASSICAL CONTROL MODEL

Taylor's and Fayol's work achieved great prominence. This was due in part to their own characteristics and reputations, the nature of what they said and wrote and time and places in which they worked. Most writers on Taylor and Fayol have concentrated upon their differences. Taylor began as a tradesman. Fayol began as a manager. Taylor withdrew from the chance of recognised full-time tertiary education. Fayol undertook full-time tertiary education. Taylor oriented his viewpoint from the lower echelons of the organisational hierarchy. Fayol oriented his viewpoint from the upper echelons of the organisational hierarchy. In seeking to understand the classical COM into which both their conceptualisations dovetailed, a myopic focussing upon such differences only obscures the crucial causes of their control concepts' compatability and social acceptance.

In fact, the writing of both men shared remarkably common socio-economic backgrounds. Both formed their ideas from working in the manufacturing sector, particularly with reference to the steel industry. In each country (France and the USA), organisation size was increasing, technology was advancing and capital was being increasingly substituted for labour (though at a faster rate in the USA). Both steel industries were primarily serving a home market, although the reasons for that differed (a large home market in the USA, a too competitive foreign market for France). In both countries there was a concern for efficiency and cost control, though again for slightly different reasons (a socially approved and technologically inspired vogue in the USA, an economic necessity in France). Finally, both Taylor and Fayol rose to influential positions in industry whereas neither automatically achieved rank through a firm of their own family dynasty, although it must be admitted that family connections undoubtedly helped. At least to some degree they were self-made men. When the common nature of their socio-economic bases is recognised in this way, Taylor's and Fayol's concepts of control certainly began with a propitious chance of being welded into a composite classical COM.

Furthermore, the question might be raised as to their separate uniqueness in their own time and locations. Were they unique with respect to the COM to which they contributed? The evidence presented in this chapter identifies them as being very much 'men of their time' in tune with the social and economic conditions of their day. Therefore rather than being categorised simply as extraordinary men whose work produced an extraordinary model, they should be accorded due recognition as reflective men whose work produced a reflective composite COM. That is to say they each reflected their socio-economic scenarios which were very similar and in doing so, came to produce the constituents of a COM which reflected the social, economic and managerial conditions and predispositions of the day.

THE CLASSICAL MANAGEMENT MODEL OF CONTROL

From the combination of both the Taylor and the Fayol models of control it is possible to identify a composite classical management COM. Both adopted a relatively authoritarian and paternalistic approach to control in particular and to management in general. Both presumed that the ultimate right of authority was vested in top management and implicitly used this as justification for authority-based control with direction and command as its integral elements. A key element of control as they saw it was the task of monitoring performance through established controls (information-based). This 'controls' element of their control models facilitated the operation of control-by-exception. Taylor and Fayol advocated the identification of weaknesses and errors and the enforcement of conformity to controls through the applicaton of sanctions (usually penalties). This approach was encompassed by their jointly-held view that employee obedience was highly desired and to be secured through discipline. Again, this fitted neatly into their authoritarian view of control.

It should be remembered by way of background scenario to the Taylor and Fayol models of control that both models were mechanistic and tended to have little regard to the human dimension of control. Furthermore, they both saw a need for their normative discussions of management and concepts of control to be enshrined in the form of moral and legal laws and principles.[16] This laid the foundation for the classical management school's orientation towards the elaboration of sets of management principles.

On the basis of the control models constructed in this study as representations of the contribution by Taylor and Fayol to management thinking on control, a further composite classical COM, to which both contributed, has been constructed. The elements comprising the model and their hypothesised relationships are outlined in Figure 2.3. Both writers contributed the concepts of disciplinary, exception, authoritarian and 'controls' control. The concept of total control was primarily contributed by Taylor whereas the concept of co-ordinative control was primarily contributed by Fayol.

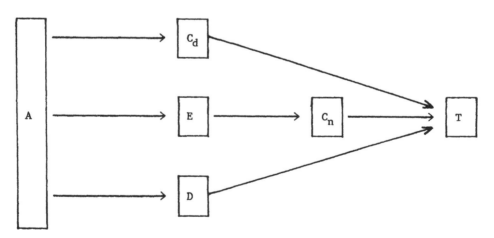

where: A   = Authority-Based Control
       C_d = Co-Ordinative Control
       E   = Exception Control
       D   = Disciplinary Control
       C_n = 'Controls'
       T   = Total Control

Figure 2.3: The Classical Management Model of Control

The composite classical COM was focussed upon the concept of total control (T) and had its source in the concept of authority-based control (A). Authority-based control operated through the agency of the concepts of co-ordinative control (C_d), exception control (E) and disciplinary control (D) in order to achieve total control. In turn, the concept of exception control operated through the agency of 'controls' in making its contribution to the attainment of total control. Such a structure reflects the necessity of utilising control through co-ordination, the invoking of discipline, and the identification and correction of exceptions in order to effectively pursue a concept of total control. Similarly, a concept of exception control could not be effectively operationalised without 'controls' against which actual performance could be compared and major exceptions identified.

CONSOLIDATING THE CLASSICAL MODEL

This classical COM became so all-pervading in the management literature, that subsequent writers up to the 1950s merely embellished and elaborated upon this basic model. Even after the management literature on control began to take new directions in the 1950s this model maintained a school of adherents right through to the 1970s. As the classical management literature expanded, writers increasingly resorted to value judgments about appropriate management principles and practices so that these principles became a mix of facts, prescriptive practice guides and ethical pronouncements [Massie, 1965]. Their approach to control remained correspondingly static and mechanistic.

The Classical Ethos

The human factor in any management or control situation still remained largely ignored. Labour as a class was still considered only to desire wages, set hours of work and security [Commons, 1921]. Management writers such as Coonley tended to approach the management of the human factor as they would the engineering control of a mechanical component.

"Science serves to separate the human from the
mechanical effort and confines within lesser limits
the psychological problems of business."

[Coonley, 1930:223]

The pursuit of efficiency too, remained uppermost in classical
management writers' thinking. Its attainment was said to be possible
through 'scientific' sharing of gains between workers and management,
through principles of authority and duty through formal definitions of
jobs and functions, through rigid co-ordination of policy and through
indoctrination [Mooney, 1937, 1947; Krupp, 1961]. Commons' [1921:145]
survey of major business establishments from Wisconsin to Maine was
representative of the mood of the period when it found that all
managements were "trying to sell efficiency to democracy".

Particularly in the 1920s and 1930s the notion of control so
dominated management writers' thinking that the task of management itself
was often defined as control. Writers such as McKinsey [1921], Mixter
[1923] and Sisson [1937] therefore tended to equate organisation and
management with control. This probably contributed to the optimistic
view that the application of science to business would render factors
more controllable [Coonley, 1930] and that some factors were potentially
completely controllable [Feiss, in Coonley, 1930]. To this end, the
preservation of centralised higher management control over the
organisation was still seen as critical for successful management
[Mooney, 1939].

The Unchanging Definition

Two leading writers of the classical management school provide
examples of Fayol's specific definition of control being perpetuated in
the management literature through the 1920s and 1930s. Gulick [1937:13]
produced a list of the elements of management entitled POSDCORB -
planning, organising, staffing, directing, co-ordinating, reporting and
budgeting. He clearly stated that his list was adapted from Fayol's
analysis. His 'planning', 'organising' and 'co-ordinating' approximated

Fayol's while 'directing' replaced Fayol's 'command'. 'Staffing' and 'reporting' were Gulick's own additions, while 'budgeting' was substituted for Fayol's 'control' [Massie, 1965] but was more narrowly defined as "all that goes with budgeting in the form of fiscal planning, accounting and control" [Gulick, 1937:13].

Of all the classical management writers it could be argued that Urwick[17] committed himself most clearly to some fundamental definition of control.[18]

> "Control consists in seeing that everything is carried out in accordance with the plan which has been adopted, the organisation which had been set up, and the orders which have been given. Maintaining the metaphor of the machine, it is the gauges and records of performance."
>
> [Urwick, 1937a:77-78]

It is apparent that this definition is very similar to Fayol's definition constructed twenty years earlier.

Authority-Based Control

The classical management school continued to subscribe to the authority-based control dimension of the classical COM. Its leading writers [Mooney, 1937, 1947; Urwick, 1937a] admired the most autocratic of institutions, the Church and the army, and sought to replicate control through formalised, militaristic authority in all organisations. Control was to be achieved through formal lines of authority and through the preservation of top management's prerogative to exercise centralised control [Werolin, 1947; Brech, 1948a].

> "The very nature of control makes it the prerogative of the managing director."
>
> [Wharton, 1947:117]

Fundamental to the exercising of authority-based control was the act
of command, a much emphasised principle among classical management
writers.   Thus control involved "the constant checking up of the results
of command in action" [Urwick, 1937a:178].   Supervision too, was equated
with control [McKinsey, 1921] and terms were quite often used
interchangeably.

> "The selection in part, but especially the promotion,
> demotion, and dismissal of men, depend upon the
> exercise of supervision or what is often called
> 'control'."
>
> [Barnard, 1938:223]

Once again, just as Taylor and Fayol had done, later classical
management writers emphasised the interrelatedness of duties,
responsibility, power and authority [Urwick, 1942a].   Within this
hierarchy top management was seen as guiding and directing the whole
organisation, restraining and governing its activities, centrally
reviewing progress and co-ordinating any delegated line authority into a
general plan of central control [Mixter, 1923; Rose, 1948; Maddock,
1949].

Disciplinary Control

Just as Taylor and Fayol had stressed the need for discipline as a
key component of the classical COM, so the later writers of the classical
management school admired the degree of control achieved by the military
through discipline and the control exercised by the Roman Catholic Church
over its adherents through laws and psychological control [Rautenstrauch
in Coonley, 1930; Urwick, 1937a].

The key to this effective disciplinary control, as its advocates saw
it, lay in the employment of techniques of indoctrination and enforcement
[Donald, 1947; Mooney, 1947].   This is especially reminiscent of Taylor's
attempts to indoctrinate the workers into the scientific management way
of thinking and to enforce their obedience to its precepts.   Over thirty

years later management writers were still advocating the use of discipline to exact obedience to top management authority.

Co-Ordinative Control

Co-ordination between different organisational functions was still considered necessary for effective business administration by classical management writers [McKinsey, 1921; Maddock, 1949]. It represented at least in part the classical management response to decentralised responsibility which had found its way into business practice. Co-ordinative control was advanced as a copy of military co-ordination through which a considerable degree of centralised control was retained [Mooney, 1947]. Co-ordination was to begin at the top of the organisation and was to be achieved through the authority of the superior and through self-adjustment between subordinates [Mooney, 1937; Urwick, 1937a; 1942b]. The mechanisms for achieving such co-ordination included specification of objectives, tasks, lines of authority, spans of control etc [Jolder, 1945; Puckey, 1948]. The classical COM and its co-ordinative control component from Fayol's work was thus simply being reiterated decades later.

'Controls'

Just as Taylor and Fayol had concentrated a considerable amount of attention upon 'controls' within the classical COM, so the classical management school continued with their interest in this dimension of the model.

> "The primary problem is one of control or lack of control, through the ability to use the instruments of control. The instruments of control have been refined and refined, and probably will continue to be refined."

> [Silcox in Coonley, 1930:24]

The emphasis upon 'controls' really amounted to a continued manifestation of the mechanistic approach underpinning the classical COM. To this end standards came to be seen as a means of controlling costs and profits [McKinsey, 1921; Coonley, 1930]. Standardisation was pursued in terms of technical operating procedures and in terms of estimated financial and non-financial performance [Commons, 1921; Mixter, 1923]. Indeed Brett [Davis, 1932:11] put the classical management position quite simply when he stated that "Standards are the operating tools of control". Management writers' pre-occupation with 'controls' extended well beyond the 1930s and was still in evidence in the late 1950s.[19]

Exception Control

Just as Taylor and Fayol had prescribed, classical management writers continued to view 'controls', for example in the form of standards, as the means for putting the exception principle (first expounded by Taylor) into practice. The concept of exception control thus continued virtually unchanged in the management literature for decades beyond its original inception in the classical COM even though the derivation was not always explicitly recognised.

Rathe [1950] for instance, saw management control as uncovering errors made while pursuing or deviating from plans. On the other hand Koontz [1958] developed a principle of strategic point control which stated that control was most effective when directed to factors that were strategic to the appraisal of performance, but admitted that it was really a refinement of Taylor's exception principle. Whether these derivations were recognised as such by classical writers or not, the concept of exception control survived intact.

A Fixed and Durable Model

The classical COM emerged as the composite result of two models of control which have been constructed from the writings of Frederick Taylor and Henri Fayol. While in some respects these two men occupied different professional roles, experienced different career patterns and developed their theories from different standpoints, they also shared many similar attributes. They worked in the same industry, came from similar class backgrounds, were subject to similar socio-economic influence (even though in different geographical locations), trained in the same profession, and worked towards similar objectives. Their models of control therefore appear to have been predisposed towards at least some degree of mutual compatibility. It is partly to this compatibility that credit must be accorded for the composite model's long period of survival. By the time writers after Taylor and Fayol began to promote and explore it, the classical model had already reached an advanced stage of analytical development just from the work of its two originators.

The well-developed state of the original classical model also provides some degree of explanation as to why the subsequent classical management school, right through to the late 1950s, only appeared to elaborate and embellish the model. Possibly no significant changes or improvements to the classical model were achieved, simply because its original authors had exhausted that basic line of thinking which focussed almost exclusively upon the development of normative principles supposedly capable of being generalised to fit all situations. The change of focus and direction required for any significant advance in management thinking on control did not appear to be within the capability of the sizeable group of writers of the 1920-1960 period known as the classical management school. For them the Taylor-Fayol inspired classical COM would hold total sway. Advancement was to come from other quarters.

NOTES

1. Henry Metcalfe, writing in 1881, developed a theory of management based on system and control.

2. Frederick Taylor first published *Shop Management* in 1903, and *The Principles of Scientific Management* in 1911.

3. Henri Fayol first published his *Administration Industrielle et Generale - Prevoyance, Organisation, Commandement, Co-ordination, Controle*, in 1916.

4. After 1918, the scientific management school emphasis shifted from the objective of making employees work harder to one of making their work more effective [Drury, 1922:9].

5. For instance, Copley [1923, Vol 1:183] cited Taylor as having stated that "If a man won't do what is right, *make him* ..." (emphasis in original). Braverman [1974] too, maintained that Taylor was in fact asserting the absolute necessity of dictating to the worker the precise manner of work performance.

6. Robert Hoxie, Professor of Political Economy at the University of Chicago, was Chief Investigator on scientific management for the US Commission on Industrial Relations. His team of investigators examined 35 shops employing scientific management during January to April, 1915, and interviewed 150 industrial leaders, labour officials and authorities such as Taylor, Gantt and Emerson [Wren, 1979:256].

7. i.e. control tools such as rules, instructions, standards, limits, etc.

8. Probably an even more telling criticism was levelled, decades later, by Aitken [1960]. He argued that while Taylor claimed he was only instituting technological and administrative changes, he was in fact disrupting an established social system and trying to build a new one.

9. In support of this interpretation, Haber [1964:24] and Aitken [1960:46] refer to Taylor's speech "Why Manufacturers Dislike College Graduates" in the proceedings of the Society for the Promotion of Engineering Education, 1909, in which he stated that workers should do what they were told promptly and without asking questions or making suggestions.

10.   The youthfulness of American steel managers was noted by English
       visitors.   Of a sample of 21 blast furnaces in 1901, 18 were
       managed by young university graduates.   Steelmasters exploited
       their vigour and enthusiasm for peak operations and promoted
       rivalry and competition between them [Brody, 1970].

11.   Résumés of Taylor's life's work are available in Urwick and Brech
       [1951] and Haber [1964].

12.   Quakerism was an offshoot of Puritanism.

13.   This was subsequently reproduced in book form by Dunod of Paris in
       1925 and translated into English by the International Management
       Institute in Geneva in 1929.   It was virtually ignored in the USA
       until it was published there in 1949, while its ideas had achieved
       wide currency in Europe long before [Urwick and Brech, 1951;
       George, 1968].   Between 1949 and 1965, his book was reprinted six
       times in the English language.

14.   Fayol's annual plan could be said to approximate the accountant's
       annual budget [Pearson, 1945].

15.   The combination of the three principles of Unity of Command, Unity
       of Direction and Subordination of Individual Interest to General
       Interest appears to have laid the (hitherto unrecognised)
       foundation for the concept of Goal Congruence which appeared in
       the accounting literature of the 1960s and 1970s.   While the
       concept has been thought to be of more recent origin, it closely
       approximates the combination of these three principles, even
       though Fayol did not use the term 'Goal Congruence'.

16.   While Taylor's desire for a moral imperative and a legal
       prescription for management operations has been well documented in
       this chapter, a similar tendency can be recognised in Fayol's
       argument that a special code of moral management laws was needed
       (as a derivative of the general principles of the church) [Fayol,
       1949].

17.   Lyndal Urwick was a British consultant who summarised and compared
       the basic ideas and concepts of other classical writers [Massie,
       1965].   His claim to fame "was that he attempted to demonstrate
       that the body of knowledge about management was sufficiently large
       that it had emerged as a more scientific and integrated field than
       had been recognised at that time" [George, 1972:142].

18. Many classical management writers never specifically defined
     control but left their interpretation of the term to be deduced
     from the totality of their work and from the cross-section of
     principles which they chose to expound.

19. Refer for instance to Koontz's [1958] discussion of controls
     reflecting organisation structure and preventing present and
     future deviations from plans.

CHAPTER 3
FOUNDATIONS OF MANAGEMENT REVISION

Following its early specification and popularity as expounded in Chapter 2, the classical management COM continued to attract a significant degree of attention in the management literature of the 1940s, 1950s and 1960s. Even in the 1930s however, change was beginning. Some writers in the classical management tradition began to consider the structural aspects of control including both its functional characteristics and its relationship to organisational structure. Another divergence from the classical COM occurred in the shape of a behavioural approach to control. This was an even more marked divergence than the structural approach.

Before considering these two new emerging models of control, recognition must be given to the major contribution to the conceptual development of control that was made by Follett. As a pioneer of management thought her work has often been ignored or misclassified. While some writers of her day (and reviewers of later decades) regarded her as solely a scientific management theorist, the analysis that follows will show her to have broken away from that tradition. Her contribution was not only an important one, but also anticipated COM development which was to take place in the 1960s and 1970s.

FOLLETT'S UNIQUE CONTRIBUTION

Mary Parker Follett, political scientist and philosopher "was, in effect, a prophet in the management wilderness" [George, 1972:139]. While the theories of Taylor and Fayol were gaining a considerable amount of attention and credence from businessmen (and, at times, the public), Follett's speeches and writings on administration, exhibiting markedly different views, were heard by a much more restricted audience.

Behavioural Control

From Follett's writings on society and business administration, elements of a behavioural COM clearly emerge. She recognised that in dealing with personnel the human and technical problems could never be completely separated and that an organisation's standards must be allowed much more elasticity than Taylor's system had allowed [Follett, 1941a]. Furthermore, Follett [1918] recognised that a worker was a complex person so that even at work he could still be a father, a citizen, a religious believer, an artisan and a businessman. Unlike Taylor, who had focussed on management's need to control the individual worker, Follett perceived the ability of groups of workers to control themselves.

In her view "Our political life is stagnating, capital and labor are virtually at war, the nations of Europe are at one another's throats — because we have not yet learned how to live together" [Follett, 1918:3]. The remedy she prescribed for politics, international order and industry, was group organisation. This she saw as the method for self-government. The collective will was to evolve through the group process of members' acting and reacting, interweaving of ideas and reciprocity of action. Thus differences would be brought out and integrated into unity. Within the group the continuous exchange of ideas and views would provide the group with self-created ideals and norms rather than individuals having norms imposed upon them by outsiders (as in the Taylor system). Furthermore, the strength of a group, in her view, did not rely upon the strength of individual members, but upon the strength of the bond between them [Follett, 1918].

From group processes therefore, came Follett's concept of democracy and indeed she argued that:

> "*Collectively* to discover and follow certain
> principles of action makes for *individual* freedom.
> Continuous machinery for this purpose is an essential
> factor in the only kind of control we can
> contemplate."

[Follett, 1941b:304]

Within this group context Follett elaborated even further on her notion of control:

> "Control might be defined as power exercised as means toward a specific end."
>
> [Follett, 1941d:99]

She was quick to point out, however, that while the term 'power' was often used to mean 'power-over', it was possible to construct a concept of 'power' as being 'power-with'. Thus power would become a jointly developed, coactive concept rather than a coercive concept. When control was defined as the exercising by groups and group members of power *with* one another, Follett [1924:187] argued that "together we will control *ourselves*". The more power that a group (or individual) had over itself, the more able it was to join successfully with another group (or individual) in developing power within the new combined unit.

Through her recognition of group processes and her notion of a 'power-with' concept, Follett had arrived at concepts of self-control and shared control. As a social process self-control allowed the exercising of free-will. The individual was not to be dominated by others because 'A' did not control 'B' nor did 'B' control 'A'. Instead, they intermingled and exchanged views and ideas in a continuing social process in order to produce the collective thought and the collective will [Follett, 1918]. The group-oriented process of shared self-control therefore constituted a major aspect of the Follett behavioural COM. Interestingly in addition to her sociological and psychological bases, Follett also developed her notion of self-control through holistic theory.

Holistic Control

Rather than treating control as a static function Follett chose to treat control as a dynamic continuous process which she called interweaving. In more general terms she saw executive decisions as a moment in a process. Similarly, to her, an order or command was but "a step in a process, a moment in the movement of interweaving experience" [Follett, 1941c:149]. Control then, was a process of continuous adjustment and continuous co-ordination [Follett, 1937, 1973a], In concentrating upon control as a process rather than as a function, Follett had anticipated the systems theory approach of dealing with connections and links between elements or functions rather than the traditional approach of focussing only upon the elements or functions themselves.

Follett also anticipated the systems approach to control in her recognition of the importance of the environment to the management of organisations.[1] Consistent with the post-1960 open systems approach she argued that:

> "Not only have self and environment acted and reacted upon each other, but the action and reaction go on every moment: both self and environment are always in the making. The individual who has been affected by his environment acts on an environment which has been affected by individuals."

> [Follett, 1918:98]

The individual then, responded not to a static, rigid environment, but to a changing environment which itself changed (in part) in response to the activity of the individual. Thus a process of mutual responses, continually being modified, was set in train [Follett, 1924]. The process became a dynamic pattern of action response and mutual adjustment between parties. 'Control' (or indeed 'control-with') was available to all participants in that process.

The goal of Follett's [1924] dynamic control process was unity. She was concerned to integrate organisational activities into a whole and drew her notion of 'wholeness' from Gestalt psychology. For her, biological, personal and social development required the study of the whole or total situation and not merely its constituent parts:

"Philosophers, biologists and physiologists tell us
that the essential nature of a unity is discovered not
alone by a study of its separate elements, but also by
observing how these elements interact."

[Follett, 1937:163]

In emphasising the need to integrate activities of the whole
organisation Follett directly referred to the biological study of
organisms and the psychobiological study of whole personalities. Under
this approach the 'whole' was more than just a sum of its parts, and
therefore integration of opposing or differing ideas and activities was
intended to achieve more than compromise. Compromise involved both
parties 'giving up' something and the continuance of an amended form of
the 'old' way. Integration allowed the contribution and 'addition' of
both parties' viewpoints (rather than the sacrifice of one viewpoint) and
the embarking upon a 'new' way of operating [Follett, 1924, 1973b].

"Most obviously, an organic whole has a spatial and
temporal individuality of its own, and it is composed
of parts each with its individuality yet which could
not exist apart from the whole. An organism means
unity, each one in his own place, everyone dependent
upon everyone else."

"Next, this unity, this interrelating of parts, is the
essential characteristic. It is always in unstable
equilibrium, always shifting, varying, and thereby
changing the individual at every moment."

[Follett, 1918:75-76]

This focus upon 'the whole' in organisational analysis led Follett
to see the two fundamental problems of business management as:

(1)   Defining the essential nature of the total situation.

(2)   Discovering how to pass from one total situation to another.

Both concerns reflected a holistic perspective in their focus upon 'the
whole' and upon interrelationships between its constituent parts.
Unified activity, in Follett's [1973a,b] view, depended not upon the

constituents alone but upon their interrelatedness. For Follett, unity itself constituted control. In her view co-ordinated control was more than a mere addition of specific controls. While unity was 'achieved control', integration, in Follett's scheme of things, was the method for securing it. Integration concentrated upon the interrelationship of organisational parts. Follett explained, for example, that while prevailing credit conditions, customer demand, output facilities and workers' attitudes constituted a given 'situation', they did so not just by their separate existence but through their interrelatedness. A change in one factor could lead to a series of changes in the others. Therefore effective control required "the co-functioning of organic inter-activities" [Follett, 1937:130], the interweaving of controls and the enlistment of co-operation of personnel involved.[2] She concluded that while co-ordination *provided* control, interacting *was* control [Follett, 1937, 1973a,b].

Just as the Follett behavioural COM incorporated self-control as one of its constituents, so the Follett holistic COM also incorporated self-control. Since she had adopted the biologists' concept of the control system as an organism, she accepted the need for self-direction and self-regulation which an organism had by virtue of the way in which its parts interacted. Thus for her control became the self-*directing* power of a unity. From the biological perspective, she considered that since every living process was subject to its own internal control, social control was generated by the process of interaction itself. Since control arose from within this unifying process she deduced that the greater the degree of integrated unity required in an organisation, the more that self-control must predominate [Follett, 1973a,b]. This tendency for an organisation, in its parts and as a whole, to move towards self-control implied for Follett [1937] some quite specific control strategies. Executives should join in a process of managing *with* their fellow men, a group of executives should self-adjust through direct contact, managers and workers should share in joint organisational control and the aim of organisations should be collective self-control.

Interrelated Models

Consistent with her philosophy of focussing upon interrelationships
between parts of the whole, the behavioural and holistic models of
control which can be constructed on the basis of Follett's conceptual
work appear to have been interrelated to a considerable degree.   The
behavioural   model,   its   component   concepts   and   their   hypothesised
relationships are outlined in Figure 3.1.   Control was group-sponsored
and group-oriented, with self-control (S) being exercised by individuals
and by groups (G).   The co-ordination of this spectrum of control loci
was to be achieved through a power 'with' or power-sharing control (P).
It   allowed   for   the   recognition   of   the   real   dispersal   of   control
throughout all levels of the organisation in contrast to the classical
management's COM which assumed that control was centralised at the top of
the   management   hierarchy.   The   link   between   G   and   S   resulted   from
Follett's perception that groups of workers could control their own
activities.   This link took place via P since Follett argued that group
members   exercised   control   *with*   one   another   (rather   than   *over*   one
another).

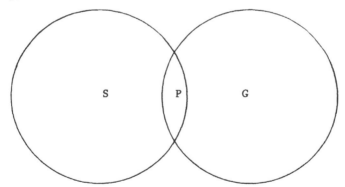

where: S = self-control
          P = power-sharing control
          G = group control

Figure 3.1:   The Follett Behavioural Model of Control

Similarly, the Follett holistic COM has been constructed and is shown in Figure 3.2. Here, the organisation is seen as consisting of innumerable cells (both group and individual) of self-control (S) which generate control not just through their own existence but also through their interaction with each other (I) and through their interaction with the environment (S <-> E). It is important to note that Figure 3.2 does not attempt to specifically represent Follett's concept of unified control (for instance, of the whole organisation). While it might conceivably be represented by the external boundaries of the 'S' sets, Follett argued that total control of the whole entity was more than just the sum of its components.

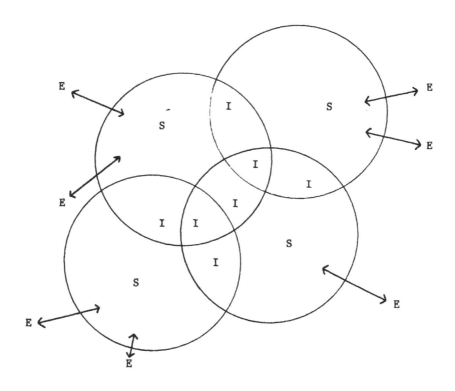

where: S = self-control
         I = interactive/integrative control
         E = environment

Figure 3.2:   The Follett Holistic Model of Control

The two models represented in Figures 3.1 and 3.2 are in both
appearance and source interrelated. Central to both is the concept of
self-control (S) and the concept of interrelatedness or sharing (P and
I). In addition, Follett saw her ideas as springing from an eclectic
source of politics, economics, sociology, law, biology, psychology,
psychobiology and philosophy. While her focus upon interrelationships
and evolving situations anticipated a systems COM to a large degree, she
also related its origins to social psychology. Similarly, while power
formed a key constituent of her behavioural COM, she also viewed it in a
holistic sense when she defined power as an organism [Follett, 1924].
Thus Follett clearly saw her view of control as an integrated whole in
itself, having been influenced by the combination of a variety of
disciplines. However for the purposes of this study, it has been
necessary to clearly identify the way in which she predated the
subsequent development of *two* models of control in the management
literature, behavioural control and systems control.

A Personal Philosophy

In 1868 Follett was born into an old New England family in Quincy,
near Boston, Massachusetts. When receiving here secondary education at
Thayer Academy in Braintree she was influenced towards idealistic
philosophical thinking (and the work of the philosopher Fichte[3]) by a
teacher, Anna Boynton Thompson. Subsequently, in 1888, she enrolled in
Harvard's Annexe for women, Radcliffe College, and was influenced by
Professor Albert Bushnell Hart (historian and political scientist) who
specialised in historical fact and political analysis. Follett's six
years at Radcliffe were interrupted by one year's study at Newnham
College, Cambridge (England), from 1890-1891, in which she read law,
history and political science and developed an abiding interest in
English life and working conditions. Returning to the USA and graduating
from Radcliffe in 1898, she then undertook post-graduate study in
Paris. In 1900 she returned to Boston and began work with the poor and
disadvantaged in Roxbury, promoting social, recreational and educational
facilities for communities into the early 1920s and founding the Boston

school (evening) centres for extended community use. From that work she
was appointed in 1912 to the first Placement Bureau Committee for
vocational guidance and identification of job opportunities. In 1917 she
was elected vice-president of the National Community Centre
Association. She was also a member of the Massachusetts Minimum Wages
Board and met regularly with representatives of employers and employees
[Metcalf and Urwick, 1941; Fox and Urwick, 1973].

Throughout her life, Follet was an active writer and speaker. Her
book, *The Speaker of the House of Representatives*, published in 1896, was
primarily developed from her Radcliffe days. Her book, *The New State*,
appeared in 1918 as a result of her community centre work, and her
subsequent book of 1924, *Creative Experience*, reflected her experiences
with employers and employees on the Placement Bureau and the Minimum
Wages Board. As a result she became recognised as a leading political
scientist and a growing authority on business administration. This
reputation she enhanced through her lectures at Metcalf's Bureau of
Personnel Administration in the city of New York in the years 1925 to
1932 and through speeches at the Rowntree Lecture Conferences (Oxford)
and at the National Institute of Industrial Psychology in the UK. From
1929 to 1933 she resided in England and studied English industrial
conditions. Her final lectures were given in January-February 1933 for
the newly formed Department of Business Administration at the London
School of Economics. On her return to the USA to attend to personal
affairs, she died on 18 December, 1933 [Metcalf and Urwick, 1941; Fox and
Urwick, 1973].

Follett's models of control quite clearly reflected her lifelong
interests and philosophy. She is said to have been skilled at engaging
in discussions with people from all walks life and at all social and
educational levels. She had an abiding interest in every individual's
experiences and mentally absorbed them as cumulative case histories. She
also read widely in philosophy, politics, jurisprudence, sociology and
psychology. This background provided ample foundation for her humanistic
and holistic-based writing. Her enthusiasm for group-based control arose
from her years of work with community groups at all levels in Roxbury,

and was first reflected in *The New State*. It was a resort to the replacement of hierarchical institutional and governing devices with a network of groups and appealed to those who were disenchanted with corruption and manipulation present in supposedly democratic frameworks. Follett's work at the Boston Placement Bureau and the Minimum Wages Board shifted her interest from political and social issues to industrial relations, particularly through her direct involvement with employer and employee representatives and through her visits to the Dennison Manufacturing Company in Massachusetts, Filene's department store in Boston, Rowntree and Co. Ltd. in York, England, and the League of Nations in Geneva[4] [Metcalf and Urwick, 1941; Fox and Urwick, 1973]. In these cases she observed the effects of enlightened personnel policies and co-ordination of international relations policies. This spawned her concept of integrating opposing points of view for overall control of the whole situation, power-sharing control at the group and individual level, and control as being affected by the organisation's environment.

Throughout her work Follett had been concerned more with philosophical and psychological foundations of management than with specific management techniques [Metcalf and Urwick, 1941], and had turned away from the classical management COM which relied to a great degree upon hierarchical direction, to advocate the cultivation of co-operation [Fox and Urwick, 1973]. While she constructed her theories on the basis of her reading and social and business experiences and observations, she was distinctly and deliberately normative in her approach. Yet much of her work has been subsequently confirmed by empirical studies of the 1960s and 1970s. From a psychological and holistic perspective she became dissatisfied with conventional means for resolving social issues, and in seeing human relations as fundamental to the effective management of organisations, advocated a psychological approach to industrial problems [Follett, 1918; Metcalf and Urwick, 1941; Fox and Urwick, 1973]. To her, matters of power, authority and indeed control, were psychological issues, critical to the search for a better ordered society and a fuller individual life. To this end the motivations of individuals and groups were her focal point for organisational analysis. She believed that the individual should learn to exercise self-control but that such freedom and self-control must come through the activities of the group [Metcalf and Urwick, 1941; Wren, 1979].

Misclassified and Neglected

Follett did not fit neatly into any one particular school of thought. In some respects she exhibited classical management school characteristics in attempting to derive principles of management and depersonalise control. On the other hand, many subsequent commentators have concentrated upon her psychological approach to management, and have classified her as part of the human relations school [Follett, 1941b; Child, 1969; Loomba, 1978]. As Wren [1979:325] has noted:

> "Chronologically, Follett belonged to the scientific management era; philosophically and intellectually, she was a member of the social man era."

All of the above classifications have their difficulties. Follett was in part a classical management writer, in part a behaviouralist, and in part anticipated systems theory.

The prescience of Follett's work has not been as widely recognised as it deserves. In some part this may be attributable to the above-mentioned difficulty in neatly classifying it. Fox and Urwick [1973] have also suggested that attention may have been diverted from her 'humanistic' work to the struggle for survival in the Great Depression. Metcalf and Urwick [1941:17] reported that in the UK "her teaching roused but little enthusiasm outside of a small circle". In the 1930s, there was little discussion of personnel behaviour in management circles and indeed Follett was misinterpreted by some as suggesting a means of management manipulation of subordinates and as only proposing a management technique. In the UK, the late 1940s and 1950s witnessed a degree of renewed interest in Follett's writings as the work of Mayo and the human relations movement attracted management attention [Child, 1969]. Nevertheless, she has remained as probably one of the most neglected of the major early management writers. This neglect would not be so significant but for the fact that many of her COM components can be

found to be consistent with the development in behavioural and systems
models of control after 1960.[5]   Her work presents a bridge spanning
decades of COM development.

THE EMERGING STRUCTURAL CONTROL MODEL

While the classical COM persisted through the 1930s, 1940s and
1950s, it played a part in spawning another COM, the structural model, as
a revision of the 'pure' classical management model.   One foundation was
laid by a group of writers concerned about the process (or function) of
management who looked to Fayol as their founder.   He identified
managerial functions such as planning, organising, commanding, co-
ordinating and controlling, and subsequent proponents of the structural
approach to management (the sector often termed the process school)
viewed these functions as a process that was carried out by the manager
[Duncan, 1975; Hodgetts, 1979; Wren, 1979].   The concept of bureaucracy
as enunciated in 1921[6] by the German sociologist Max Weber laid another
foundation for the structuralist school [Huse and Bowditch, 1973; Duncan,
1975; Pugh, Mansfield and Warner, 1975].   Unlike Taylor and Fayol, Weber
was not a practical man but a social scientist whose intention was to
describe organisational phenomena as objectively as possible.   He
focussed on legitimate and illegitimate power, labelling legitimate power
as authority and then moved on to distinguish between traditional
authority, bureaucratic (i.e. rational-legal) authority and charismatic
authority.   Weber[7] described the fundamental characteristics of
bureaucracy [Parker, 1978] which appeared to be remarkably consistent
with key concepts of the structuralist school as they had developed much
later [Duncan, 1975:341].

Beyond the post-Weberian development in the theory of bureaucracy,
the structuralist school expanded its concerns to include the vertical
and horizontal structure of organisations in terms of both design and
impact.   This work had its origins not only in bureaucracy but also in
classical management principles of delegation and span of control.
Literature on organisation structure expanded considerably from the 1950s
onwards [Luthans, 1977].

Developing a Structural Model of Control

> "I desire to confine myself strictly to the static or
> structural aspect of the subject. In this sense the
> term organisation can be defined very simply as
> determining what activities are necessary to any
> purpose and arranging them in groups which may be
> assigned to individuals. It is concerned purely with
> correct grouping of activities."
>
> [Urwick, 1942a:8]

The structural approach to control concentrated upon the matching of control to an organisation's structure and upon the control of functions in the management process. As a static structure the organisation was seen to be an arrangement of parts which should act as one body. Accordingly, the focus of management efforts at control were to be upon organisation charts, span of supervisor's control,[8] channels of authority, and elaborateness of organisation structure [Puckey, 1948]. This perpetuated classical management's unitary principle and emphasised the need for controls design to reflect organisation structure [Maddock, 1949; Koontz, 1958].

Through emphasising the importance of tailoring control to an organisation's structure, the structuralists almost inevitably had to grapple with the question of location of control in decentralised organisations (which were to become quite commonplace by the 1940s). Some recognised that centralised control located in the hands of top management had been most appropriate to the owner-manager and small-scale business and that even when such businesses had grown, pride, family tradition, the fear of lost power or status and the penchant for independence had often perpetuated 'one-man' control [Dale, 1953]. On the other hand, the danger of hasty, ill-informed or delayed management decisions, and of conflict between vested interests among top management, was recognised by others. Nevertheless, contrary to what might have been expected, these fears do not appear to have stimulated the development of any significant decentralised COM by the structuralists.

Instead, structuralists saw the delegation of authority down the line and the encouragement of initiative at various levels of the decentralised organisation as a problem to be overcome by a return to centralised control. Delegated line authority was to be co-ordinated into a general plan of central control [Mooney, 1947] and assembly and review of control information was to be centralised [Maddock, 1949]. It could indeed be argued that while structuralists recognised the dangers of centralised control, they feared the problems of decentralised control even more, and since they were more experienced in dealing with the former they chose to continue to develop the classical management school's centralised concept of control.

> "The very nature of control makes it the prerogative
> of the managing director."
>
> [Wharton, 1947:117]

Thus many structuralists wished to locate control at the top of the organisation structure [Werolin, 1947; Brech, 1948a]. In this scheme of things control continued (as in the classical model) to be equated with directing, restraining and governing [Werolin, 1947; Rose, 1948]. As Fayol had done in his COM, the structuralists saw co-ordination as a prerequisite to centralised control but then argued that control activities, by relating activities to each other, themselves provided part of the means for co-ordination [Maddock, 1949]. Thus, great emphasis was placed upon achieving co-ordination through the authority of the superior directing subordinates to conform to centrally determined objectives [Urwick, 1942b; Mooney, 1947].

The co-ordinating structure facilitating the control process was to include a definition of objectives, description and assignment of tasks and specification of lines of authority [Jolder, 1945]. All activities were to be subject to control so that specialised functions such as sales control and production control would be related to the whole organisation [Bliss and McNeill, 1944]. Indeed control was seen as an all-inclusive concept built into the authority and responsibilities of every key position in the organisation:

> "Control itself can be defined as the making of
> decisions and taking of actions required by the
> responsibilities of each position, i.e. the proper
> performance of each executive according to the
> requirements of his position."
>
> [Emch, 1954:94-95]

To the structuralists, organisation and control were inseparable.

Due to their concern with control of process structuralists
discussed the relationship between planning and control. In the main
they appear to have argued that planning and control were interrelated
rather than quite separate from each other [Brech, 1948b; Rathe, 1950].
While Emch [1954] saw planning as an effective basis for a separate
concept, control, Koenig [1951] treated planning as a subset of control,
Urwick [1956b:84-85] thought that "Planning enters into process with
Direction and the effect is Control", and Koontz [1958:48] saw planning
and control to be "so closely connected as to be singularly inseparable".

In the 1940s and 1950s, the structural school of management thought
had moved some distance from its classical management and bureaucratic
theory forebears and from the concepts identified in the foregoing
discussion, a structural COM can be constructed. Control was built
around organisational structure and focussed upon functions at each level
of the hierarchy. The resulting model, including its component concepts
and their hypothesised relationships, is represented in Figure 3.3. The
model represents an organisational hierarchy with the flow diagram
matching a hierarchical organisation structure. Centralised co-
ordinating control (CC) is vested in top management and exacted by means
of directives (D) to successive subordinate levels of management who each
in turn exercise authority-based functional control ($A-F_1$ ... $A-F_n$) over
their subordinates. Authority (A) is based upon position/rank in the
organisational hierarchy, while functional control (F) represents the
various tasks and responsibilities of that position over which control
must be exercised. The required conformity of control to organisational
structure is represented by the structure (replicating an organisational
chart) of the model itself.

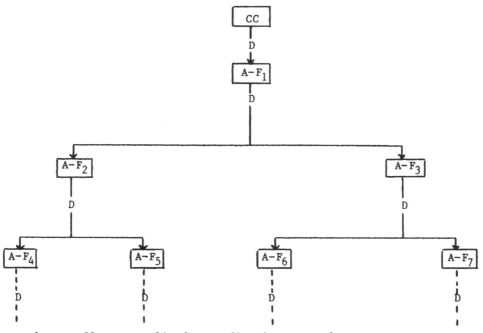

where: CC = centralised co-ordinating control

         D = directive control

A-F$_1$ ... A-F$_n$ = authority-based functional control

         (where n - number of department)

--------------- = lines of control down to successive layers of departments

         in the organisational hierarchy

Figure 3.3:   The Developing Structural Model of Control

This developing structural model retained many of the characteristics of its classical predecessor. Authority-based (including directive) and co-ordinative control remained common to both models. Change was evident, nonetheless, in the more overt emphasis given to centralised control, to functional control, and to the required conformity of control to organisational structure in the structural model.

The Influence of Enterprise Scale

The growth in size of orgnisations, especially after World War II, stimulated structuralists to continue their study of management, particularly through the process approach [Wren, 1979]. In the USA a third wave of mergers[9] had begun in the mid-1940s and continued through the 1950s. These mergers were, however, of a different character to those which took place in the 1920s, and often occurred between firms with unrelated product lines whereas earlier merger waves had involved vertical and horizontal integration. The post World War II growth in enterprise scale therefore took the form of large-scale conglomerates [Tuttle and Perry, 1970; Brownlee, 1974]. In the UK too, business enterprises grew in scale. Standardised products, advertising, productive techniques and efficiencies of scale caused a marked growth in incorporated companies between the two World Wars and the predominance of large firms became even more marked after World War II. This trend was aided by a resumed merger movement which gathered momentum in the 1950s [Murphy, 1973; Youngson, 1976].

While the nature of these large-scale organisations may have been more diverse, their sheer size no doubt prompted the structural school to emphasise the conformity of control to complex organisation structures and to emphasise centralised, co-ordinating and authority-based control as key components of their COM. In the face of growing complexity of corporate structure and operations, and the accompanying difficulties in managing such enterprises, this type of model must have had at least some logical appeal.

The structuralists observed the growth of decentralised (or divisionalised) organisations, but in the main chose to stress the need for centralised control. What factors may have led to this? Chandler [1976] has alleged that UK firms adopted multi-divisional structures much later than US firms. Of the sample writers used by this study to derive a structural COM, those advocating centralised control were mostly UK-oriented authors.[10] This may partly explain the incorporation into the model of centralised rather than decentralised control. Nevertheless, some US-oriented structural theorists also advocated centralised control, so that the UK-US organisational differences cannot be regarded as the sole explanatory factor. Chandler [1966] noted that in the USA organisations had been slow to formally change to decentralised structures (some time after operations called for such a move), and that even when they did divisionalise the change in structure did not automatically lead to a complete relocation of decision-making powers, and in effect, control. Indeed, that much centralised control was effectively retained by top management in divisionalised structures is evidenced by Chandler's following observation.

> "But these decisions were to be made within the framework set by the broad policy guides and financial budgets through which the general executives determined the present and future allocation of the resources of the enterprise as a whole and within the carefully defined interrelationships between the operating units and the general office as indicated by the company's structure."
>
> [Chandler, 1966:385]

Thus the structuralists, in pursuing a centalised, co-ordinating control concept within the structural COM, may have been reflecting the real location of effective control even in the decentralised corporations of their day. The retention of some significant degree of centralised, authority-based, directive control in organisations may also have been prompted by the replacement of family management by professional managers, by the specialist expertise required of top management and higher level administrators, and by a tendency towards bureaucratic management in US organisations after World War II [Chandler, 1966; Handlin, 1975].

The probable factors influencing the development of the structural COM, particularly in the 1940s and 1950s, therefore appear to have acted in combination. The growth in organisational size, delays in the divisionalisation of large organisations, the rejection of divisionalised structures by organisations in some industries, the growth of a technical and bureaucratic elite in corporate management, and the observed retention of a significant degree of centralised control in many divisionalised organisations, all had a clear opportunity to influence the development of the structural COM.

THE EVOLVING BEHAVIOURAL MODEL OF CONTROL

The behavioural school of management thought can be traced back to the Harvard group of Mayo [1933], Whithead [1938], Roethlisberger and Dickson [1939] in the Hawthorne experiments between 1927 and 1932. These experiments began as a result of earlier scientific management-based studies in order to determine the effect of intensity of lighting on worker productivity, but in failing to confirm such a relationship, moved on to consider psychological and sociological variables. This laid the foundation of the human relations movement. It was from the human relations beginnings that the subsequent tradition of the behavioural school of management thought continued. This school focussed upon the study of management in terms of interpersonal relationships at the levels of both individual and group behaviour. Just as the classical management and structural schools concentrated upon technical, economic and structural variables, so the human relations school began to focus their attention on psychosocial variables [Silverman, 1970; Kast and Rosenzweig, 1979].

Barnard [1938] contributed to the behavioural school through his interest in authority, communication, and the informal (versus the formal) organisation as well as motivation and decision-making [Hodgetts, 1979; Wren, 1979]. Another noteworthy 'father' of the behavioural school was Abraham Maslow [1943, 1954] who provided one of the now best known theories of motivation in terms of a hierarchy of needs which prompted further research into motivation at work over subsequent decades and encouraged promotion of management strategies designed to improve employee mental health [Massie, 1971; Tosi and Carroll, 1976; Hodgetts, 1979].

Davis [1957] studied the informal organisation, combined economic, psychological and social dimensions of organisational life and stressed the importance and complexity of societal factors [Wren, 1979; Thierauf et al, 1977]. March and Simon [1958] published *Organizations* which proposed a theory of organisation which recognised employees' (management and workers) limited rationality and argued for recognition of all participants' needs and goals. Rather than studying 'economic man' or 'emotional man', they attempted to build an aggregate picture of 'real-life man' [Pollard, 1978; Wren, 1979]. Further writing on motivation was produced by Herzberg, McGregor, Likert and Argyris. Herzberg [1959] set out his two-factor 'motivation-hygiene' theory of motivation. McGregor [1960] argued that managers' assumptions about human nature dictated their management style of which he created two categories, X and Y. Argyris [1957, 1960, 1962, 1964] also followed these influencing pioneers and argued that the formal organisation treated adults like immature children. Classical management and structural school principles of chain of command, unity of direction, and span of control were all seen to be inhibiting self-control. This constituted a mismatch between the requirements of an organisation and the needs of a healthy personality [Wren, 1979; Hodgetts, 1979; Pollard, 1978].

The behavioural school of management thought developed in an observably more eclectic fashion than most other schools of management thinking, before or since. From the human relations era it had incorporated inputs from sociology, social psychology, anthropology and political science initially as a reaction to the confident, rigid, mechanical absolutes of classical management thinking. It had begun by trying to bring humanity to work, moved on to consider how variables such as motivation, attidue and social environment affected performance, and by the late 1950s and early 1960s had begun to consider the intricate interactions between personnel, organisations and society.

A Control Model Takes Shape

The behavioural school principally rebelled against what it saw to be the static, mechanical, de-humanised classical management approach to control. Classical and structural model components such as authority, chain of command and span of control were regarded as inappropriate bases for an effective COM and as potentially counter productive [McGregor, 1960; Argyris, 1957]. For instance it was argued that classical control strategies could make individuals passively dependent upon superiors and leave them little control over their own working environment. They would thus be driven to immaturity and dissatisfaction at work rather than being allowed the adult process of personality maturation. With morale jeopardised, negative feelings about controls might grow amongst subordinates, and produce cheating, distortion of information, interdepartmental strife, avoidance of control systems,[11] excessive concern for departments to the detriment of the organisation and ultimately the formation of resistance groups [Argyris, 1957; Roethlisberger and Dickson, 1939].

> "The impact of management controls is similar to that which the formal organization and directive leadership have upon the subordinates. Management controls feed back upon and give support to directive leadership as both 'compound the felony' committed by the formal organization every hour of the day and every day of the year."
>
> [Argyris, 1957:138]

In this sense the behaviouralists considered the classical COM to be potentially self-defeating.

In contrast to the classicists and structuralists, how did the behaviouralists conceptualise control? They argued that human needs had to be taken account of in the effective application of control techniques [Brech, 1948b]. A set of controls was seen as interacting with individuals' attitudes and surrounding situational factors to produce a particular level of motivation [Davis, 1962]. Thus effective control only came from the *interaction* of several variables (including behavioural and environmental). Control was therefore conceived as the modification of an individual's ability to achieve his or her goals and needs [McGregor, 1960] subject to the understanding that authority for exercising control (and hence its potential effectiveness) ultimately relied upon the acceptance or consent of individuals subject to it [Barnard, 1938].

While behaviouralists argued for account to be taken of human reactions to the formal organisational control system, they also recognised that this formal, hierarchical control system (as conceived by the classicists and structuralists) did not encompass all spheres of human activity in an organisation since a range of personnel interactions, known as the informal organisation, lay outside its scope [Mayo, 1946]. This informal organisation could not be subject to formal hierarchical management control. Instead authority and control were seen to be earned and to be granted permissively by those who would be the object of informal control [Davis, 1962].

The two major concepts which behaviouralists began to develop between the late 1930s and the end of the 1950s, could most appropriately be termed social control and self-control. One of the earliest observations of social control were made in the Bank Wiring Observation Room portion of the Hawthorne studies [Roethlisberger and Dickson, 1939]. Groups maintained their own internal self-discipline where the group exacted conformity to mutually agreed internal norms or standards by its members and at the same time protected members from outside interference. Deviations from agreed norms were controlled by a variety of subtle group-induced pressures ranging from quiet warnings to exclusion from group membership.

> "The men had elaborated, spontaneously and quite unconsciously, an intricate social organisation around their collective beliefs and sentiments."
>
> [Roethlisberger and Dickson, 1939:524]

In this way a group could informally compel changes in motivations of its individual members, outside the scope of the formal management control system [Barnard, 1938]. Accordingly behaviouralists recognised that the classical belief in formal authority as the only source of 'power to control' was a misconception [McGregor, 1960]. Group co-operation and communication were essential prerequisites for effective social control [Barnard, 1938; Davis, 1962].[12]

Allied to the concept of social control, the concept of self-control had begun to emerge (though still in its infancy) by the close of the 1950s.[13] Though primarily identified with the classical management and structural schools, Urwick [1942a] must be credited with having recognised that co-ordination was achievable in part through 'self-adjustment between subordinates' and that discipline was organised self-control. The concept of self-control recognised that the only person who, in the final analysis, could 'directly control' activities, was the one directly responsible for them [Emch, 1954:97]. Therefore it could be argued that control should be available at each level where action was to be taken, so that directives from higher management or hierarchical control should only be necessary where action required was not readily apparent to lower level personnel. Self-control required the granting of at least some degree of authority to the individual to facilitate his or her control over their own behaviour with respect to self-imposed norms or standards [Vickers, 1958]. The behaviouralists emphasised that self-control could be put into effect by various strategies which involved the conditioning of managers' and subordinates' attitudes and beliefs rather than any propagandising or form issuing [McGregor, 1960].

From the control concepts identified in the behavioural literature it is possible to construct a developing pre-1960 behavioural COM. The model, including its component concepts and their hypothesised relationships, is represented in Figure 3.4. The focal point of the model was motivation to act (M). Situational (S_i) and cognitive (C_o) variables influenced the formation and maintenance of self-control (S_e), social control (S_o) and hierarchical control (H) which in turn jointly interacted to produce in each individual involved, the motivation to act (M). It must be stressed that this model was still very much in its infancy before the 1960s and that its components had only been explored to a limited degree by a small number of writers. Motivation to act (M) had not been delineated in any great detail, situation (S_i) and cognitive (C_o) variables had been specifically applied to hierarchical control (H) but related to self-control (S_e) and social control (S_o) more by inference. The behaviouralist model had, however, moved some distance from both the classical and structural models of control. It had rejected their authoritarian emphasis, had added an input of situational and cognitive factors, had added informal concepts of control to the formal concepts already in existence, and had replaced the focus upon all-inclusive top management control with a focus (however vaguely expressed) upon motivation to act.

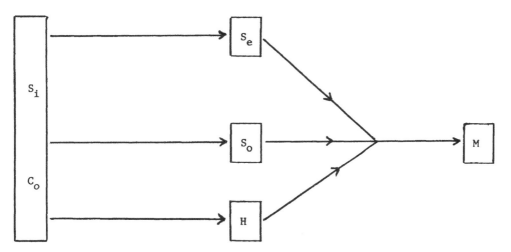

where: S_i = situation variables C_o = cognitive variables
        S_e = self-control (informal) S_o = social control (informal)
        H = hierarchical control (formal) M = motivation to act

Figure 3.4: The Developing Behavioural Model of Control

While hierarchical (formal) control had not been entirely abandoned as a concept, its advocated style of operation had been amended by the behaviouralists. Furthermore, clear recognition was paid to the importance of informal control concepts and to the potential for exercising effective control over organisational activities that existed at lower levels of the hierarchy. Behaviouralists began to express the hope that both formal and informal control concepts could be jointly utilised for the benefit of the organisation.

The Economic, Political and Social Impetus

To what events and conditions might the behavioural COM's development between 1930 and the late 1950s be attributed? Wren [1979] has argued that the foundation laid by Mayo and Barnard was in part a response to the economic malaise of the Great Depression. Society suffered a psychological as well as an economic depression, as faith in the free enterprise system, the primacy of profits, the goal of wealth and the creed of self-sufficiency were severely shaken [Murphy, 1973]. The Great Depression induced to some degree the replacement of achievement needs by affiliation needs, the substitution of government assistance for self-help, and the loss of social esteem for businessmen. The behaviouralists aimed to rebuild social solidarity and the social skills of management through expression of concern for the 'little man' in bottom-up control notions, participative decision-making, the fostering of worker groups, and the seeking of job satisfaction.

The way was also laid open for a behavioural COM by the pro-labour attitude of government, particularly in the 1930s. In the USA this attitude hastened the growth of trade unions and added further impetus to the consideration of employee behaviour in any consideration of control concepts and strategies [Robertson, 1964]. Government attitudes in the USA were backed up by social welfare and labour legislation[14] which provided for assistance to the aged, a guaranteed minimum hourly wage for certain workers, some unemployment insurance, and the right of workers to organise in unions and engage in collective bargaining [Handlin, 1975; Wren, 1979]. Union membership grew steadily from the 1930s into the 1950s as a socially acceptable form of employee self-protection. Initially, after the shock of the great depression, unions in the US and the UK exhibited a hostile attitude to employers, and while this did not persist in its vehemence indefinitely, World War II witnessed another concerted drive by American unions for improved wages and conditions [Kast and Rosenzweig, 1970; Tuttle and Perry, 1970; Youngson, 1976]. Such developments appeared to be outside the traditional formal framework provided by a classical management COM and clearly called for some conceptual changes which the behavioural school appeared to be offering.

Not only did employees organise, but over time the types of employees in organisations perceitibly changed. This became particularly noticeable with the advent of World War II. In the USA economic activity quickened and the long-term unemployed found themselves back at work. Prospects of education, professional and management careers improved. In the UK new industries had been growing and employing newcomers from different locations in the country with different habits and social backgrounds. Here too, employee expectations were rising, a growing number of women joined the workforce, and the war created new products, demanded new technology and called for a more broadly-based and skilled workforce. The subsequent growth of multinational corporations and advanced technology industries through the late 1950s and the early 1960s further complicated employee variety[15] and required more sophisticated models of motivation, control and behaviour in general [Roebuck, 1973; Handlin, 1975; Tosi and Carroll, 1976].

Changing social mores and attitudes in the USA and the UK could also be seen as having encouraged the development of a behavioural COM. After the great depression people began to place a higher value on financial security[16] than prospects of wealth, and tended to reject the individualism and achievement-orientation of capitalism for the psychological security of work, religious, political and social group membership. Education began to prepare students for fitting into social groups and employees valued group membership as an adjustment to their individuality in such large industrial organisations. Workers' economic and social aspirations were rising and the advent of World War II reinforced an ideology of equal opportunity and rewards based on merit. Their working hours too, were falling and their leisure time was increasing. After World War II college and university enrolments in the

US increased markedly and holiday provisions for the average employee improved even further [Robertson, 1964; Handlin, 1975; Wren, 1979].

Similar social trends were experienced in the UK. The inter-war years saw a rising level of people's expectations, both economic and social. The working classes gained greater self-esteem and demanded a greater share of national wealth. Living standards were rising. Women assumed new roles such as factory workers, artists, political workers, professionals, etc. The working class approached the middle class in terms of wealth, leisure, paid holidays, and shorter working hours. All this created a less deferential social climate in the UK, where title, rank and family name declined in influence and industry spawned a white collar middle class which managed industry rather than owning it. By the late 1940s employment was being sustained at high levels and, as in the US, education was being pursued by growing numbers of students at all levels [Roebuck, 1973].

These social and economic changes had rendered organisational life far more complex than the classical management COM had assumed. Their advent was so marked that many elements must have been clearly recognised by behavioural researchers. The behavioural COM's self-control concept reflected the greater confidence, education and self-esteem of employees, its social control concept reflected the marked tendency to group affiliation in society and the impact of union legislation and organisation, while the rejection of authority-based concepts in classical management's hierarchical control reflected the number of changes in social ideology that had permeated America and Britain by 1960.

THE SEEDS OF CHANGE

By the close of the 1950s the management literature on control had moved a considerable distance from the work of Taylor and Fayol. That is not to say that their influence had been lost. Far from it! Their classical management COM remained an influential force in management thought, with an array of adherents and proponents who were prepared to elaborate upon the model at length. Their embellishments however, were largely in the nature of repetition rather than constituting any significant improvement upon the original model.

The classical management school played a significant part in spawning the structural COM. Here the management literature was presented with a model which concentrated its attention upon particular aspects of the classical COM and applied them to the hierarchical authority structures of large-scale organisations. To some degree this has been construed as an adaptive response of the classical school to the increasing size of companies and to the growth in number of such companies operating in the USA and the UK. Nevertheless, it represented a school of thought and a model which was uniquely identifiable, quite separate in its constitution from the classical COM.

An even more dramatic divergence from the classical COM was to be observed in the behavioural COM. As a reaction to the technical and structrual obsessions of the classical and structural models, the behavioural model focussed upon psychosocial factors in an attempt to encompass a 'proper' degree of recognition to the importance of human behaviour to the objective of securing and maintaining effective management control. The potential impact of self-control and social control upon personnel motivation had begun to achieve prominence in management thinking to what, in the 1940s and 1950s, amounted to an unprecedented degree. It marked a continuing change in economic and social circumstances of the post World War II workforce and partly in response to those circumstances was to maintain its impetus on into the 1960s. With the approach of the 1960s the management literature could boast three major models of control at various stages of development. While that development was by no means complete, the seeds of change had been well and truly sown.

NOTES

1.   Wren [1979] noted her advocacy of recognising the relationship of
the firm to its environment of creditors, stockholders, customers,
competitors, suppliers and the community. It constituted a larger
than traditional view of the firm and its environment.

2.   While T. Burns and G.M. Stalker (*The Mangement of Innovation*,
London, Tavistock Publications, 1961) decades later, classified
organisational systems as mechanistic or organic, Follett had
already exhibited a marked organic orientation in her analysis.
She envisaged control as being a horizontal rather than vertical
process [Follett, 1941b, 1973a]. Her idea of central control was
that of co-ordinating the many controls throughout the
organisation [Follett, 1937] with control being exercised by
cross-relations between department heads rather than vertically
down the line through the chief executive. Krupp [1961]
recognised her work as being "rooted in organicism" and Massie
[1965] too, noted her definition of authority (and control) as
being pluralistic rather than simply flowing down from the top of
the organisation.

3.   Johann Fichte (1762-1814) was a German philosopher who advocated a
nationalist system in which the freedom of the individual was a
subordinate component of group will [Wren, 1979].

4.   What politicians were attempting to apply to the world (e.g. power
sharing and democracy) in general, Follett sought to apply in a
business context.

5.   This view is also held by Krupp [1961] and Massie [1965].

6.   Weber wrote on bureaucracy with respect to power and authority
primarily in his *Wirtschaft und Gesellschaft* published
posthumously in 1921.

7.   Significant developments in the study of bureaucracy subsequent to
Weber included R.K. Merton in 1940 (a model of bureaucracy based
on control imposed from the top of the hierarchy of authority),
P. Selznick in 1949 (a model of bureaucracy concentrating on
delegation of authority) and A.W. Gouldner in 1954 (concentrating
on the use of general and impersonal rules as a control
mechanism). This area of work is discussed in more detail in
Parker [1978].

8. The notion of 'span of control' is originally attributed to Urwick [1944].

9. Peterson and Gray [1969] have provided the following data on mergers:

    Mergers in Manufacturing and Mining Industries (USA)
    (Five-Year Totals)

1895-99	1,649	1920-24	2,235	1945-49	1,505
1900-04	1,363	1925-29	4,583	1950-54	1,424
1905-09	440	1930-34	1,687	1955-59	3,365
1910-14	451	1935-39	577	1960-64	4,366
1915-19	625	1940-44	906		

    First wave peak 1895-99
    Second wave peak 1925-29
    Third wave peak 1955-59

10. Writers on centralised control included:

    (UK) E.F.L. Brech in *British Management Review*
    (UK) J. Maddock   in *British Management Review*
    (UK) L. Urwick   in *Industry Illustrated*
    (UK) K.J. Wharton in *The Accountant*
    (USA) J.D. Mooney in *The Principles of Organisation*
                          (published in New York)
    (USA) A.E. Werolin in *Advanced Management*

11. Orders were observed to be fulfilled, 'in the narrow sense', but not in terms of conduct and manner of execution. Rules and regulations were not obeyed. Information flowing upwards was distorted by job trading, mutual help of workmates, stalling, and excessive work claims.

12. Hence they argued that management should not attempt to undermine or defeat social control, but should accept its existence, try to understand its *modus operandi*, to avoid any formal activities which might threaten it and to attempt to integrate social control with formal hierarchical control [Davis, 1962].

13. The pioneering work of Mary Parker Follett had much earlier taken the concept a considerable distance along its developmental path.

14.   Part of President Roosevelt's 'New Deal' programme.   These
        included:

            The Social Security Act 1935
            The Fair Labor Standards Act 1938
            The Railroad Unemployment Insurance Act 1938
            The Federal Anti-Injunction Act 1932 (Norris-La Guardia Act)
            The National Labor Relations Act 1935 (Wagner Act)

15.   For example, increasing numbers of professionals were being
        employed by large organisations. Multinationals began to embody a
        whole range of cultural backgrounds and behaviour patterns in
        their workforce.

16.   For example pension plans, social insurance, etc.

CHAPTER 4

THE ACCOUNTING MIRROR

Accounting theories of control followed initiatives taken by contributors to management theories of control and up to the close of the 1950s closely mirrored the classical management school. The classical COM in the accounting literature was to be largely expressed through the budget, with its roots planted firmly in the engineering and scientific management tradition. As will be seen it gained an even more dominant position in accounting theory than it had achieved in the management theory literature.

Traditionally accounting has been viewed as a key instrument of administrative control, both in terms of past events and in terms of planning for future profits [McKinsey, 1919; Scott, 1973]. To many accountants management and administrative control also embraced cost control [Lukens, 1932; Peck, 1938]. Indeed the emphasis upon cost control in the accounting function gained even greater currency among accountants in the 1940s and 1950s [Crossman, 1953]. For instance Dugdale [1953:347] argued:

> "The function of control is integral in the techniques
> of management accounting. Such techniques, in fact,
> now constitute one of the major tools of economic
> management."

Accounting writers of the 1940s spoke of the passage from 'record accounting' to 'control accounting', from mere cost determination to cost control, and saw the financial records as a key source of management control [Rose, 1941; Hill, 1945; Matz, 1945]. The budget was seen to be the most effective means available for controlling operations and costs. This view became so prevalent that in fact the terms 'budget' and 'budgetary control' came to be used synonymously [Coonley, 1925; Hecox, 1929; Davis, 1932; Ashworth, 1935]. Certainly the two terms were only ever vaguely defined, if at all.[1]

ADOPTING THE CLASSICAL MODEL

An investigation of the accounting literature between 1900 and 1960 reveals all too clearly that the classical management COM as shown in Figure 2.3 constituted the only model to secure general adoption by accounting writers. In common with their scientific management forebears accountants preferred to specify principles of control, to build simple step-by-step processes, to attach responsibility in terms of the hierarchy of authority, to focus upon measures of performance and efficiency, and to report according to the principle of exception [Hill, 1945; Matz, 1945]. The extent to which accounting writers followed classical management thinking will become evident from a brief outline of the following classical control concepts (already identified in Figure 2.3) which they expounded.

Authority-Based Control

To most accounting writers control required clearly laid down lines of authority and classification of responsibility at each point of the organisational hierarchy. Specified lines of authority were a critical prerequisite for fixing responsibility and for enforcing so-called budgetary control. Within the budget, authority, responsibility and hence control were to be specifically assigned to individuals or departments [Davis[2], 1932; Theiss, 1932, 1935; Morris, 1936a]. In fact it was argued that control should be centralised at the highest level of authority. Top management authority was to be strengthened[3] through a centralised accounting system designed to provide a unified machinery of control, specifically in the shape of the budget [Coonley, 1925; Tobey, 1925; Drucker, 1930; Lukens, 1932; Scott, 1973].

This authority-based concept of control was further expressed by accounting writers in terms of 'responsibility budgeting' [Matz, 1945; Dugdale, 1951]. Cost-centre budgets were to be set up for each department head as a means of exercising expense control. A primary value of the budget was seen to lie in its supplying top management with information about actual versus desired performance of subordinates and the means of fixing responsibility for undesired performance upon individual supervisors [Kassander, 1942; Muth, 1947].

Essentially accountants were promulgating a concept of control that was centralised, and enforced by top management direction and the assignment of responsibility, all through the allocation of authority.[4] This represented a replication of the classical management concept of authority-based control.

Disciplinary Control

As early as 1912 Franklin [1912e:705] spoke of the organisational cost system as "offering, urging, and indeed forcing, methods of improvement and control". By the 1930s accounting writers were advocating the enforcement of control through the budget to keep department heads 'on their toes' [Hovey, 1931; Theiss, 1932; Perry, 1938]. Accounting records were thought to be vital to the task of directing operations [McKinsey, 1919; Gessner, 1936].

Direction by itself however was not sufficient. The disciplinary concept of control relied also upon regulation, limitation or restriction and even outright prohibition. Control by regulation was pursued through the budget and affected areas of activity such as production, sales and administration expenses [Coonley, 1925; Hecox, 1929]. Cost control came to be viewed very much as a task of regulation [Matz, 1945] and included limitation or restriction of expenditure or action. Expenses were almost treated as an invidious disease to be contained in order to avoid an undesired 'breakout' [Franklin, 1912d]. Indeed it was argued that they should be *rigidly* controlled within budget estimates much in the manner of a motoring speed limit [Helm, 1930; Peck, 1940; Kassander, 1942]. So firm was the accounting commitment to disciplinary control that the National Association of Cost Accountants as early as 1922 [p.13] had listed 'proper control of expenditures' as a desired product of budgetary control, and recommended that it be achieved by the prohibition of expenditures in excess of departmental estimates. Such a view maintained its popularity from then onwards [McGladrey, 1934; Kassander, 1942].

Again, the disciplinary control concept of the pre-1960 accounting literature conformed with its classical management predecessor. Enforcement, direction, regulation, limitation, restriction and prohibition were its hallmarks.

Co-Ordinative Control

Co-ordination was also recognised as a component of control by accountants [N.A.C.A., 1922]. McKinsey [1919] for instance argued that if accounting was to serve as a basis for functional control it should co-ordinate the functions of sales, purchasing, stock control, production planning, plant maintenance and funding of credit, into a well formulated business programme. From another view of the organisation it was argued that the control function of accounts connected and unified technological operations with the business administration that controlled and directed production [Scott, 1973]. Clearly this view treated control as in part a co-ordinating activity. Some accounting writers were quite content to refer specifically to 'control by the co-ordinated budget' [Hovey,[5] 1931:105]. Here too, the accountants' concept of co-ordinative control was notable for its consistency with the classical management concept of the same name.

'Controls'

While the classical management COM emphasised the importance of 'controls' as tools for the achievement of control, the accounting model relied at least as heavily on 'controls' particularly in the form of the budget and its component standards. To accountants the budget became the best method of controlling costs [Davis,[6] 1932]. As Theiss [1932:13] expressed it:

"For example, it is quite clear that the modern budget must be more than a restricting and restraining device for cash outlays, a few unusual expenses, and production costs; it can and should provide also a control of sales and selling expenses and we may add, it can and may, before many years, provide a means of measuring and controlling the costs of management. This last mentioned objective would mean a control of the administration by the owners of the business."

Indeed, such importance was attached to the budget as a control tool by accountants that to many it became synonymous with control (as a concept) itself [Theiss, 1935]. Nevertheless, many accounting writers saw in the budget and its component standards a mechanism for providing the means for orderly attainment of effective control of operations and costs, particularly in large firms where it could provide a substitute for sole owner-manager control of a small business [McKinsey, 1921; Theiss, 1932, 1935; Hawkins, 1935; Makin, 1940a; Klein, 1942; Werolin, 1947; Benninger, 1950]. This emphasis upon 'controls' in the form of budgets and standards not only conformed to the classical management model but paved the way for accounting writers' emphasis upon the concept of control by exception.

Exception Control

Great importance in the accounting literature on control was attached to checking for expenditure excesses [Anon, 1917]. As early as the 1920s budgeting was regarded as a venue for providing "proper control of expenditures" through checking actual operating results against estimates [N.A.C.A., 1922:13]. Check-ups on policy execution, checks for unfavourable trends, and so-called scientific checks on salaries were widely advocated [Coonley, 1925; Hecox, 1929; Drucker, 1930]. In this light the budget was seen as an alarm system which would automatically sound when predetermined figures were exceeded [Hawkins, 1935]. The notion of checking up on subordinate performance via the budget persisted as an integral part of accounting thought on control into the 1950s [Edey, 1949; Barrett,[7] 1959]. In the UK the Institute of Cost and Works Accountants defined budgetary control as:

> "Budgetary control is the systematic control of
> business operations by means of predetermined
> statements prepared in minute detail and assembled
> into a comprehensive programme, in order to provide a
> basis of comparison with actual performances and
> costs, with the object of obtaining the final results
> indicated in the programme."
>
> [Makin, 1940:229]

The statements of minute detail, in effect, were budgetary standards, the
key operating tools of control in the budgetary system [Fletcher, 1922;
Hovey,[8] 1931; Davis,[9] 1932; Ashworth, 1935; Peden, 1937] facilitating the
identification of exceptions. Exceptions were measured by variances of
actual operating results from standards and were mostly seen to denote
inefficiency and weakness which must be identified and corrected
[Longmuir, 1902; Baker, 1918; Holden, Fish and Smith, 1951].

For exception identification the budget allowed "the efficient
factory manager to place his finger very speedily on factory
inefficiencies" [Gairns, 1949:81]. Corrective action followed:

> "The subject of control takes on a significance that
> should not be minimized, if corrective influences are
> to be set in motion ... ."
>
> [Peck, 1938:417]

Indeed all too often the onus for unfavourable variances was placed upon
managers and supervisors personally:

> "If the allowance on a job is two hours and the
> machinist requires three, the foreman knows at once
> that he has exceeded his standard and that he has
> failed in his control."
>
> [Kassander, 1942:4]

The accounting concept of exception control was complete in its
conformity with the classical management concept.

A Classical Model Replica

The accounting literature between 1900 and 1960 quite clearly chose to adopt the classical management COM. What might be termed the resulting 'classical accounting' COM matched its management counterpart virtually concept for concept. Authority-based control, disciplinary control, co-ordinative control, 'controls', and exception control formed the foundation components of both models. While the original classical COM derived from Taylor and Fayol's work did include a concept of total control (primarily contributed by Taylor), in the consolidated classical management COM expounded by subsequent management writers from the 1930s onwards this concept received less direct attention, although by implication it underpinned other concepts and represented their summation. Similarly, total control was not directly discussed in the accounting literature.

The result of this analysis of accounting thought on control before 1960 is that a 'classical accounting' COM identical to its classical management counterpart, as shown earlier in Figure 2.3, can be constructed. Once again as in the classical management COM the classical accounting COM was focussed upon the concept of total control (even if more by inference than direct assertion) with the primary source being the concept of authority-based control. The intervening concepts contributing to total control were disciplinary control, co-ordinative control, and exception control. Once more, as in the classical management COM, exception control contributed to total control through the agency of 'controls'.

For the accounting literature on control before 1960, this classical COM achieved even more pre-eminence and pervasiveness in accounting thought than it achieved in the management literature from which it apparently stemmed. Accounting writers added nothing significant to the model and indeed appeared well satisfied to continue propounding and reiterating its component concepts, rather than exploring any new ground, into the 1950s.

THE ROOTS OF DETERMINATION

Prima facie, the relatively detailed matching of the management COM by the accounting COM suggests that accounting writers may well have replicated the model from their management counterparts. A further question then arises as to what factors may have predisposed them to adopt this approach. Several key factors appear likely to have acted in concert and were, in the main, budget-related, since the majority of accounting writers discussed control within the context of budgeting.

Aspects of Budget Development

The notion of control through limitation and restriction by those in higher authority may in part have been founded in the origins of both the term 'budget' and its practice. The Gallic word *'sack'* was Latinised as *'bulga'*,[10] and appears to have been first used in Romanised France. From this came the old French term of *'boge'* or *'bouge'* which became in modern French, *'bougette'*, meaning 'little bag'. This appeared as the terms *'bogett'* or *'bougett'* in Middle English from which finally the Modern English term 'budget' appeared [Toby, 1926; Theiss, 1937; Rautenstrauch and Villers, 1968]. Subsequently the term 'budget' was used to include not only the container but also its contents. Hence it could be argued that the early use of the term 'budget' began in the restrictive sense of containing something.

As early as 1760 the Chancellor of the Exchequer presented the national budget to the English parliament at the commencement of each fiscal year. Indeed the first use of budgets was made by governments for the purpose of controlling (i.e. restricting) their expenditures. The budget was adopted to check or limit the king's power to levy taxes and to limit or restrict the expenditures of public officials [Theiss, 1937; Rautenstrauch and Villers, 1968].

In the USA the budget did not achieve prominence until it was adopted for business use.[11] Even after papers presented to the Taylor

Society, the release of a US Chamber of Commerce brochure and the publication of several books on budgeting, all in the early 1920s, general business interest in the budget did not gather momentum until nearly 1930. When business use of the budget did become commonplace it emphasised the same restrictive and authority-based concepts of control as English government use had done. Indeed, business budgeting began by concentrating upon the restricting and limiting of advertising, welfare, research, personnel and plant extension expenditures [Theiss, 1937; Potts, 1977].

Industrial engineers concentrated upon standardising factory operations and securing operational and cost efficiency. They assisted plant managers in preparing factory budgets or prepared budgets themselves and helped establish the importance of restrictive cost control [Theiss, 1937]. The early dominance of business budgeting development by engineers has been suggested by Sutcliffe [1976] who contends that Harrington Emerson[12] saw the original role of efficiency engineers as one of developing records to measure the difference between actual and standard performance and to eliminate that difference. From this viewpoint the role of the accounting system was limited to recording, in money terms, the engineer's progress in moving towards the ideal 100 percent efficiency state. This interpretation was suported by Theiss [1937] who saw accountants' primary contribution to the early development of business budgeting as being their recording of business transactions and the provision to managment of information on past performance. Accountants' interpretation of budgetary estimates, results and variances did not really become common until at least the late 1930s. It can therefore be argued with some conviction that business budgeting owed its early development first to the engineers. Thus the classical management COM and its replica, the classical accounting COM shared the common ancestry of the engineers' approach to control, which was expressed through the scientific management school.

Scientific and Efficiency Concerns

That the engineering background of budgeting may well have influenced the accounting COM to follow the classical management COM is further evidenced by the frequency of accounting references to the scientific management approach. While accountants were in favour of classical concepts such as "centralised control of the highest type" [Coonley, 1925:64], they also identified information as a basis of control and called for scientific administration through the proper application of correctly interpreted information [McKinsey, 1919][13].

> "Budgeting has merely aided business management to realize its profit objective by providing a scientific technique for forecasting business operations and establishing standards."
>
> [Theiss, 1937:48]

The budget was said to prove in financial terms the benefits of scientific management [Frazer, 1922][14] and to provide a scientific basis for centralised authority and adequate control. Furthermore, it was argued that businesses required scientifically recorded costs as a foundation for future estimates and investigation of causes of events [Rightor, 1917; Harrison, 1924; Frazer, 1933]. While a writer such as Theiss [1935:158] observed the scientific method to be "generously applied, both in the preparation and enforcement of the budget", Weger [1926] went so far as to claim that scientific management contemplated and embraced a budgetary system of control as one of its component strategies. Later, Urwick and Brech [1957] similarly argued that the post-World War I development of budget standards was a refinement of scientific management techniques rather than a pioneering stage in itself. The apparently definitive scientific framework offered by scientific standard setting appealed to accountants as a substitute for nebulous ideals, with the engineer determining the standards and the accountant measuring the performance results. Thus standard costs and budgeting came to be advocated as a natural corollary to scientific management [Scovell, 1914; Harrison, 1924; Tsuji, 1975].

Accountants also shared the scientific management concern for efficiency.

> "The modern cost-accounting fundamentals are Standards, Efficiencies, Equivalents."
>
> [Emerson, 1913:389]

Emerson advocated that in the ideal form of organisation for industrial efficiency, specialists would formulate underlying principles and relentlessly reveal their observance and neglect. Gantt [1916] called for a cost system that would reduce to a financial expression the difference between efficient and inefficient operations. Just as Taylor had sought daily reports on operations, so writers such as Peden [1937] began to argue for daily rather than monthly control by issuing daily reports to foremen on their production efficiency, labour control and economy in use of materials. Thus, efficiency became a key concern of accountants as a scientifically inspired object of control:

> "Finally, a word to Cost Accountants in particular. Do not be scared of the term 'budgetary control', forget 'budgetary' if you like and only remember 'control', 'standard', 'estimate' or any other term you like. Go out after the main idea, 'efficiency' - efficiency in selling, efficiency in manufacture."
>
> [Hawkins, 1935:227]

Accounting records were seen as an agent of control in the pursuit of efficiency, fighting the tendency towards waste through scientifically determined standards [Franklin, 1912a,c,d; Scovell, 1914]. By the mid-to-late 1930s the budget was being 'sold' to accountants and managers as a mechanism for keeping departments operating at maximum efficiency with budgetary control causing departmental managers to discover errors and correct inefficiencies [Wight, 1934; Hawkins, 1935; Banks, 1937].[15] This scientific management concern to control for efficiency appears to have influenced accountants' adoption of the exception control concept. Through the budget, control was to be "effected by a system of variations which disclose inefficiencies, and operates on the principle of exceptions, whereby normals may be neglected and attention focussed on the exceptional cases" [Morris, 1936b:925]. The accounting concern for efficiency continued through the 1940s and 1950s [Klein, 1942; Taylor, 1946; Gillett, 1949; Bentley, 1959].[16]

> "The developments in accounting technique for management purposes have expanded the accounting function until it well nigh covers control as defined by Fayol."
>
> [Morrow, 1949:508]

> "In manufacturing, for example, we have management accounting, budgetary control, full-scale costing, and all the other modern techniques which have been devised to aid scientific management. You may well ask why this has come about. It is because in the manufacturing industry the accountancy profession has been welcomed and encouraged by managements to assist in obtaining maximum efficiency."
>
> [Barrett, 1959:105]

Accounting Perceptions of the Budget

Since much of accounting writers' analysis of control took place within the budgeting context, further understanding of the accounting COM's replication of the classical management COM can be gained by considering accounting perceptions of and attitudes to the budget. In the first instance, in addition to the influences earlier discussed, at some points of time (particularly during the 1920s and 1930s), accountants stressed the need for budgeting in order to cope with depressed economic conditions. While planning for profitability was seen as one budgetary advantage in this respect, control (i.e. restriction)[17] of expenditure through budgeting was empahsised rather more [Banks, 1937; Loncar, 1956]. The budget was seen to be a counter measure to the uncertainties of a fluctuating cycle of business and economic activity, while the likelihood of future business catastrophes was supposedly to be reduced by the control of expenses [Lazarus, 1924; Vieh, 1925; Hensel, 1937].

Any attempt to gain a first impression of accounting perceptions of the budget itself through accounting definitions of budgeting or so-called 'budgetary control' provides a largely superficial impression. Indeed, few attempts were made at specific definition:

> "It does not seem possible to lay down a general ruling on the literal interpretation of the term 'Budgetary Control'."
>
> [Dunkerley, 1935:26]

It was variously defined as foreseeing problems, accomplishing planned results and developing and controlling a business programme [Coonley, 1925; McGladrey, 1934; Perry, 1938]. The search for the accounting perception of budgeting must therefore go beyond basic definitions.

Accountants were concerned to direct management's attention to the need for profit and considered the budget to be a means of projecting desired profit and controlling activities with a view to achieving desired profit [Dunkerley, 1935; Morris, 1936a; Perry, 1938; Klein, 1939]. The question then arises as to the means by which accountants thought budgeting could encourage profitability? The answer lay in control which was seen as the prime function of budgeting and expressed in terms of centralised control of costs and expenses by higher management exercising ultimate control over subordinates, activities and expenditures through the budget [Tobey, 1925; Colgan, 1928; Theiss, 1932; Ashworth, 1935]. Indeed some saw the one advantage or purpose of budgeting as control so that they tended to concentrate upon the control function to the exclusion of all else[18] [Hawkins, 1935; Hensel, 1937; Theiss, 1937]. This pronounced emphasis upon control continued in the accounting literature into the 1950s [Rose, 1952; Edey, 1959].

This emphasis upon control in the budgeting literature was also to be found in budgeting practice. Coonley [1923] described the production and inventory control practices of the Walworth Manufacturing Company and found that control via the budget emerged as a key focus of that company's management system. Theiss [1932] provided a summary of budget practice from a survey of approximately 250 industrial, wholesale and retail businesses, public utilities, railroads and financiers throughout the Middle West of the USA, and from a survey of 40 of the largest department stores in the USA. The types of budgeting systems found were classified as cost control, sales promotion, financial management or executive, and analytical accounting control. With the exception of the sales promotion type all of the budgeting categories were concerned largely with securing centralised, authority-based control. A survey by Dunkerley [1935] provided similar findings. Firms surveyed came from industries such as confectionery, hosiery, motor vehicles, steel, glass, rubber, boots and shoes, musical instruments and patent medicines. Almost every reply to one particular question, "Exactly what use is made of the budgets by managment?",[19] centred upon the control function. This was referred to directly as 'control' or indirectly as 'policy', 'regulation', 'limiting' or 'co-ordinating'. Both in theory and in practice it is clear that the accounting perception of the budget was that it was an instrument of control and a venue for exercising control.[20]

This emphasis in the accounting literature has not always been recognised by accountants. In July 1930 the International Conference on Budgetary Control hosted by the International Management Institute was held in Geneva, Switzerland, at which theories underlying the exercising of budgetary control were considered [Dunkerley, 1935]. Two hundred delegates from 27 countries heard papers presented by executives from the USA, UK, Canada, Belgium, Germany, Switzerland and France [Theiss, 1937]. At that conference, the following definition of budgetary control was adopted:

> "Budgeting is not merely control: it is not merely forecasting: it is an exact and vigorous analysis of the past and the probable and desired future experience with a view to substituting considered intentions for opportunism in management."

> [Stone, 1952:31]

This more balanced emphasis upon control and planning represented a significant departure from the control emphasis in the budget-related accounting literature of the period but had little effect on subsequent accounting literature which continued to emphasise control. Even the Geneva definition itself suffered from reinterpretation when in 1935, Hawkins [1935:271] argued that 'budgetary control' was a term generally adopted after agreement at Geneva and that it was understood to cover any system of *general control*[21] of a business activity by predetermined yardstick or budget. Such a control emphasis was clearly inconsistent with the intention of the original Geneva definition.

A Derivative Model

Based upon the preceding analysis it appears highly probable that accounting writers adopted a derivative of the classical managment COM due to a combination of factors. While the factors discussed may not comprise all the influences on the accounting COM's development, they appear to have been significant contributors.

The derivation of the term 'budget' had emphasised both the 'controls' and the disciplinary concepts of control, while early government use of budgeting had concentrated upon authority-based and disciplinary concepts of control. Thus some critical components of the classical model were already entrenched in the budgeting tradition which accountants took up. Since accountants considered concepts of control primarily in the context of budgeting, they followed the earlier involvement of engineers in budgeting. Budgeting was imbued with a scientific management philosophy and accounting writers openly embraced that philosophy.

Accountants' sharing of a concern for efficiency with their scientific management colleagues and forerunners allowed the exception control concept to take root in the accounting COM just as surely as it had done in the classical management COM. Finally, accountants' perception of the budget focussed largely on its control function, particularly in terms of centralised, authority-based co-ordinative and disciplinary control concepts. The path had been cleared for an accounting replication of the classical management COM.

RECOGNISING THE BEHAVIOURAL DIMENSION

Quite a number of accounting writers between 1920 and 1960 began to recognise that budgets had an impact upon human behaviour and that the results might be of some significance for the organisation. What they observed were the types of problems in terms of manager and subordinate reactions which a budget system could induce.

A few writers noted the growing unpopularity of the budget. McGladrey [1934:488] noted for budgets that "their value is about in inverse ratio to their popularity". Such unfavourable attitudes were observed to exist in businessmen and laymen alike, particularly where budgets has been used to exert relentless pressure for improved performance. For many, budgets had become a symbol of oppressive action to be regarded with suspicion and mistrust [Peck, 1938; Bronner, 1953; Loncar, 1956]. Yet the writers who observed such budgetary unpopularity often failed to recognise the associated range of causes. Discussion of causes mostly came from others who did not appear to have considered to what extent the resulting problems had caused budgetary unpopularity.

What sort of behavioural problems had accounting writers begun to recognise in budgeting? Makin [1940b:289] noticed the tendency of managers "to shift the blame on to 'the other fellow'" when things went wrong, but merely saw it as an inherent "singular reluctance to shoulder responsibilities" rather than as a reaction to the budgetary system. Yet some other writers had begun to recognise budgeting administration problems that caused negative subordinate reactions. Theiss [1937] pointed to the overemphasis on the negative idea of restricting expenditures through budgeting, while Hawkins [1935] and Bunge [1946] expressed concern about the propensity for the budget to be used in a rigid and arbitrary fashion by higher management. Such rigidity, they felt could destroy executives' initiative and result in the full expenditure of all budget allowances, even when savings could have been achieved relatively easily. One further budgetary problem recognised by a small group of accounting writers was that of pressure for increasingly demanding performance targets. This, it was argued, would cause dissatisfaction and resentment among various management levels with foremen and other managers setting up defences against those administering budget controls [Hawkins, 1935; Bronner, 1953; Loncar, 1956].

In a more positive sense a very small number of authors considered what positive actions could be taken in administering budgets in order to diminish observed behavioural problems. There was some recognition of the need for a degree of lower level management self-determination in the budgetary process [Wright, 1927; Muth, 1947; Holden, Fish and Smith, 1951]. However, there was no detailed analysis and behavioural matters did not rate any mention by the vast majority of accounting writers.

Two accounting writers made more exceptional contributions to the fledgling literature on behavioural effects of budget administration than their contemporaries. Dent's [1931] paper entitled "Budgetary Business Control in Practice" represented a significant and apparently conscious departure from the conventional accounting wisdom about budgeting at that time. He particularly stressed the psychological and human factor in budgetary control and argued that an organisation's psychological resistance had to be recognised and efforts made to convert it into co-operation. Accordingly he [Dent, 1931:549] argued that "on psychological counts budgets should be built up from below". The budget need not limit initiative but should promote co-ordination between organisation members, through patience, tact, understanding and goodwill.

The other exceptional pre-1960s writer on behavioural aspects of budgeting in the accounting literature was James Peirce [1954] who saw the budget as resting on principles that had more in common with concepts of human relationship than with rules of accounting. He argued that when the budget was associated with paucity and niggardliness, it would be surrounded by criticism, recrimination and mistrust, and accordingly would be bound to fail. In response, he suggested that planning be emphasised in budgeting, with conrol as the complement. To Peirce [1954:60] it was "in the control area that the colossal mistakes of budgeting are made". Poorly trained subordinates were censured for exceeding budgets, subordinates concealed actual results and padded budgets "to give themselves breathing room", and staff men usurped authority. Thus Peirce [1954:61] proposed that control in budgeting take the form of "self-discipline - voluntary, unified and co-operative".

The accounting recognition of the behavioural dimension of budgeting however, was still very much in its infancy before 1960. What recognition had occurred was mostly related to the budget rather than to any concept of control and of those writers who did recognise behavioural factors in budgeting, the majority were primarily contributors to the classical accounting COM making behavioural observations as minor 'asides' from their main classical themes rather than attempting to construct new control concepts.

SIGNS OF A DEFECTIVE MIRROR

The accounting literature on control between the years 1900-1960 has been found to have acted as a mirror, reflecting the classical management COM. Yet the accounting mirror was a defective one. It failed to reflect the management literature's emerging structural COM and similarly failed to reflect the management literature's behavioural COM. Some accounting writers began to discuss the behavioural dimensions of budgeting in general but there was no sign of any attempt to devise a behavioural accounting COM prior to 1960. The accounting approach to control had quite clearly begun to 'mark time', particularly in the 1940s and 1950s. Significant revisions in management theory approaches had begun in the early 1940s but were not apparent in the accounting literature even in the late 1950s. Moreover, accountants had not initiated any other new approaches to the study of control on their own account.

NOTES

1. As an example of vague definition, Robson [1949:199] tried to explain "what the accountant really means when he uses the terms 'standard costs' and 'budgetary control'". This, he said, was "the most flexible accounting device for controlling the expenditure of money in the carrying out of any particular function".

2. Argued by Alden C. Brett, the then comptroller of Hood Rubber Co. Inc., Watertown, Massachusetts, when commenting on a paper by R.J. Davis.

3. Refer also to Furukawa [1961].

4. For instance, Werolin [1947:125] argued that "progressive companies" used budgets to allow top management to delegate authority to divisional and departmental managers without sacrificing overall control.

5. Argued by Arthur W. Marshall, assistant production manager, General Asphalt Company, Philadelphia, when commenting upon F.F. Hovey's paper.

6. Budget officer for the Hills Brothers Company.

7. Barrett [1959] defined control (through accounting) in terms of selective checking of an organisation's personnel more for dishonesty than for error!

8. Comment by Arthur W. Marshall.

9. Comment by Alden C. Brett.

10. Described as a leather bag or knapsack for carrying food.

11. A national budget was not adopted in the USA until 1921 [Rautenstrauch and Villers, 1968].

12. A renowned engineering writer.

13. This approach is also reflected in Hecox [1929] and Ashworth [1935].

14. This view is consistent with Sutcliffe's [1976] thesis that the accounting system was originally intended to measure the financial effects of the efficiency engineer's work.

15. That accountants followed classical thinking in seeking efficiency via control is further confirmed by Dunkerley's [1935, Appendix II(d)] survey of budgetary practice. Later, Holden, Fish and Smith's [1951] empirical survey revealed that all companies studied, stressed the importance of cost reduction and control but few were particularly well organised for achieving it.

16. It seems evident that in the minds of a significant number of accounting writers, cost control for efficiency included the pursuit (not unlike Taylor) of cost reduction [Franklin, 1912b; Matz, 1945; Fiske, 1947; Muth, 1947; Bronner, 1953].

17. Restrictive practices included arbitrary reductions of personnel, expansion of supervisory workloads, and cost reduction programmes [Loncar, 1956].

18. For example, planning or supply.

19. Question 10 [Dunkerley, 1935, Appendices 1(a), 1(b)].

20. Some authors did at times recognise a more balanced role for both planning and control in the budget [McGladrey, 1934; Perry, 1938; Makin, 1940; Bunge, 1946; Wilks, 1947; Stone, 1952; Loncar, 1956] but they still represented a minority group in the accounting literature.

21. At the same time, Hawkins [1935:271] demonstrated a rather *laissez-faire* attitude to the question of budget nature or emphasis in stating that "for so long as we all understand what is meant by the term 'budgetary control', it does not matter what people call it."

PART TWO

MANAGEMENT AND ACCOUNTING APPROACHES TO CONTROL: 1960-1979

CHAPTER 5
MANAGEMENT MODELS: EXPLORING AND MATURING

After 1960 the classical COM continued to attract some management writers' attention but came under increasing criticism. The structural model was consolidated and revised to a degree, and the behavioural COM expanded through revision and addition of component control concepts. During this period, the sytems approach to control also emerged. The developmental progress of these structural, behavioural and systems models of control will be examined within the context of the schools of thought from which they arose and set against the background of their socio-economic environment.

FOLLETT: BELATED RECOGNITION

The 1960s saw a belated recognition of the importance of Follett's contribution to management theory. When recognition had occurred it usually took the form of an attempt to classify her as purely a scientific management theorist.[1] Krupp contended that while Follett was normative[2] as compared with the generally positive approach of more recent, particularly behavioural, theorists, their final products were not very different. For instance, he argued that Follett, Barnard and Simon all shared a common perceptual framework in their treatment of organisations. He also recognised her concern with organisational processes and systems and defined her work as "rooted in organicism" [Krupp, 1961:86-91].

Savitt [1962:20-21] acknowledged Follett's notion of (an organisation's) 'functional relating' that could create a unity with value beyond the mere addition of its parts. Out of this 'dynamic management' concept he saw control appearing as a major aspect. Savitt considered that recent management thought was beginning to emphasise voluntary human action in the Follett mode, rather than coercive control.

Further direct[3] references to Follett's work appeared in the mid-1960s. Livingstone [1965:41] acknowledged Follett's 'law of the situation' for taking orders from the requirements of the specific situation rather than simply from the organisation's hierarchy of authority, and for expanding feedback beyond just a downward flow of information through the organisational hierarchy. Massie [1965] saw Follett's view of management as significantly different from the views of Fayol, Mooney and Sheldon. He saw Follett's orientation as having been primarily in the areas of psychology and sociology and her ideas as having been far ahead of her time.

Follett anticipated some essential elements of subsequent management models of control. Ahead of the structural theorists, she viewed planning and control as being integrated rather than totally separate. She anticipated the systems COM by treating the organisation as a whole and control as a process rather than as a static element and focussed upon the interaction of organisational parts rather than only with the parts themselves. In advance of the behavioural COM she accepted the need for organisms to exercise self-control and hence advocated that executives should manage *with* their fellow men, should be allowed to self-adjust and that organisations should allow collective, self-control. In addition she saw the organisation as being pluralistic (rather than stressing authoritarian, hierarchical control) and stressed two-way feedback of information as well as both lateral and vertical co-ordination of controls. Finally her argument that the unity could have a value greater than the sum of its parts in some respects covered ground that Tannenbaum [1964, 1968] and others would tackle later with respect to the distribution of control in an organisation.

Thus many control concepts identified with control models of the 1960s and 1970s were anticipated by Follett's conceptualisations. Her influence upon the present-day concepts of control has been uncontestably significant and rivalling the long-standing influence of such giants as Taylor and Fayol.

THE CLASSICAL CONTROL MODEL: UNDER PRESSURE

That the classical COM continued to attract adherents through the 1960s and 1970s is evident, if only from the number of references to Fayol's early definition of control or from the number of definitions which virtually replicated it. A typical definition of the period read as follows:

> "Controlling is determining what is being accomplished, that is, the performance, evaluating the performance, and, if necessary, applying corrective measures so that performance takes place according to plans."
>
> [Terry, 1964:591-592]

This may be compared with Fayol's definition:

> "In an undertaking, control consists in verifying whether everything occurs in conformity with the plan adopted, the instructions issued and principles established. It has for object to point out weaknesses and errors in order to rectify them and prevent recurrence."
>
> [Fayol, 1949:107]

The similarity between the two definitions is quite striking. Other writers of the 1960s and 1970s either quoted Fayol's definition directly or specifically referred to it [Lindberg, 1972:143, 147-158; Mockler, 1972:1-11; Luthans, 1973:257]. However, these were still only attempts to define how to exercise conrol rather than its nature as a concept.

The component concepts of the classical COM continued to be restated, but came under increasing criticism. Authority-based control was still seen to require the "asymmetric, one-way control from a single source at the top of the organization" [Cartwright, 1965:2]. Direction, domination and supervision still figured largely in this concept [Drucker, 1964; Gross, 1968; Reeves and Woodward, 1970]. Goals set by top management were still accorded pre-eminence [Livingstone, 1965; Wright, 1965; Lorange and Scott Morton, 1974]. On the other hand

management writers were beginning to discuss goals in terms of rendering
major collective goals and individual employee aspirations mutually
compatible while control was beginning to move away from the
authoritarian notion of 'enforcement of goals' towards a notion of
'reconciliation of goals' [Atkinson, 1964; Lowe and McInnes, 1971; Lawler
III, 1976].

The disciplinary concept of control too, came in for critical
review. While regulation and policing still attracted attention, writers
began to adopt a more critical approach [Terry, 1964; Berlo, 1975]. This
was constrasted with approaches to control that placed greater reliance
upon voluntary human action [Savitt, 1962]. Control that relied upon the
direct use of force and force-based authority was increasingly being
regarded as obsolete.

Co-ordinative control also was referred to after 1960 [Litterer,
1965; Murdick, 1970] though the number of management writers concerning
themselves with this concept did appear to have declined. Indeed Machin
[1973] focussed attention upon the difficulty of achieving it in large
organisations.

Originally classical management theorists had been greatly concerned
with the employment of 'controls'. Their emphasis began to change in the
1960s. While the potential usefulness of information-based control was
still acknowledged, its complexities were also recognised. Some
measurements used as performance criteria inadequately reflected the full
dimensions of performance, some aspects of performance defied measurement
and other measures risked becoming unjustifiably reified [Gross, 1968;
Strong and Smith, 1968]. It was suggested that information-based control
could be located throughout the organisation rather than remaining the
prerogative of top management (as classical management theorists had
previously assumed). In addition, behavioural science findings had begun
to show that misleading and invalid information could be fed through
control systems by employees [Berlo, 1975; Lawler, 1976].

Finally, exception control continued to be expounded as an aid to pinpointing weaknesses and failure [Terry, 1964; Wright, 1965; Stokes, 1968]. However, the possibility that this could antagonise employees and encounter non-compliance and resistance was, in the 1960s, being considered. Writers such as McGregor [1967] had begun to argue that this type of control implied mistrust and the threat of retribution and could provoke negative responses from subordinates.

The classical COM, while continuing into the 1960s and 1970s, had come under increasing critical pressure [Stephenson, 1968; Urwick, 1971]. No longer did management writers see control in terms of a set of inviolate principles or in terms of a simple definition. No single definition of control had dominated the management literature [Fleming, 1972],[4] ambiguity abounded [Reeves and Woodward, 1970] and confusion about the nature of control persisted. "No universal agreement as to the precise meaning of the word" [Luneski, 1964:592] appeared to exist after all. The classical world of certainty was evaporating. Tannenbaum [1968] concluded that the changing nature of society and its organisations had begun to highlight some of the limitations of those earlier classical ideas. The questioning of authority, the growing importance of skills and specialsit knowledge and the introduction of industrial democracy were some of the factors contributing to this change. In addition, management theorists had begun to recognise that solutions ignoring interpersonal relations could be dangerously simplistic [Stephenson, 1973]. Thus by the early 1960s, other control models had already begun to supplant the previously dominant position of the classical management COM.

THE STRUCTURAL CONTROL MODEL: FURTHER EVOLUTION

The structural COM continued into the 1960s and 1970s, with its focus on power relationships, the distribution of authority, and working procedures, while attempting to manipulate these factors to achieve maximum organisational performance [Pugh, Mansfield and Warner, 1975]. Indeed the structuring of official positions, the allocating of functional activities and the co-ordinating of relationships remained very much in the Weberian tradition [Weiss, 1969]. Solutions to problems of job allocation and co-ordination were seen to lie in a range of continuous processes so that structuralists emphasised the process[5] approach to control. The structural COM therefore considered organisations in terms of size, division of authority and centralisation of power and on the other hand (from a process perspective) in terms of power, conflict, leaderhip, decision-making and communication [Weeks, 1973; Duncan, 1975; Hodgetts, 1979].

An Expanded View of Process

The allocation and co-ordination of functional activities were seen by structuralists to be essential to organisational maintenance [Weiss, 1969]. For them organisational performance was the end. In pursuit of that end organisational control was defined by Etzioni within a process perspective as:

> "... a distribution of means used by an organization to elicit the performances it needs and to check whether the quantities and qualities of such performance are in accord with organizational specifications."
>
> [Etzioni, 1965:650]

For Etzioni, hierarchical organisational structure was essential to his concept of conrol which could be achieved through physical, material or social processes.

With respect to control, particular attention was paid to diagnosing the "situation in order to define the control problem and the method for dealing with it" [Mockler, 1972:17]. Probing for causes of problems or deviations and collecting related facts considered essential as an adjunct to corrective processes [Luthans, 1973].

> "Exercising control involves more than just sitting back and 'correcting' a deviation. Such steps as

uncovering the exact cause of a deviation and devising
the most economical information system are demanding
and challenging tasks, and essential to effective
management control."

[Mockler, 1972:20]

The process of corrective action was also fundamental to the structural
view of control and included not only remedies for performance but also
remedies for the control system itself.[6] Correction need not be aimed
merely at securing subordinate compliance, but could be aimed at
stimulating improved performance through a combination of constructive
criticism and education of subordinates.

Structuralists also paid more attention to the relationships between
alternative control processes (or functions). Child [1972] replicated[7]
the Aston study [Pugh et al, 1968] of organisation structure in order to
test the proposition (based on the Weberian theory of bureaucracy) that
specialisation, rules, procedures, paperwork and an extended hierarchy
would all be positively interrelated and negatively related to the
centralisation of decision-making.[8] His results indicated that as
organisations adopted increasingly formal procedures for regulating
activities they tended to develop less centralised forms of control.[9]
Structuralists also considered the potential influence of organisational
size upon control processes adopted. Rushing [1969] tested the
hypothesis[10] that with an increase in organisational size, dependence
upon control through formal rules and records increased at a faster rate
than dependence upon supervision.[11] Analysis of results revealed a
negative correlation between organisational size and the surveillance-
formal rules index, so that it was suggested that with organisational
growth, formal rules and records increased at a faster rate than
surveillance procedures. This question was also considered by Salaman
[1979] who pointed out that Weber's bureaucracy had prescribed tight
specification of activities (formal rules) *and* hierarchical control
(centralisation of authority via supervision). Again it was noted that
the evidence pointed towards centralised control in small organisations
and formal rule and records-based control in large organisations. Thus
the structuralists appeared to be moving towards general agreement that

as organisation size grew, direct centralised control declined and indirect rules and records-based control became more common.

As they had done before the 1960s, structural theorists continued to consider the nature of the relationship between planning and control. While earlier writers had been almost unanimous that planning was a subset of control, structuralists in the 1960s and 1970s appeared to either treat planning and control as indivisible or alternatively as quite distinct. Those who considered the functions indivisible cited their common decision-making characteristic, their joint functioning in the design of control system policies, procedures and decision rules, and their combined role in setting short-term directions for an organisation [Bonini, 1964; Anthony, 1965; Lorange and Scott Morton, 1974]. The alternative view was that the functions were distinct because they were part of a step-by-step operation in which planning preceded controlling [Terry, 1964; Mockler, 1972]. While obvious disagreement on this point persisted in the 1960s and 1970s, the supporting arguments were relatively superficial. Writers simply assumed their particular view to be 'logically' correct, or made only token efforts at arguing the reasonableness of their case. The lack of rigorous or convincing argument on this question left the matter unresolved.

The Model Revised

The greater emphasis accorded by structuralists to the role of control process requires a partial revision of the pre-1960 structural COM represented in Figure 3.3. This revision is incorporated in a post-1960 model whose component concepts and their hypothesised relationships are represented in Figure 5.1.[12] While the basic framework of the revised model remained unchanged from that of its pre-1960 predecessor, the notion of directive control (D)[13] was re-expressed in terms of the alternatives of surveillance control (S) or rules-and-records control (R).[14] The degree of centralised control (CC) exercised, was thought to be a function of organisation size, as was the choice between the alternatives of surveillance control (S) and rules-and-records control

- 126 -

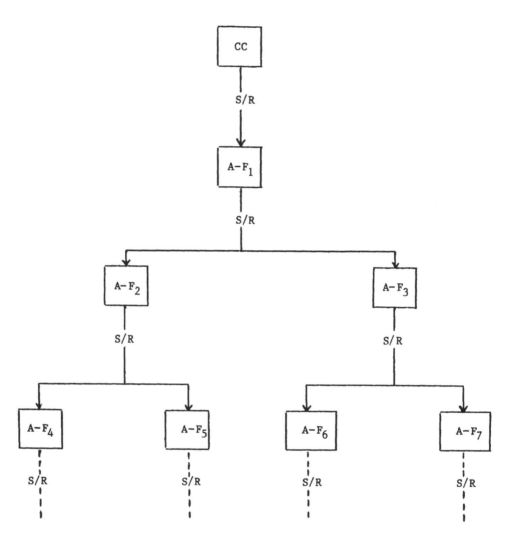

where: CC = centralised co-ordinating control
          S = surveillance control
          R = rules-and-records control
        S/R = either S or R depending on organisational size
A-F$_1$ ... A-F$_n$ (where n = number of departments)
--------- = lines of control down to successive layers of
            departments in the organisational hierarchy

Figure 5.1:   The Revised Structural Model of Control

(R). While these processes were specified in more detail than they had been in the earlier model, they remained fixed to a framework of hierarchical control in the strict Weberian bureaucracy sense. Thus each official position in the hierarchy exercised authority-based functional control $(A-F_1$ to $A-F_n)$ over its subordinates and their activities.

Just like its pre-1960 predecessor, the post-1960 structural COM retained its likeness to a hierarchical organisation structure with the concept of centralised co-ordinating control located in the hands of top management. Authority-based functional control continued to be vested in each official position in the organisation's hierarchy of authority, with each position exercising control over subordinates through either surveillance or rules-and-records control.

The Continuing Impact of Scale

The influence which the growing size of organisations had on the development of the structural COM in the 1940s and 1950s appears to have continued to influence the work of the structuralists in the 1960s and 1970s. The 1960s witnessed both growth and mergers of major firms in the US and the UK [Youngson, 1976; Tuttle and Perry, 1970]. By the 1970s great American corporations differed significantly in size from their predecessors, with capitalisation of more than a billion dollars and annual sales of similar proportions no longer exceptional [Handlin, 1975]. It is reported that in 1947 the largest 200 US corporations produced 30 percent of the value added to manufacturing output, but by 1970 the top 200 produced 43 percent of the value added [Tosi and Carroll, 1976].

The spread of each corporation's operations over a range of industries also continued unabated for many. Disparate activities were combined in vast conglomerates. As Brownlee put it:

> "The private sector has refined its fundamental
> institutional structure, placing a contemporary
> emphasis on diversifying products and markets,

especially among industries such as electronics and chemicals ... ."

[Brownlee, 1979:324]

Vast financial resources were accumulated in these organisations which frequently had diverse and complex structures and major problems in planning and control [Kast and Rosenzweig, 1970; Handlin, 1975; Youngson, 1976].

Not only did organisations grow in size but many became multinational. In the 1960s and 1970s particularly, many large firms commenced operations in foreign countries or engaged in joint ventures or licensing arrangements with firms in other countries. Overseas operations of such large organisations included not only investment in foreign operations or the use of foreign selling outlets, but also included the setting up of full-scale operations abroad (including manufacturing) [Murphy, 1973; Tosi and Carroll, 1976; Youngson, 1976].

Both the post-1960 growth in company size and the increasingly multinational character of many provided a stimulus to the continued efforts of structuralists to refine the structural COM. The associated complexity of organisational operations and structure maintained the impetus for structuralists' efforts to build a hierarchically-structured control system revolving around a centralised control authority which sought control over the whole enterprise through co-ordination. The likelihood of increased difficulty in achieving this in large (and particularly multinational firms) would have constituted a major reason for structuralists' interest in studying the relationship between organisational size, surveillance control and rules-and-records control. In attempting to maintain the relevance of their control structure to larger organisations they had attempted to improve the specification of its process components.

THE BEHAVIOURAL CONTROL MODEL: NEW DIMENSIONS

The work which contributed to the behavioural COM continued its momentum into the 1960s and 1970s. Moving on from their human relations roots behavioural scientists became transactional in orientation, studying all aspects of human behaviour and interrelationships in organisational life and particularly concerned themselves with the potential conflict between worker satisfaction and 'efficient' organisation. The behavioural approach to the study of control remained essentially interdisciplinary, including the psychology of the individual and the sociology of the group [Silverman, 1970; Duncan, 1975].

Where the classical and structural models of control had focussed upon control structures, functions and mechanisms, the behavioural COM continued to emphasise the human organisation:

> "Therefore, a valid philosophy of managerial control utilizes the premise that even the most complete of *quantitative* control must be consonant with the *qualitative* control provided by the human organization."
>
> [Powell, 1966:56]

Behavioural research became concerned with the relationship between control bases and satisfaction [Ivancevich, 1970], between employee perceptions of control and their performance [Todd, 1977] and between types of organisational control and emotional well-being [Ouchi and Johnson, 1978]. Control itself was seen to have special psychological significance for individuals and might imply superiority, inferiority, dominance, submission, guidance, help, criticism or reprimand [Tannenbaum, 1964].

Self-Control

> "It is important that deviations be reported to the employee himself. By making progress reports available to those who are actually doing the work, a

climate is created where they can adjust their own
performance instead of being told to do so."

[Scanlan and Keys, 1979:553]

In its simplest form, self-control was suggested to be a first line of
control where an individual could be allowed to control his or her own
activities and participate in managing the work situation. This involved
a social contract of personal trust between superiors and subordinates
[Murdick, 1970; Berlo, 1975]. Such a concept of self-control was deemed
by some to be a prerequisite to joint sharing of information and joint
decision-making in a participative management scheme [Luthans, 1973;
Warmington, 1974].

Considerable attention was paid to the question of how an
individual's self-control could be encouraged. On one hand it was seen
to be a form of learned behaviour. The individual could examine
alternative actions and their associated outcomes and choose an action
leading to a preferred outcome, rather than behaving rashly and
implusively with undesired consequences. Behaviouralists recognised that
the strength of an individual's opposition to attempts at external
control over him depended upon the match or mismatch between his own
beliefs, attitudes and behaviour and those required by management. On
the other hand, the degree of self-control exercised by an individual
depended upon his cognitive, motivational, social and personality
characteristics. External, contrived controls need not be resorted to so
frequently when the individual developed characteristics of a
psychologically mature person. Nevertheless, it was argued that control
could be learned in both the perceptual and motivational senses. In the
perceptual sense it depended on the employee's capacity to discriminate
patterns of stimulation requiring different responses, while in the
motivational sense it depended upon the extent to which effective
performance was a goal or seen as a means of attaining some goal [Vroom,
1964; Cartwright, 1965; Luthans and Kreitner, 1975].

Lawler [1976] marshalled evidence from a number of studies to
suggest that self-control was more likely to be exercised by individuals

when they received feedback on their performance, when they accepted goals that were moderately difficult to achieve and when they participated in control system design. It was also contended that self-control was most likely to be present in people who desired intrinsic rewards. In addition, it was often argued that participative management schemes allowed individuals to feel a greater degree of influence over events, to become more 'ego involved' and hence encouraged them to exercise self-control. However, the evidence on this point was not entirely unanimous.[15] Indeed, some uncertainty also existed with regard to the role of an individual's cognitions and attitudes in predisposing him or her to exercising self-control. It was argued that an individual believing in external control viewed events as being independent of his own actions and dependent upon fate, chance or other influences. While some studies cited by Szilagyi et al [1976] found that internal control believers were better informed about their work, believed more strongly in their control over job achievements and rewards, were more satisfied with their work, expected higher performance and rewards for themselves, responded to environmental contingencies more consistently, and performed better in incongruent, stressful situations than internal control believers, other studies cited by them revealed little significant difference in performance or satisfaction between each type.

By the close of the 1970s self-control was specified in a more sophisticated form than it had been prior to 1960 and had begun to be seriously considered as a substitute for authority-based, hierarchical forms of control in certain circumstances. Nevertheless its relationship to 'motivation to perform' was still not completely clear and indeed those factors which encouraged self-control still required further investigation.

Social Control

In the 1960s it continued to be apparent that in relation to control, people's opinions, beliefs and attitudes were conditioned and indeed validated for them by similar beliefs, opinions and attitudes of their reference groups [Cartwright, 1965].   Such group cognitions and behaviour could provide a powerful pressure upon an individual towards conformity.[16] The power of this social control was said to be a function of the degree of attractiveness or cohesiveness of the reference group.

Social control appeared to be a bilateral concept. In any social system control was not simply exercised in one direction, from the top of the hierarchy downwards, but could also be exercised upwards through an organisation.   Subordinates could also influence superiors, particularly through the agency of their reference groups. Furthermore, the important distinction was made that in whatever direction control was said to be exercised, it was in reality only effectively exerted to the extent that it was *either* perceived to be exerted by organisation members [Whisler et al, 1967; Kast and Rosenzweig, 1970].   Thus the classical notion of unilateral, 'top-down' control was supplanted.   An organisation member was no longer considered to *either* control *or* be controlled but could be in both situations at the same time.   This phenomenon was particularly evident in the context of social control.[17]

The social control concept arguably allowed this notion of mutual control to go a step further in spawning the idea of multidirectional control.   Control could be exercised vertically and horizontally (each in both directions), since every organisation member was controlled by impulses from many sources (not just the formal hierarchy of authority) and each had varying degrees of control over many other people in the organisation besides direct subordinates.   Reciprocal informal control could be exercised by groups and individuals in many directions, including control over formal superiors.   Groups were also seen to have the ability to exercise social control over other groups [Tannenbaum, 1964; Rhenman, 1968].

Social control thus remained as a well established component of the behavioural COM and had helped foster a recognition of the scope of influence open to informal means of control, the mutuality and multidirectional character of control, and the inadvisability of sole reliance upon the formal control mechanisms of the classical management COM.

Formal Control

After 1960, while still maintaining their earlier interest in dysfunctional impacts of hierarchical control, behaviouralists paid further attention to the manner in which hierarchical control could be exercised. This somewhat broader perspective provided sufficient justification for considering the concept to have extended itself in the 1960s and 1970s, so that it could more appropriately be termed formal control.

Positive and Negative Aspects

While hierarchical control had been treated by the classicists as involving direction, commands and 'top-down' supervision, formal control considered the manner of exercising superiors' control over subordinates in a less simplistic way. In the first instance persuasion was recognised as a means of control. It could be employed in formal channels of communication, meetings and personal interactions. Bases for successful persuasion included: access to communication channels, prestige, credibility, expertness or objectivity of the persuader, and skill in constructing messages [Cartwright, 1965].

However persuasion was also seen to be a technique for leading people to attitudes predetermined by the persuader to be in his own best interests. It was argued that persuasion was a form of control that had the appearance of being co-operative and voluntary but was in fact a surrogate for force [Berlo, 1975].[18]

What behaviouralists also came to recognise about formal 'top-down' control was that it could be exercised in either a positive or negative manner. Many organisational control systems were considered to have been structured or administered in a negative sense [Scanlan and Keys, 1979] by exerting pressure as a basis for enforcing compliance with externally imposed standards. Financial rewards, promotion prospects and praise were seen as positive sanctions but also had negative implications in the implied threat of their withholding or withdrawal should the required behaviour not eventuate. Conversely, negative sanctions such as reprimands, fines, demotion and suspension also had positive implications in their inference that such deprivations would be avoided or removed by subordinate adherence to required behaviour patterns [Fox, 1971].

Luthans and Kreitner [1975] went on to argue that positive reinforcement strengthened behaviour by the presentation of a desirable consequence, while negative reinforcement strengthened behaviour by the withdrawal of an aversive stimulus.[19] Thus a reward might or might not be perceived as such by a potential recipient. It only could be termed a positive reinforcer when it significantly increased subordinate response frequency. Punishment was not the equivalent of negative reinforcement, because it weakened behaviour while negative reinforcement strengthened behaviour through the termination of punishing consequences. Even when reinforcers were correctly identified it was argued that a universal reinforcer did not exist. The manipulation of punishing consequences as a means of negative-style control was observed to be popular amongst management.[20] However, punishment was held to be temporary in its effect, to generate emotional reactions and to induce subordinate inflexibility. A positive style of formal control was recommended as a preferable alternative.

The Role of Controls

Whereas the classical COM had emphasised the importance of controls in securing organisational control, behaviourally oriented management literature took care to make the point that an array of 'controls' did not automatically guarantee effective control:

> "In the grammar of social institutions the word 'controls' is not the plural of the word 'control'. Not only do more 'controls' not necessarily give more 'control' - the two words, in the context of social institutions have different meanings altogether."
>
> [Drucker, 1964:286]

'Controls' (i.e. control tools) were seen rather as a means and 'control' as an end. Thus while controls were designed "to constrain idiosyncratic behaviour and to promote conformity with organizational norms" [Livingstone, 1965:37], the possibility of their failure was recognised. Indeed it was argued that too many controls in an organisation might provide too little effective control [Powell, 1966].

What the behaviouralists came to realise was that controls tried to prescribe preferred behaviour, but often were interpreted as stipulating minimal behaviour patterns. Indeed, since discretionary or informal behaviour appeared to be an immutable part of organisational life, it was argued that organisational control would at times be rendered more effective by the substitution of informal co-operation for formal controls [Salaman, 1979]. Reeves and Woodward [1970] found that control could range from personal to mechanical. At the mechanical end of the control continuum the hierarchy of authority became less important (with line managers acting as supplements to the 'controls') and activities of directing and motivating became separated from those of detecting and correcting deviations. At the personal end of the control continuum such activities became 'inextricably interwoven'. Ouchi and Maguire [1975] reconsidered the distinction[21] between behaviour control (based on direct, personal surveillance) and output control (based on measurement of outputs) and found that output control served organisation-wide control needs, while behaviour control served control needs of the individual manager. Further, they observed that output control was often used in response to demands for simple, quantifiable controls, but that such controls were often used when least appropriate, in the face of complexity, interdependence and lack of expertise.

While 'controls' were not rejected outright by behaviouralists, they were no longer seen as a simplistic 'cure-all' as had been the tendency in earlier decades. Their dysfunctional consequences were increasingly being recognised.

Dysfunctional Effects

It became apparent to behaviouralists that the administration of controls could antagonise personnel at all levels of the organisational hierarchy and could induce their resistance or non-compliance as well as unreliable information [McGregor, 1967]. Underlying this were observed conflicts between accuracy and imprecision of control instruments, short-run manager rewards and long-run organisational health, individual needs and management pressure, workers' and supervisors' desire for control, and performance aspirations and 'tight' budgets [Livingstone, 1965]. Such conflicts could occur throughout the organisational control system [Bhattacharyya, 1969].

When controls were avoided or circumvented due to such conflicts, closer supervision and higher associated administrative costs were observed to result, as well as even more vigorous attempts by employees to circumvent controls. Controls were perceived as traps and pitfalls rather than as guidelines or checkpoints and tighter supervision implied that employees were 'at fault' or untrustworthy. This caused 'controlees' to focus attention on their own department even if at the expense of the whole organisation, to 'beat the control system' through burying or disowning problems, and to attempt to out-manoeuvre 'controllers' [McGregor, 1967; Dawson and Carew, 1969]. Formal control systems were thus observed to suffer considerable distortion and evasion [Fox, 1971; Dubin, 1974].[22] In addition to 'buck passing' blame for failures and outright resistance to control, subordinates were observed to be feeding invalid data [Lawler III, 1976] into the formal control system, 'fudging' the records in their own interests and attempting to disrupt any new control systems [Argyris, 1957]. Such resistance was interpreted by behaviouralists to stem from the employees' perception that any new formal control system could pose a threat to the satisfaction of their needs.

An Expanded Concept

The concept of formal control after 1960 had expanded considerably upon its predecessor, the hierarchical control concept. Researchers had recognised both the positive and negative manner in which such control could be exercised, had distinguished between 'controls' and 'control' more carefully than others before them, and described the possible dysfunctional results which careless application of formal control could produce. While behaviouralists were not overly keen to rely heavily upon a concept of formal control, they nevertheless laid the groundwork for its more intelligent employment.

Power-Based Control

After 1960 behaviouralists also began to see control in terms of a power-based concept of control. Unlike the classical management school which had tended to view power only in terms of the formal hierarchy of authority, the behaviouralists took a rather broader view. Power was not required to be vested solely in a formal position of authority, but was seen to be 'a capacity to control' available in varying degrees to *anyone* in the organisation.

> "A number of authors prefer to distinguish power from control by defining power essentially as the ability or capacity to exercise control, that is, as 'potential control'."
>
> [Tannenbaum, 1968:5]

> "In this paper, control is interpreted as any process in which a person or a group influences the behaviour of another person or group. This definition conforms closely to what other researchers mean by power and influence."
>
> [Ivancevich, 1970:428]

It was argued that power (and associated control) was desired by individuals partly because for many it was synonymous with prestige, status, social eminence or superiority [Tannenbaum, 1964].

Through power being defined in more general terms behaviouralists were able to recognise it as residing in informal[23] as well as formal groups within an organisation. The types of power identified as providing the force to control others and to obtain their compliance [Tosi and Carroll, 1976; Hodgetts, 1979] were classified as coercive, persuasive, reward, legitimate, referent, identitive and expert power[24] [French and Raven, 1960; Gilman, 1962; Etzioni, 1964, 1965; Tosi and Carroll, 1976]. Through these various bases attempts could be made for instance to physically control organisational members, to persuade them, to control their gains and losses, to control the information available to them, to influence their attitudes and to manipulate their social or physical environment. This predisposition was neatly summarised by Cartwright [1965:7]:

> "Whatever the ultimate reason for wanting power, a person may exercise influence in order to augment his resources and thereby strengthen his base of power; he uses power to acquire power."

The power to control, according to the behaviouralists, did not reside exclusively in the official positions of authority in the organisational hierarchy. For instance it was pointed out that when a subordinate was formally encouraged by superiors to improve his performance, normative power was being used as the basis for control, but that when that individual was influenced or controlled through the medium of his peer group, normative-social power was being used as the basis for control [Hodgetts, 1979]. This could be reinterpreted as superiors using legitimate power to pursue formal control over the individual and colleagues in his workgroup using identitive power to pursue control over him.

The distribution of power to control events through the organisation was characterised by some behaviouralists in terms of the 'control or influence pie'.[25] One of the first to argue in this manner was Likert [1967] who claimed that high producing managers had been observed to increase the size of their 'influence pie' through the leadership methods they employed. Better leaders with cohesive groups, efficient

communication and the capacity to exert upward influence, gave
subordinates and their managers more influence and therefore increased
the total amount of control in the organisation. Thus it was argued that
the organisational control 'pie' was not fixed in quantity, but could be
increased or decreased in total and that the increase in control gained
by one party would not necessarily be at the expense of reducing the
control exercised by another party [Livingstone, 1965].

The most notable proponent of this view of the distribution of power
to control was Tannenbaum [1964, 1968]. According to him the total
amount of control in an organisation could increase, and the participants
could each acquire "a share of this augmented power". This could take
the form of increased exchanges of resources in return for compliance,
including employees more fully in the organisation or promoting greater
orderliness within the organisation. A key vehicle for inducing these
sorts of expansion in total control was said to be employee participation
in decision-making. This might involve the exercising of more mutual
than unilateral control as well as the exercising of social control by
cohesive groups.[26] The notion of the distribution of power to control
and the variability of total control appeared to be confirmed by
empirical studies of amount of organisational control in relation to
organisational effectiveness and employee attitudes and performance
[Smith and Tannenbaum, 1972; McMahon and Perritt, 1973; Todd, 1977;
Smith, 1978]. High amounts of total control were linked to better
performance ratings, interunit co-operation, cost reduction, improved
communication and accomplishment of organisational objectives.

Power-based control provided behaviouralists with the vehicle for
breaking away from the classicists' restrictive assumption that the power
to control was solely vested in and confined to official positions in the
organisation's hierarchy of authority. Through a more detailed
consideration of the nature and distribution of power, it allowed them to
conceive of a far broader base of potential control in organisations than
had previously been thought possible.

Expectancy Control

Beginning in the 1960s expectancy theory expounded the view that the degree of an individual's motivation to perform was a function of:

1. The likelihood of his achieving the required level of performance.

2. The likelihood that required performance will generate the promised rewards.

3. The degree to which he values the extrinsic or intrinsic rewards offered.

[Tosi and Carroll, 1976; Hodgetts, 1979; Scanlan and Keys, 1979]

In 1964 Victor Vroom outlined the basic parameters of expectancy theory as:

$$Force = \Sigma \text{ Valence } x \text{ Expectancy}$$

Force was synonymous with motivation to perform, valence referred to a person's (strength of) orientation towards a particular outcome, and expectancy described the probability which the person attached to his actions producing the planned outcome [Hodgetts, 1979; Scanlan and Keys, 1979].

Vroom's theory of expectancy was subsequently expanded by Porter and Lawler [1968] who argued that performance resulted in rewards, which if considered by the individual concerned to be just and equitable, would cause high levels of employee satisfaction. This sense of satisfaction influenced the linkage between effort and reward. Thus instead of adopting the commonly held management assumption that worker satisfaction led to better performance, Porter and Lawler argued the reverse:

Rewards in this instance could be intrinsic (such as personal feelings of accomplishment) or extrinsic (an externally generated payoff, such as a bonus). This expectancy theory was somewhat more complex and comprehensive than Vroom's, as a simplified version in Figure 5.2 shows:

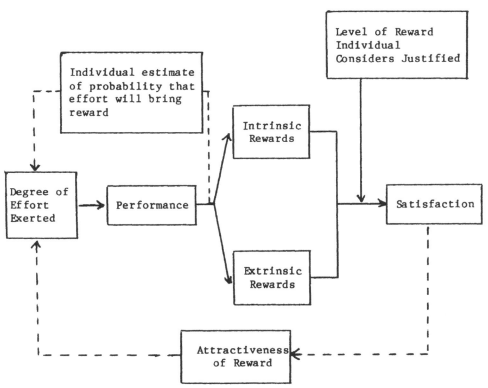

**Figure 5.2: A Basic Version of Porter and Lawler's
Expectancy Theory**

While these two theories were quite highly regarded by behaviouralists, the controversy over the direction of linkage between performance and satisfaction continued throughout the 1970s [Duncan, 1975; Hodgetts, 1979].

Some behaviouralists considered the implications of expectancy theory for organisational control. Since expectancy theory incorporated an individual's perception of the probability of his effort yielding required performance and the probability of that performance yielding desired rewards, the higher those probabilities, the greater his motivation to perform. Thus it was argued that the control system designer must ensure that control maximises these expectancies for personnel. The object of control became that of strengthening the linkages between effort, performance and rewards[27] [Ansari, 1977]. Turcotte [1974] studied two large government agencies differing in effectiveness, relating the difference to their observed characteristics. He found that sustained high motivation and performance occurred when executive and legislative branches held precise performance expectations for the agency, these expectations were demanding, widely understood and frequently caused output targets to be adjusted, and when the formal control system emphasised and helped achieve high output.

Kopelman [1976] studied the interrelationships between organisational control system responsiveness, expectancy theory and work motivation across three organisations, all claiming to reward employees on the basis of merit. In summary he found that subjective and objective indicators of control system responsiveness appeared to converge, significant inter-organisational differences in motivation appeared between the three companies and were positively related to differences in organisational control system responsiveness which itself appeared to affect job performance indirectly through intervening variables such as expectancy theory constructs. Machin [1973] constructed expectations-based programmes for measuring the effectiveness of an organisation's management control systems which he argued was a function of the accuracy with which appropriate actual expectations were achieved. The extent of mismatch between mutual expectations which parties held of each other's performance was conceived as a simple measure of that effectiveness. This approach was verified by subsequent application to 35 organisations [Machin, 1979].

The concept of expectancy control appears to have involved the design of an organisational control system which was responsive to and attempted to maximise employees' expectations, as well as attempting to match the expectations of different groups in the organisation. This required clearly defined, demanding and uniform (but flexible) expectations for all persons involved.

The Advancing Model

From the concepts of control discussed by behaviouralists in the 1960s and 1970s, a model can be constructed that has developed quite considerably from its pre-1960 beginnings. The pre-1960 model recognised situational (S_i) and cognitive (C_o) variables as affecting self-control (S_e), social control (S_o) and hierarchical control (H), which in turn combined to influence motivation. This model had differed from classical and structural models in identifying motivation as a focus. By the close of the 1970s, the concept of self-control (S_e) had attained a decidedly more sophisticated specification, social control (S_o) had been elaborated, the concept of hierarchical control (H) had been broadened to reappear as formal control (F), and the concepts of power-based control (P) and expectancy control (E_x) had been added. Power-based control brought with it a new acknowledgement of the wide distribution of power to control throughout the organisation. Expectancy control had attempted to deal more clearly with the effort-performance-reward link, and while not solving it, incorporated individual perceptions and expectations more directly into the behavioural COM.

A revised (post-1960) behavioural COM has therefore been constructed and is outlined in Figure 5.3. It retained motivation to perform (M_p) as its focal point. Situational (S_i) and cognitive variables (C_o) influenced the new expectancy control concept (E_x) as well as the concepts of self-control (S_e), social control (S_o), and formal control (F).

While expectancy control was thought to act directly upon motivation to perform, self-control, social control and formal control could be conceived as influencing individual and group motivation to perform through the agency of the more recently-recognised power-based control

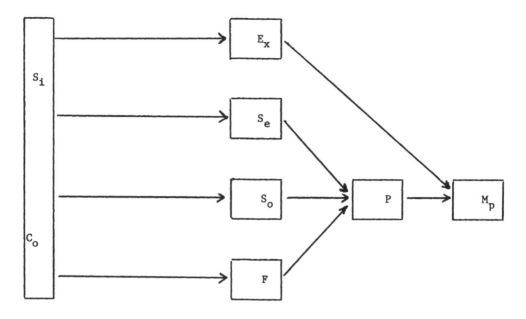

where: S_i = situational variables C_o = cognitive variables

S_e = self-control S_o = social control

F = formal control   P = power-based control

E_x = expectancy control M_p = motivation to perform

Figure 5.3:   The Advancing Behavioural Model of Control

(P).   The argument for power-based control acting as the newly emerged
intervening concept (between self, social, formal control and motivation
to perform) can be made out on the following basis.   Self-control was
recognised as being activated through an individual's ultimate power to
control his or her own activities.   Social control was seen to be
activated, for instance, through the use of social or workgroup norms and
sanctions which conferred upon group members the power to control each
other's activities.   Formal control was deemed to be activated through
officially conferred (largely by higher management) power-to-control.
Expectancy control, on the other hand, was thought to act directly upon
motivation to perform through the expectations of outcomes, associated
penalties or rewards and the values placed upon each.   Overall, by the

close of the 1970s, the behavioural COM was still developing, but had made considerable advances in its attempt to incorporate the complex array of human behaviour patterns in its design.

Socio-Economic Impetus Maintained

This continuity of interest in a behavioural COM can be attributed to the impetus provided by continued social and economic change. Technology grew in sophistication and complexity, best epitomised by the advent of the 'space-age'. Such technological research spilled over into many areas of industry, particularly through automation and computerisation, bringing new types of employees into organisations and affecting their structure. Technological change also affected social relations among workers and their types of work. Electronic data processing required improved co-orindation of work and allowed less autonomy to some work groups. While the advent of scientific management had introduced a preoccupation with the mechanics of organisational operations to the virtual exclusion of the human element, the dramatic advances in technology of the 1960s and 1970s brought with them an equal concern for their impact upon employees and their work [Kast and Rosenzweig, 1970; Wren, 1979].

The post-1960 development of the behavioural COM reflected a relatively democratic stance, with formal control being subject to detailed critiques, with the concepts of self- and social control being expanded and consolidated, and with the potential for power-based control being accorded to all levels of employee in the organisation. These developments reflected changing social attitudes. In both business and society, experiment, innovation and an "almost neurotic pursuit of novelties" had become fashionable [Youngson, 1976:173]. The corporation became the new predominant social institution, capable of promoting quite radical changes in society. Motor vehicles, television and automation became commonplace [Kast and Rosenzweig, 1970] and changed employee roles, perceptions and expectations.

The civil rights movement and student activism promoted a questioning of social institutions and values, a revival of interest in philosophy and ethics, a change in attitude to authority, and an upsurge of interest in 'bottom-up, power-equalizing humanism' [Wren, 1979:478]. Students and young employed began to place less emphasis upon security and promotion, and more emphasis upon autonomy and interesting work. The rights of the individual and of disadvantaged groups received particular attention with calls for power equalisation programmes to alleviate poverty, pollution control, unemployment reduction, employment of minority groups and so on [Kast and Rosenzweig, 1970; Tosi and Carroll, 1976]. The democratic conception of the behavioural COM, with its emphasis on self-control, social control, and the distribution of power-based control, therefore reflected prevailing social attitudes.

Corporate profit was no longer considered to be the sole measure of organisational performance, business was seen to operate not only in an economic environment but also in a social one, and further measures of an organisation's social effectiveness were sought [Tosi and Carroll, 1976; Youngson, 1976; Wren, 1979]. That the pre-1960 concept of hierarchical control should be broadened and subjected to more critical appraisal and that 'power-to-control' should be accorded to all types of formal and informal groups in the organisation appears to have been a logical outgrowth of the broadening of managements' perspectives. Such developments also reflected the changing composition and nature of the labour force. Changing technology had required the organisational employment of professionals such as engineers and scientists with their own professional allegiances and expectations, and requiring some altered management and leadership approaches. For the existing workforce, work organisation had become an important substitute for traditional forms of human organisation common in previous social periods [Kast and Rosenzweig, 1970; Peaker, 1974; Wren, 1979].

Larger disposable incomes had also allowed more students to undertake secondary and tertiary level studies so that organisations in the 1960s and 1970s were facing a workforce of significantly improved education levels.[28] This prompted a rise in the workforce's expectations of job conditions as well as aspiration levels for personal autonomy, work satisfaction and participation in decision-making. All this was accompanied by reduced working hours, increased leisure time, and more paid vacations. Increasing educational levels rendered social divisions less clear, social pressure induced organisations to employ more workers from disadvantaged and minority groups, and racial and educational barriers were increasingly surmounted in both business and society. As a result social mobility increased at a significant rate and opportunities for merit-based advancement in organisations were much more readily available [Robertson, 1964; Tuttle and Perry, 1970; Roebuck, 1973; Tosi and Carroll, 1976].

The attention paid to concepts of self-control, social control, power-based control and expectancy control, appears hardly surprising given the environment which spawned it. Organisations experienced major shifts in technology, social attitudes, workforce composition and expectations, objectives and distributions of power. The behavioural COM provided a clear presentation of this mood of change.

THE SYSTEMS CONTROL MODEL APPEARS

The early beginnings of systems theory was characterised by the pioneering work of Ludwig von Bertalanffy [1950, 1952, 1968, 1972] a theoretical biologist, who first began articulating the General System Theory in the 1930s. It was advanced as a general model of common characteristics of entities integrating knowledge from physical, biological and social disciplines. From this dynamic, multi-disciplinary synthesis, whole systems and their interrelatedness with other systems and subsystems could be studied. Thus social organisations came to be viewed as open systems, open to external environmental influences as well as internal factors, receiving inputs and transforming them into outputs, engaged in a process of continuous adjustment to environmental changes and regulating their activities with a view to achieving a state of dynamic equilibrium [Bowey, 1976; Wren, 1979; Parker, 1980].

While some have attributed a systems orientation to the writings of Barnard [1938] and Selznick [1948], the application of systems theory to the study of organisations did not begin until the 1950s when Homans [1950] and Parsons [1951] studied social groups, organisation structure and processes using a systems approach. At the same time, Trist and Bamforth [1951] initiated the Tavistock Institute's studies of the relationships between technical and psychosocial systems in the organisation. The 1960s however was the period during which the systems school of organisational study and management thought truly flourished. Johnson, Kast and Rosenzweig [1963, 1967] integrated the general systems theory approach with the process approach to management, Brown and Jaques [1965] identified several social systems within the organisation, Etzioni examined organisations in terms of social systems [Silverman, 1970], and an open systems perspective of organisations was advocated by Katz and Kahn [1966] and Miller and Rice [1967].

From the open systems perspective also emerged the so-called socio-technical systems theorists who considered that in reacting with its environment, the organisation operated as a socio-technical system integrating the human social system and technological systems. This approach was represented by Burns and Stalker's [1961] identification of mechanistic and organic organisational systems, and Emery and Trist's [1960], Woodward's [1958, 1965] and Lawrence and Lorsch's [1967] studies of the relationships between technology and organisation. Decision theorists headed by Cyert [1963], March [1965] and Simon [1957, 1964] also worked in the systems theory tradition and conceived the organisation as encompassing a complex information-processing and decision-making system.

Introducing Control from a Systems Orientation

Systems theory as applied to organisations stressed the importance of studying the organisation as a whole rather than treating it as an arrangement of independent parts. Instead the parts were seen to be interrelated and susceptible to integration. Indeed each system would be factored into a hierarchy of less complex subsystems with interaction occurring between these subsystems. Such systems were defined as open systems where the environment influenced the acitivities of organisations which in turn themselves affected the environment, and where the attainment of organisational equilibrium was really a process of balancing internal and external forces at work. Thus control, from a systems viewpoint, would shift from a static, functional or structural emphasis, to a dynamic focus upon the interaction between activities and people [Emery, 1969; Silverman, 1970; Wren, 1979].

Control was no longer confined to the identification and correction of variations from higher management plans and instructions but was being recognised as an organisation or system-wide concept, inherent in interlocking subsystems throughout the organisation. Nor was it confined to a top management prerogative but was intrinsic to tasks and functions at all levels of the organisational hierarchy [Whisler et al, 1967]. In addition control was seen as contributing to the maintenance of the organisational system's equilibrium:

> "Control is used to regulate the organization and maintain a state of equilibrium which is dynamic (subjective) and sensitive to changes both within as well as outside the 'company walls'."
>
> [Strong and Smith, 1968:3-4]

Control was conceived as a dynamic mechanism for coping with change and as being continually exercised by *all* components (including individual members) of the organisation. It provided the organisational system with information, decision rules and means of corrective action [Strong and Smith, 1968] largely through mechanisms such as the 'information feedback control loop' [McGregor, 1967:116-117]. Indeed control itself was seen as a system encompassing numerous interlocking subsystems [Litterer, 1965]. While a few writers had begun to consider this approach to the study of control in the late 1950s [Koontz, 1958; Vickers, 1958], it was not until the 1960s that systems writing on control emerged in the management literature to a marked extent.

The Control Cycle

Control was treated in the systems-oriented management literature as a cybernetic system which while primarily applied to mechanistic engineering problems, was also seen as applying to social systems [Haberstroh, 1969; Kast and Rosenzweig, 1979]. Communication and control were held to occur in physical, biological and social systems such that all systems exercised self-control through the feedback of information which revealed where results fell short of goals and initiated corrective action to restore equilibrium. The equilibrium-seeking characteristic of the control cycle was derived from the general systems theory characteristic of homeostasis, of which the ability of the human body to self-regulate the temperature of blood was an oft-cited example [Litterer, 1973]. It was emphasised however, that the so-called equilibrium which a control cycle continually attempted to reach was not necessarily a fixed point but constituted a series of possible balance points along a continuum, since organisations were dynamic rather than static and unchanging [Huse and Bowditch, 1973].

Quite a number of formulations of the specific nature of the organisational control cycle appeared in systems theory writing. The most often quoted cycle was the thermostat-type control cycle [Litterer, 1965; Koontz and O'Donnell, 1976]. When house temperature dropped below a predetermined minimum the thermostat (sensor) detected it, closed an electrical circuit, turned on the furnace, heated the house and increased house temperature. When the predetermined maximum temperature was attained, the thermostat detected it (discriminator) and opened the circuit, thus stopping the furnace (decision-maker) and reducing house temperature. In organisational terms this control cycle was recast for example as in Figure 5.4. It began with the setting of organisational objectives and ended with their attainment, while in the interim, performance standards were to be developed, actual and standard performance compared, and unacceptable variations from standard corrected. This control cycle was not simply an ordered path of sequential steps but involved overlapping activities, back and forth movement along cycle paths and different parts of the cycle at times being performed simultaneously [Stong and Smith, 1968; Mockler, 1972].

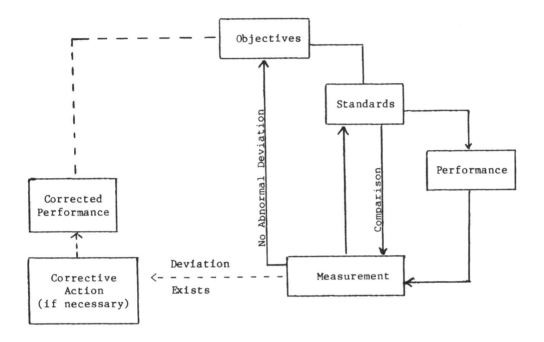

Figure 5.4: The Management Control Cycle

[Mockler, 1972:21]

Modifications to the management control cycle included corrections to plans as well as corrections of actual performance as shown in Figure 5.5.[29]

Further modifications included the interface between long- and short-range planning and associated control factors [Lorange and Scott Morton, 1974]. These took the form of the control variable identification process, the short-term direction setting process and the short-term plan accomplishment tracking process. These components were linked not only to each other but also to the long-range planning process in assessing last year's performance and determining next year's plan.

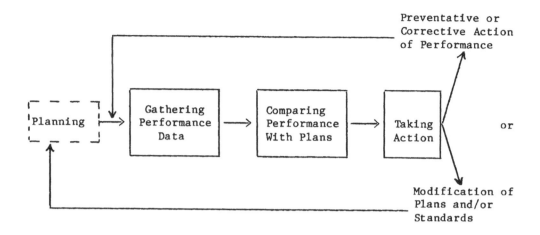

Figure 5.5: A Modified Management Control Cycle

[Fleming, 1972:57]

The control cycle was conceived as being either closed or open
[Litterer, 1973:532-533].   Figure 5.4 and 5.5 were classified as closed
control loops.   In these cases current performance provided information
that was used to control future performance.   The alternative, an open
control loop, allowed activities to change in accordance with a plan or
programme but provided no automatic mechanism for evaluating current
performance or modifying future performance.   Instead, corrective input
came from outside the loop rather than from within [Scanlan and Keys,
1979] (as in the case of the sensor, discriminator and decision-maker of
the closed loop).   However it was recognised that in the case of the
closed loop, its critical component, feedback, could either reduce or
aggravate the error or variance from standard [O'Shaughnessy, 1966].   The
closed and open control loops are represented in Figures 5.6 and 5.7.
The control cycle was even more complex than just being either open or
closed.   Organisations were in addition viewed as containing a
progression of standards and control loops, or in fact, control loops
within control loops [Litterer, 1973].

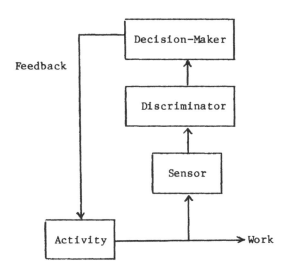
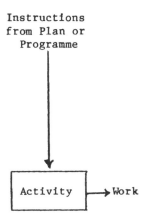

Figure 5.6: A Closed Control Loop
          [Litterer, 1973:533]

Figure 5.7: An Open Control Loop
          [Litterer, 1973:533]

Any discussion of the cybernetic control cycle concept as developed in the management-systems literature of the 1960s and 1970s would not be complete without reference to the significant work of Eilon [1971]. He concentrated upon the controller's relationship with the control system and with other controllers and examined control as a closed loop system in which the controller was a decision-maker whose task was to analyse information transmitted to him and to make a decision to affect the future state of the control system in some specific way. Using matrix analysis he concluded that a correspondence between a system and its controllers was an essential feature of the control function.[30] Having conceived the manager as a controller employing a closed loop control system, Eilon treated the communication of control information between controllers as central to the control process, being a 'vehicle of control' and linked to the manager's decision-making role.

Some management writers criticised the control cycle concept because of the mechanistic, impersonal 'human engineering' approach to control which it involved. Eilon's approach, seen in this light, was more

concerned with the mechanical workings of control systems than the
underlying complexities of behavioural interactions and environmental
influences [Phillips, 1972; Thayer, 1972]. In particular the mechanistic
nature of the feedback loop [Fleming, 1972] was not considered by some
writers to be identical to the transfer functions of individual decision-
makers in a man-machine system. The engineering treatment of transfers
in the control cycle centred upon efficient servomechanisms for keeping
key variables "in control" [Livingstone, 1965:38]. Similarly, the
biologically-based systems theory dealt with predictable outcomes of
interactions between cells and between organisms [Silverman, 1970].
Management control systems were seen to differ from such certainty of
outcomes due to the complexity of human behaviour and due to deficiencies
in available methods of financial performance measurement.

Open and Closed Control Systems

From the closed systems perspective the organisation was treated as
a self-contained entity disregarding environmental factors such as social
custom, political events and technological change. For instance, the
human relations theorists adopted a closed systems approach by
concentrating their attention on the workgroup and ignoring technology.
The closed systems view of organisations paid attention to internal
variables such as supervision, the reward system and internal structures
designed to maximise internal efficiency rather than being concerned
about adaptation to change [Silverman, 1970; Duncan, 1975]. The
alternative open systems view of the organisation, envisaged it as
adapting to its environment by continually modifying its internal
structure and processes through acceptance of inputs from the environment
(such as raw materials, labour and information), operation on those
inputs, and production outputs to be distributed back into the
environment which would change and provide further inputs to the
organisation. Organisational survival depended on this continual inflow,
transformation and outflow. In this scheme of thing's adaptability to
uncertainty and change became equally as important as efficiency
[Silverman, 1970; Duncan, 1975; Kast and Rosenzweig, 1979].

Many systems writers recognised that the distinction between open and closed systems might often be less than 'clear-cut' and that to a degree systems could be closed off from some environmental factors by their boundaries. For purposes of studying organisations it was admitted that a partially-open systems view could allow attention to be given first to an organisation's internal variables, introducing external variables as constraints at a later stage of study [Silverman, 1970; Kast and Rosenzweig, 1979].

Litterer [1965] pointed out that control systems such as production-control and budgets were sometimes designed as closed systems on the assumption that no external influences had to be considered. The open system concept of control, however, recognised the impact of external influences and recognised that an organisation's dynamic environment contained forces that were beyond management's scope of control [Hodgetts, 1979]. With respect to those variables within an organisation's power to control, it was emphasised that the organisational system did not simply exist within its environment but by means of it. Thus control could in part be derived from the organisation's relating to and integrating with its environment. The manipulation of variables within management's scope of control must, it was said, be directed towards adaptation to environment with a view to organisational survival [Lowe and McInnes, 1971].

In the open systems concept of control, adaptation was required as a response to the internal and external environment and so-called 'maintenance' was required to moderate the rate of organisational change, thus keeping the organisational system in balance [Hodgetts, 1979]. This control concept therefore included maintenance and managerial subsystems.[31] The maintenance subsystem was directed towards eliminating problems in operating other subsystems and monitoring their day to day workings (via performance standards). Maintenance activities included training, socialisation, indoctrination, supervision, performance assessment and reward mechanisms. The mangerial subsystem was seen as primarily engaged in determining general policy and strategy for organisational interaction with environment with a view to ensuring long

term organisational survival.   Internal subsystem conflict resolution
also came within its scope of responsibility [Tosi and Carroll, 1976]

One further dimension of the open systems control concept deserving
mention related to the organisation's boundary spanning subsystems, which
carry out environmental transactions including the securing of input and
disposing of output.   Boundary exchanges between the organisational
system and the environmental supra-system was seen as a critical factor
in the pursuit of survival and efficiency [Silverman, 1970].   As such,
boundary controls were said to be essential for protecting the conversion
process from excessive environmental requirements and sought to allow
transactions between the organisational system and its environment that
were essential to the performance of its tasks [Miller and Rice, 1967].

Control Timing Systems

Historically, classical and structural writers had discussed control
mainly in terms of ex post control.   This involved the identification of
operating results, evaluating results to determine whether actual
performance matched objectives or standards, and correcting relevant
behaviour for future situations.   It was an 'after-the-event' view of
control [Litterer, 1965; Kast and Rosenzweig, 1979].

On the other hand, systems theorists conceived of ex ante control
(or pre-control) where the controlling effort occurred prior to the
activity to which it was directed and was concerned with avoiding or
preventing undesired events or results from occurring.   Ex ante control
encompassed the development of plans, policies, rules and procedures as
well as uniform value systems among organisation members [Luthans, 1977;
Kast and Rosenzweig, 1979].   It was argued that while A's influence upon
B might depend upon the resources that A could marshall, such influence
or control could be exercised prior to any transmission of resources
through the promise to reward B or through the threat to punish B
[Cartwright, 1965].   Information too, was defined as being 'before-the-
fact' or 'after-the-fact'.   End result measurements provided 'after-the-

fact' information which was of limited predictive value, while periodic measurement of causal and intervening variables could provide 'before-the-fact' information, allowing early adjustments of strategies and reducing the need for emergency action [Likert, 1967].

An extension of the ex ante notion of control took place in the form of so-called feedforward control which allowed for preventive control action in preference to corrective control action. This form of control was to be activated at the time of initial input into the system and was then to be operated continuously so that preventive action could be taken before a significant difference between planned and actual performance occurred. Means of achieving this included using the latest available information to produce frequently revised forecasts and adjusting the plans of action accordingly, examining the interaction of inputs into a system and adjusting them before output was produced, and considering the factors which influenced system inputs themselves. While it was recognised that feedforward control really still involved the process of feedback, the information feedback was said to occur at the input point of the system so that corrections could be made before output would be affected. Nevertheless, consistent with the open systems concept of control, this approach to control acknowledged that disturbances to the system outside the scope of specified inputs could upset the system and affect output and that management must therefore be watchful for unanticipated or unprogrammed input variables [Ishikawa and Smith, 1973-74; Koontz and O'Donnell, 1976; Luthans, 1977].

A further classification of the time-based concept of control was entitled real-time (or current) control. This involved the adjustment of performance currently taking place in order to achieve the desired objective or standard. On one hand it was argued that this was a highly desirable form of control for maintaining dynamic equilibrium in an organisation. Measurements, comparisons and adjustments could be made as the system continued to function and before any major deviations of actual performance from standard occurred. In this way real-time information could facilitate real-time control. On the other hand it was argued that the feedback cycle of performance management, comparison with standard, identification of deviations, analysis and correction of causes were usually time-consuming operations. Thus some doubt was cast upon the feasibility of securing real-time control in many situations [Litterer, 1965; Koontz and O'Donnell, 1976; Kast and Rosenzweig, 1979].

Systems theorists therefore generated a time-based concept of control which included ex ante, ex post and real-time control. It was through their specification of ex ante control and the associated idea of feed-forward control however, that systems theorists advanced furthest relative to their classical and structural predecessors.

Contingent Control

Contingency theorists argued that there was no one best way to manage or structure an organisation but searched for functional relationships between situational elements and performance, so that the contingency notion was one of 'if' this situation pertains 'then' take the following action [Luthans, 1977; Wren, 1979].

> "The contingency view seeks to understand the inter-relationships within and among subsystems as well as between the organization and its environment and to define patterns of relationships or configurations of variables. It emphasizes the multivariate nature of organizations and attempts to understand how organizations operate under varying conditions and in specific circumstances. Contingency views are ultimately directed toward suggesting organizational designs and managerial actions most appropriate for specific situations."

> [Kast and Rosenzweig, 1973:313]

Thus contingency theorists argued that an organisation's structure and management patterns are contingent upon and must be tailored to its tasks and environment. Organisations that faced more stable, certain environments could be less differentiated (i.e. adopt less segmentation in organisational subunits), could achieve integration (i.e. co-ordination for unity of effort) through more formal means, and could operate in a more centralised manner. Organisations facing unstable, uncertain environments would need to seek integration through more flexible means and would probably require a more decentralised structure (i.e. a differentiated firm to match a differentiated environment) [Wren, 1979].

In summary contingency studies revealed that:

1. Differences in organisation of subunits reflected their adaptation to different environments.

2. The more stable and certain the environment, the more bureaucratic the departmental organisation.

3. A high degree of organisational differentiation required a greater amount of integration.

4. The relative effectiveness of a manufacturing organisation depended on the extent to which it achieved the required degree of differentiation.

5. Appropriate organisational structure depended upon the task, the environment, interpersonal relationships and other factors.

[Scanlan and Keys, 1979]

The contingency approach to organisations had its foundations in the socio-technical systems approach which regarded organisations not as either a social system or a technical system, but as a socio-technical system concerned to structure and integrate human activities around various technologies. The technologies affected the inputs and outputs of the organisation, while the social system determined the effectiveness of technology utilisation [Kast and Rosenzweig, 1973]. The leading researchers in the socio-technical and contingency approaches to organisational study were Burns and Stalker [1961], Woodward [1965], Miller and Rice [1967], Trist [Trist and Bamforth, 1969; Emery and Trist, 1969] and Lawrence and Lorsch [1969]. These writers have been classified at various times as being part of both the socio-technical systems and contingency schools of thought.[32] Their common roots, however, lay in the open systems approach to organisations, especially as many of them were affiliated with the Tavistock Institute of Human Relations in London which was a strong proponent of the open systems approach. the argument that organisations, as open systems, were intimately related to their environment remained a common theme in open systems, socio-technical and contingency theory writing. Thus contingency theory had evolved as a gradual modification within systems thinking [Kast and Rosenzweig, 1970, 1973; Bowey, 1976].

In the eyes of the contingency theorists no one optimal technical solution was available for the problems of organisation and control system design. Due to the mutual influences of technology, behaviour, structure and environment, a wide range of possible solutions existed [Warmington, 1974]. Thus in formulating their concept of control, contingency theorists treated information, people and technology as *both* independent and dependent variables [Ansari, 1977] with control as existing along a continuum ranging from personal to mechanical and from unitary to fragmented [Reeves and Woodward, 1970]. The more control became mechanical the more line managers and supervisors would become adjusters and supplementers of the control process with mechanisms for correction being built in at the planning stage. When control became more personal, it was argued that performance mechanisms (such as motivating and directing activities) and adjustment mechanisms (such as detecting and correcting deviations from standard) became almost indistinguishable from each other (whereas they became rather more separate with mechanical control). Unitary control involved an organisation combining different departmental standards, performance and adjustment mechanisms into a single integrated system of managerial control whereas when control was fragmented, departmental standards were set independently and not related to each other.

How did contingency theorists' view of the technological environment affect their concept of control? The degree of personal control exercised through direct supervision could be influenced by the production technology employed[33] [Silverman, 1970] with less predictable work being less susceptible to close supervisory control [Bell, 1969]. In unit and batch production, the work and its results were less predictable and more difficult to control than continous flow production where factors likely to affect production could more easily be taken into account [Charns, 1972].   On the other hand, mass production, when employing largely unskilled workers, was held to require specialsiation, routinisation and tight control of work [Kast and Rosenzweig, 1979].

The   leading   contribution   to   the   discussion   of   technological environment   and   its   relationship   to   control   was   made   by   Woodward [1965].   She found that in unit production firms, control remained with skilled craftsmen, whereas in mass production organisations, control over work   passed   from   operators   to   the   technostructure   and   became   more formalised and impersonal.   In mass production organisations management became obsessed with control by close supervision at all levels of the organisation.   Automation however, drastically reduced the number of unskilled operators so that rules, regulations and standards were built into machines and the need for control by direct supervision disappeared, leaving   professional   system   designers   controlling   their   own   work [Mintzberg, 1979].

While Woodward's 1965 study had concluded that technology influenced behaviour in organisations, a review of that work [Reeves and Woodward, 1970] suggested that control might be an intervening variable between technology and industrial behaviour.   Originally, the South Essex study showed   that   in   respect   of   some   organisational   characteristics,   unit production firms resembled process firms, while in others, they were at opposite ends of the scales being used.   A re-analysis in Table 5.1 suggested   that   similarities   between   the   two   types   of   firm   could   be attributed   to   the   predominance   of   unitary   control   in   both   and   that differences   arose   from   personal   versus   impersonal   control predominating.   Further it was noted that mass production firms using predominantly personal control approximated the organisation structure of unit production firms while mass production firms with predominantly impersonal control approximated the structure of process production firms.   Thus Reeves and Woodward suspected that the control system might be   the   underlying   variable   linking   organisational   behaviour   with technology.   Indeed management processes were suspected of being a function   not   so   much   of   technology   as   of   the   control   system   in operation. The control system itself was seen to depend upon both technology and social and economic factors [Charns, 1972].

		CONTROL SYSTEM			
		Unitary/ Personal (%)	Fragmented/ Personal (%)	Fragmented/ Impersonal (%)	Unitary/ Impersonal (%)
FIRM	Unit and Small Batch Production	75	25	–	–
TYPE	Large Batch and Mass Production	15	35	40	10
	Process Production	–	–	5	95

Table 5.1: Control Processes and Technology

A further exploration of control was undertaken by contingency theorists on the basis of Burns and Stalker's classification of mechanistic and organic organisations[34] [Burns and Stalker, 1961; Kast and Rosenzweig, 1973; Dessler, 1977] as summarised in Table 5.2. Mechanistic organisations, with their relatively routine and predictable operations were seen as commonly having a narrow span of control whereas organic organisations with their more ambiguous and unpredictable environment exhibited wider spans of control.

In the mechanistic organisation control was seen to operate through a command-based hierarchy with participants' work being externally controlled, structured and more closely supervised. In the organic organisation control assumed the shape of a flexible network dispersed throughout all areas of the organisation, reciprocal by nature and freely self-imposed by relatively autonomous participants. The mechanistic

Control Characteristic	Mechanistic Organisational System	Organic Organisational System
Span of control	Narrow	Wide
Supervision	Close	General
Locus of Control	Hierarchical/ Externally Imposed	Network/Self-Imposed
Control of Task Environment	High Degree	Low Degree
Time Horizon	Short Term	Long Term
Degree of Personality and Rule and Regulation Control	Impersonal/High Degree	Personal/Low Degree

Table 5.2: Control in Mechanistic and Organic Organisations

organisation was characterised by a high degree of control over its task environment and exercised control with a short time horizon. The organic organisation had a low degree of control over its task environment and exercised control with a longer time horizon. Finally, mechanistic organisations were observed to employ impersonal means of control, resorting more to procedures, rules and regulations than organic organisations which relied on few rules and procedures (usually unwritten and informal) but rather exercised control through interpersonal contacts [Kast and Rosenzweig, 1973, 1979; Hodgetts, 1979].

The contingency theorists had therefore begun to develop a dynamic, multidimensional control concept which could be classified by certain key characteristics (e.g. unitary or fragmented, personal or impersonal) and according to the type of organisation in which it operated (i.e. mechanistic or organic). Furthermore, control had tentatively been identified as an intervening variable between technology and organisation structure.

An Emerging Model

The systems theory school identified control not as something externally imposed upon an organisation but as a natural outcome of interlocking systems and their interaction with one another [Mantell, 1973]. Control, in an organisation-wide sense, was seen as intrinsic to organisational tasks and functions and a means of negating the entropic tendency of the organisational system [Stokes, 1968; Tannenbaum, 1968]. Managers and control system designers were called upon to focus (largely from a man-machine system perspective) upon sources of possible disturbance to the system not simply in order to correct past performance failures but to improve the organisation's reaction and adaptation to change [Roberts, 1969; Mantell, 1973; Ansari, 1977].

The systems approach was not without its critics and problems. Control systems could have their effectiveness jeopardised by incomplete design, time-lags in feedback of information, distortion of messages communicated through the system and overly simplified and inflexible systems [Litterer, 1965]. Undue emphasis upon elaborating internal control systems could yield diminishing returns [Powell, 1966]. Differing individual motivations and group norms could render an organisation's social subsystem less behaviourally predictable than a biological organism [Silverman, 1970]. Indeed, critics became concerned that systems theory had in a sense returned to the mechanistic perspective of organisations and control which it had so earnestly sought to avoid [Fleming, 1972; Phillips, 1972; Thayer, 1972]. Nevertheless the systems school contributed significant innovations in the management literature's approach to the study of control.

From the control concepts already identified in the systems literature, a systems COM which outlines the hypothesised relationships between its component concepts can be constructed. The resulting model is represented by Figure 5.8. The cyclical control (C_y) concept, with its open, closed, or progressive loops, appears to have provided the foundation for a systems perspective of control. Once a cyclical control system could be designed or identified, it could prove to embody either a

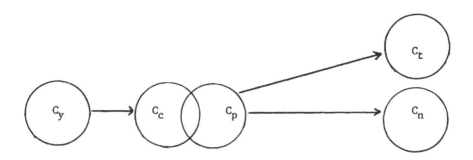

where: C_y = Cyclical Control C_t = Timing Control
        C_c = Closed Systems Control C_n = Contingent Control
        C_p = Open Systems Control

Figure 5.8: The Systems Model of Control

closed systems control concept (C_c) or an open systems control concept (C_p). Hence the connection $C_y - C_c/C_p$ was made. While a control system could be described as either open or closed, some writers argued that a control system could be a mixture of the two concepts, partially open and partially closed. This relationship is represented in Figure 5.8 as the intersecting circles, C_c and C_p. It was the open systems control concept which gained most in favour amongst systems theorists and from the open systems control perspective, the concepts of timing control (C_t) and contingent control (C_n) were developed. This open systems concept of control facilitated the environmentally adaptive character of the concepts of timing and contingent control. By the close of the 1970s it was the contingent control concept that was continuing to receive further attention in the management literature, as researchers attempted to explore its implications for organisational management and control, and as critics debated its future prospects.

The Environmental Scenario

The systems-based study of control in management theory began with just a few researchers in the 1950s, but really blossomed from the early

1960s and reflected to a large degree the socio-economic environment in developed western countries during that period. For instance the 1960s and 1970s witnessed the rise to prominence of multinational firms which began operations in a number of countries or took part in various foreign joint ventures or licensing arrangements, thus expanding their boundaries and encountering a wide diversity of operating environments. With different countries exhibiting a wide variety of market forces, government policies, cultural mores and community attitudes, the multinational organisation was faced with adapting to a much more complex and dynamic environment. A systems COM clearly had its attractions for this type of operation, especially as the organisation could be dealing with differences between host nations regarding the employment of women, the provision of support facilities in remoter areas, the need to conform to national business customs, the availability of an appropriately skilled workforce, their susceptability to government controls, the degree of political instability and even the prevalence of 'questionable' payments. Conversely, national manufacturers began to face more intense foreign competition either from multinationals in their own country or from overseas imports [Tosi and Carroll, 1976; Kast and Rosenzweig, 1979; Davis et al, 1980]. Thus the market environment for many national firms also became more volatile and this too would have enchanced the attractiveness of a systems approach to issues such as control.

In the 1960s and 1970s organisations generally faced an increasingly turbulent technological environment particularly as a result of advances through nuclear energy and the National Aeronautic and Space Administration programmes. Not only did large-scale complex organisations develop to service defence and space research programmes, but the technological developments that ensued spilled over into industry accompanied by significant growth in research and development expenditure in American, European and Japanese industry. Thus with respect to production process and end product, organisations faced an increasingly volatile scientific and technological environment requiring more flexible operational responses [Kast and Rosenzweig, 1970; Tosi and Carroll, 1976]. Further technolgical innovation occurred in response to the world energy problems of the 1970s with declining sources of petroleum and natural gas, increasing production and transportation costs, and changing levels of productivity [Wren, 1979].

In industry the onset of automated production processes led the trend towards the greater complexity and sophistication of systems for the production of goods and towards a change in the type of labour force employed. Even existing managerial roles began to change with supervisors taking on roles of mediation and integration rather than simply direction. Increasing specialisation of work roles at times made the integration of operations quite complex. Electronic data processing provided an impressive array of sometimes previously unavailable information much more quickly than previously thought possible. Masses of data could be processed at speed, planning models could be built to greater levels of sophistication, and detailed feedback was available on many dimensions of organisational performance. Indeed it was argued that technological change fed upon itself to produce even more technological change [Robertson, 1964; Toffler, 1971; Davis et al, 1980].

Such a highly charged and turbulent technological environment provided yet another fertile base for the rapid growth of the application of systems thinking to problems of organisational design and management. A systems approach to control was almost inevitably forstered by the need for organisations to adapt continuously to rapid changes in production, product and information technology. Yet social changes also contributed to the scenario. The workforce was becoming, on average, better educated, while organisations employed more skilled and professional employees who required changed patterns of man-management. General social attitudes and values were undergoing a marked shift as well. Many young employees began to value autonomy and interesting work more highly than security and promotions and no longer accepted the demands of those in authority without question. Many in society had become disenchanted with industrialisation and urbanisation. Productivity and efficiency no longer held pride of place as accepted cultural goals. Issues such as unemployment, housing the poor, environmental pollution and energy conservation became major social concerns [Tosi and Carroll, 1976; Brownlee, 1979; Davis et al, 1980].

How was corporate management to cope with this environment of social change? It required changed business ideologies, new legal and structural procedures, and more developed managerial skills. Corporate management was forced to consider the relationship of organisational structures and strategies to more than just the shareholders and consumers. Furthermore they recognised that their organisations operated within a total ecosystem so that environmental impact became a key concern in many strategy discussions [Tosi and Carroll, 1976; Kast and Rosenzweig, 1979]. This represented a significant change in the 'rules of the game' compared with the pre-1960s period. There was also a marked increase in the influence of and interaction between government regulatory bodies and business organisations. Organisational decision-making came under the influence of tariff policies, government defence expenditures, product regulation, wage and price guidelines, antitrust legislation, employment protection, pollution control and consumer protection, all through agencies of government control. Indeed by the late 1960s, government provision, government subsidy, government contract and government regulation were the order of the day and impinged on innumerable aspects of organisational operations [Youngson, 1976; Kast and Rosenzweig, 1979; Wren, 1979; Davis et al, 1980].

Instead of treating the organisation as a closed system and concentrating upon internal factors influencing its efficiency and productivity, management became outward-looking and much more concerned with organisations' socio-economic environment, either through self-enlightenment or through social and government pressure. For many management theorists the organisation had become a complex of interlocking subsystems whose interface with the external environment brought a new realisation that the organisational system was part of a much larger social system [Davis et al, 1980]. The scene was effectively set for the development of a systems approach to control focussing upon the need for faster adaptation to changing conditions. The increased turbulence of the organisational environment was particularly conducive to such concepts as cyclical control, open system control and contingent control which all contributed to the creation of an adaptive systems COM.

AN EXPANDED VIEW

The seeds of change in mangement thinking about control had been sown particularly in the 1950s. That they bore fruit in the 1960s and 1970s is quite evident from the analysis of models undertaken in this chapter. The classical COM persisted in certain sectors of the management literature, but came in for increasing criticism. Its offshoot, the structural COM, was revised in the post-1960 period with respect to some of its components, although it had largely been developed before 1960. The behavioural COM however, presented quite a different story. While it had already been quite well developed before 1960, a wealth of research and study by behaviouralists in the 1960s and 1970s produced a model with old concepts elaborated and broadened and significant new concepts added. Finally, after some stirrings of interest in the management literature of the late 1950s, the systems approach to control attracted a considerable amount of interest and attention. The resulting model, while still in the process of development at the close of the 1970s, had achieved a remarkable degree of sophistication in a relatively brief period.

In the management literature of the 1960s and 1970s control had undergone a wealth of conceptual development. A formidable array of concepts had emerged from several major schools of thought and formed the components of the major models of control just examined. These models did not develop in isolation from one another and indeed were spawned in many instances under the influence of common socio-economic factors. Furthermore these models were interrelated through links between their conceptual components.[35] Not only had the management literature therefore produced a significantly expanded view of control by the close of the 1970s, but it had produced conceptual developments which contributed to a logical framework of interrelated models of control.

NOTES

1. While part of Follett's approach was characteristic of classical management thinking, the bulk of her writings reflected a significant departure from that school. This has already been argued in Chapter 3.

2. As was the custom of her day.

3. Some arguments mounted by post-1960 management theorists, indirectly reflected a Follett view without acknowledging the connection (probably because the author was unaware of this). For instance, Litterer [1965:233] stated at the very outset of a chapter on control processes and systems that "The essence here is on directivity and integration of effort, required accomplishment of an end". Even the terminology was reminiscent of Follett. McGregor [1967:130-133] advocated a systems-based "organic approach to control systems" which, to all intents and purposes, corresponded with Follett's 'law of the situation'.

4. For the classicists, the control definition to achieve widest acceptance was Fayol's.

5. Although the process school was considered by many of its critics to be too static and simplistic to be useful, it was better received by practitioners than most other schools of management thought [Hodgetts, 1979].

6. This included re-evaluation of subunit objectives, reconciling individual and organisational interests and improving the communication of control information.

7. In modified form.

8. Child [1972] studied separate business organisations stratified by size and selected from six industries, with samples drawn from the main industrial areas of England and Scotland.

9. The reverse relationship was also implied.

10. Again based upon Weberian bureaucracy.

11.   The measure of supervisory personnel adopted was mean number of foremen and inspectors per industry. The index number and extent of formal rules adopted was mean number of file clerks per industry. These were combined to form a surveillance-formal rules index. Twenty industrial categories were studied.

12.   The planning-control interface has not been incorporated into the model because of the lack of general agreement concerning the degree of interrelatedness between the two concepts, evident among the structural theorists of the 1960s and 1970s.

13.   See notation of Figure 3.3.

14.   Refer to Figure 5.1.

15.   While studies referred to by Lawler [1976], as well as studies conducted by McMahon and Perritt [1973], Camman [1976] and Todd [1978], supported the argument that employee perceptions of greater self-control benefited such variables as their work performance, chosen goals and organisational effectiveness, other study results cited [Lawler, 1976; Parker, 1979] were not so supportive and at times provided evidence to the contrary.

16.   Conformity of his cognitions and behaviour to the group's cognitions and behaviour.

17.   It appeared that the two-way flow of control between superior and subordinate accorded some greater degree of satisfaction to both parties [Ivancevich, 1970].

18.   It was further contended that while persuasion was still a much practised form of control, its popularity was declining since subordinates were becoming less naive, less trusting in the competence and trustworthiness of superiors and increasingly averse to manipulation or external control [Berlo, 1975].

19.   An example 'close to home' is that of the tantrum-throwing child. The mother offers the child a biscuit and is negatively reinforced by the cessation of the unpleasant screaming. Meanwhile, the child having been pacified by the biscuit has been positively reinforced for throwing tantrums.

20.   Such popularity was suggested to stem from the 'eye-for-eye' notion of justice and from the possibility of administrators of punishment being negatively reinforced by terminating the annoying behaviour of others.

21.   Also made by the structuralists.

22.   This included 'banking' work to smooth out dips in activity,
        'storming' production towards the end of a quota period,
        sacrifices of maintenance to minimise short-run production costs,
        covert supervisor deals with workgroups, workgroup sanctions on
        rigorous inspectors, workgroup frustration of supervision through
        slowed working pace, and manipulation of job tickets and
        production records.

23.   Informal groups were defined as associations of personnel (e.g.
        social groups, peer groups, lobby groups, national groups) which
        existed outside the groups and relationships formally prescribed
        by the organisational rules, manual of procedures, job
        descriptions and hierarchy of authority.

24.   Coercive power was based on a subordinate's or group member's
        perception that someone could punish him. Persuasive (or
        manipulative) power was based on a capacity to convince
        subordinates or enlist their conscious or unconscious co-
        operation. Reward or utilitarian power was based on the use of
        material means for control purposes (e.g. goods, services,
        money). Legitimate or authority-based power relied upon the
        internalised belief, held by a subordinate, in a superior's
        legitimate right to control and in the subordinate's obligation
        to accept this control. Referent power was based on the desire
        of a subordinate to identify with a particular superior.
        Identitive power relied upon the use of symbols for control
        purposes (e.g. prestige, esteem, love, acceptance). Expert power
        relied on the individual perception that a leader had some
        special knowledge or expertise in a given area.

25.   This study has classified the literature on distribution of
        control and total amount of control as a component of the
        behavioural COM's component concept of power-based control. The
        behavioural classification is also supported by Jackson and
        Morgan [1978].

26.   Indeed Tannenbaum [1968] argued that a "fixed pie" assumption
        about the total amount of available control in an organisation
        might constitute a self-fulfilling prophecy. Organisation
        members who assumed the total amount of organisational control to
        be fixed, might attempt to restrict the control available to
        others and thus limit or reduce the total control available in
        the organisation.

27.   Both extrinsic and intrinsic.

28.   In the UK, the number of university students rose from 82,000 in 1954-5, to 211,000 in 1968-9, with 17 universities in 1945 and 44 by the close of the 1960s [Roebuck, 1973:175]. In the USA, the student rush to university campuses was such that their faculties increased from 38,249 in 1962 to 46,539 in 1964 [Tuttle and Perry, 1970].

29.   This cycle of control was sometimes referred to as a control feedback process in which data on performance was 'fed-back' for comparison with plans.

30.   In reaching this conclusion, Eilon had examined:

    a.   Relationships between different control systems in the organisation.
    b.   Relationships between controllers and control systems.
    c.   Relationships between controllers themselves.

31.   Organisational subsystems included production, adaptive, boundary-spanning, maintenance, managerial [Tosi and Carroll, 1976], technical and psychosocial subsystems [Kast and Rosenzweig, 1979].

32.   Members of this group have been classified as:

Socio-technical systems theorists by:	Contingency theorists by:
Lorsch [1969:325]	Huse and Bowditch [1973:254-255]
Kast and Rosenzweig [1970:117]	Kast and Rosenzweig [1973:314]
Silverman [1970:111-118]	Duncan [1975:381]
Allen and Gabarro [1972:18]	Bowey [1976:52]
Charns [1972:28]	Dessler [1977:168-177]
	Stoner [1978:322-331]
	Kast and Rosenzweig [1979:486-491]
	Scanlan and Keys [1979:340-341]
	Wren [1979:465-466]

33.   Trist [and Bamforth, 1969] found this in his study of coal mining techniques. Mechanical coal cutting and specialisation of workers by shift required closer supervision than the previous multi-skilled, self-selected, largely autonomous workgroups.

34.   Mechanistic organisations were characterised as operating in stable technologies, in an atmosphere of certainty, with a low degree of environmental impact on the organisation, having programmable decisions, with objectives set at the top levels and handed down the hierarchy, knowledge being specialised, low interdependency of tasks and a short time horizon.

        Organic organisations were characterised as operating amidst dynamic technology, in an uncertain environment with a high degree of environmental impact on the organisation, having non-programmable decisions, with participation of all levels of the hierarchy in objective setting, knowledge highly generalised, high interdependency of tasks and a long-term time horizon, [Hodgetts, 1979].

35.   These links, and the framework which they created, will be explored more fully in Chapter 7.

CHAPTER 6: PIECEMEAL PROGRESS IN ACCOUNTING

What little there was by way of 'state of the art' reviews of the historical development of accounting literature on control was not always particularly detailed or reliable. Villers [1969] briefly reviewed the history of control but effectively equated financial control with budgeting in general, so that the specific issue of control was side-stepped in favour of a brief reference to the past popularity of the budget in American companies. A more substantial review of approaches to budgeting and control was undertaken by Drinkwater [1973] who classified budgetary thought into the traditional school (pre-1950), the behavioural school (early 1950s), the quantitative school (1950s) and the structural school (post-1960).[1]

Other accounts of what control really meant were even narrower and more susceptible to confusion. Hoverland and Strickland [1967] attempted to classify control as either management control or accounting control. In their view management control was action-related and was the dominant concept, while accounting control was limited in its meaning to the provision of control information and provided merely the capacity to act. Buckley and McKenna [1972] began a brief discussion of "The Roots of Management Control" by contending that authority-based control procedures were being superseded by more enlightened, democratic control procedures but that it was questionable whether control procedures were changing in sympathy with more participative (or democratic) styles of management. From this apparently self-contradictory beginning they said little more about control concepts specifically. Bierman and Dyckman [1971] went little further than recognising that the history of cost control had been dominated by the view that the primary incentive for employees was economic and that management accounting had traditionally been viewed as the primary means for controlling and reducing cost.

At best the accounting literature's treatment of its own developmental history with respect to the concept of control was relatively superficial. Accounting researchers were left to proceed in their deliberations without the benefit of organised, conscious and informed hindsight. The paths which they took from 1960 to 1979 are the subject of the analysis that follows.

THE PERSISTENT CLASSICAL MODEL

A broad spectrum of accounting writers continued quite uncritically to expound the constituent concepts of the classical management COM which continued to predominate in the accounting literature on control during the 1960s and 1970s. For instance many accounting definitions of control during those decades were not only classical management in orientation, but closely approximated Fayol's early definition of control. For example:

> "Control, the other management function, involves the process of ensuring that the alternatives chosen are accepted and the plans for implementing them are carried out."
>
> [American Accounting Association, 1966:45]

> "A Management control system might be briefly defined as a system of organisational accountability and feedback designed to ensure that the work behaviour of an organisation's members is measured and compared with a set of operational sub-goals (which conform with overall objectives) so that the discrepancy between the two can be reconciled and accounted for."
>
> [Lowe, 1970:766]

> "Controlling implies that the plans which have been set will be achieved only if there is a means of ensuring satisfactory performance, checking performance against plans, and taking executive action."
>
> [Matheson, 1970:549]

> "Hence the term 'control' is assumed to include at least the following three elements:
>
> 1. Setting targets at the appropriate level to achieve the required performance.

2. Measuring actual performance and comparing this
    with target.
3. Taking corrective action in the event of actual
    results deviating from target results."

[Morris, 1974:383]

Similar sentiments were expressed by Jaedicke [1962:181-182], Shillinglaw
[1970:307-308] and Dew and Gee [1973:33].   When such definitions of
control are compared with Fayol's original definition restated below, it
is clear that quite a number of accountants either consciously or
unconsciously reflected Fayol's original conception first published in
1916:

"In an undertaking, control consists in verifying
whether everything occurs in conformity with the plan
adopted, the instructions issued and principles
established.   It has for object to point out
weaknesses and errors in order to rectify them and
prevent recurrence."

[Fayol, 1949:107]

Authority-Based Control

Accountants continued to advocate top management's authority and
control over the operations of the whole organisation.

"Having made a decision and given orders which will
implement the chosen plan, managers rely upon
accounting or other reports to control operations."

[Vatter, 1969:5]

They continued to worry about closing the 'management control gap' as the
growth of specialisation in large organisations strained top management's
ability to maintain close personal control over operations [McDonough,
1971].   In this regard accountants remained concerned that managers
should understand what their superiors regarded as successful performance
so that managers would not take 'wrong' actions or come to 'wrong'
conclusions [Dew and Gee, 1973:31].   In this sense also, control via the

budgetary system was still regarded as the direction and restriction of behaviour of organisation members [Dunbar, 1971].

The authority-based concept of control was also expressed in the accounting literature in terms of 'responsibility accounting'. It was assumed that people had a responsibility to achieve the firm's goals and that accounting could appropriately measure and report on that responsibility [Benninger, 1973].

> "The essence of responsibility accounting is the accumulation of costs and revenues according to areas of responsibility in order that deviations from standard costs and budgets can be identified with the person or group responsible. Reports prepared along responsibility lines are in effect 'report cards' which inform the head of each area of responsibility and his superior how well he has performed in terms of costs and profits."
>
> [Ferrara, 1964a:11]

Thus the responsibility of each manager was to be clearly defined for control purposes and with particular emphasis upon each manager's responsibility for cost control [Ferrara, 1964b; Matheson, 1970].[2]

Disciplinary Control

While this classical concept continued in the post-1960 accounting literature, it received less attention than in earlier decades. The practice of budgetary control was seen as a *disciplined* effort to follow the plan or to explain deviations from it. Management control signified *regulation* of business affairs within established standards and accountants remained firm in their concern to restrict or reduce any tendency towards excessive cost incurrence [Anderson, 1963; Surana, 1969; Matheson, 1970].

Congruent Control

In contrast to the concept of disciplinary control, the concept of co-ordinative control reappeared in a somewhat changed form after 1960, under the title "Goal Congruence". Accounting writers considered that control was essential for achieving uniformity of purpose within the organisation and for contributing towards the attainment of objectives. So that managers should not work at cross purposes, accountants advocated a control system designed to suit an organisation's formally specified objectives [Horngren, 1967; Vancil, 1973; Imdieke and Smith, 1975; Jarvis and Skidmore, 1978]. They also argued that a personal commitment to formally stated organisation objectives should be required of and secured from all personnel. Top management's task in this framework was to create harmony of effort by trying to reconcile intra-organisational differences and conflicts in the allocation of resources, policies, effort and time [Brown, 1972; Buckley, 1973; Welsch, 1976]. Controls from this viewpoint were "devices designed to motivate action toward the attainment of stipulated goals" [Benninger, 1973:20]. For most accountants the manifestation of organisational goals imposed by top management was the budget and control was introduced to ensure that those (budgetary) goals were attained [Stedry, 1960; Welsch, 1971].

What was unique about the congruent control concept, and what distinguished it from co-ordinative control, was that it extended down the organisational hierarchy to include the personal goals and aspirations of all organisation members. The stated object of control was to ensure a congruence between personal and organisational goals. Thus some accounting writers argued that the control effort should be directed towards creating a situation in which each individual, in attempting to satisfy his own personal goals, would be making the maximum possible contribution to the attainment of organisational goals [Sizer, 1975; Searfoss, 1976; Welsch, 1976]. Congruent control also appeared during the 1970s accounting literature, expressed as goal and subgoal consistency. The collective contribution of organisational subunits to organisational goals was sought through control to ensure consistency of subgoals with organisational goals and control to ensure consistency of behaviour with goals and subgoals [Lowe, 1970; Wilson, 1970; Baumler, 1972].

While this goal congruence-based concept of control emerged after 1960 as an accounting embellishment of the classical management concept of co-ordinative control, in fact it was not a new concept in itself. Fayol [1949] had anticipated this concept in his combination of principles known as Unity of Command, Unity of Direction and Subordination of Individual Interest to General Interest.[3] He saw these three principles as prerequisites to command which in turn influenced his concept of control. While Fayol did not use the term 'goal congruence', the combination of his three principles closely approximate the meaning which accounting writers later imputed to the term. Furthermore, congruent control was distinguished from mere co-ordinative control by its concern to align personal goals and motivation with formal organisation goals set by top management. In arguing for his principle of Subordination of Individual Interest to General Interst, Fayol ostensibly used this interpretation and introduced a quite separate concept of co-ordination into his COM. Accordingly while the accounting literature of the 1960s and 1970s produced an amendment to the co-ordinative control concept of the classical management COM in the shape of congruent control, it had in fact reverted to the control concept of one of the founding fathers of the classical COM, Henri Fayol.

'Controls'

The reliance upon a 'controls'-based view of securing effective control persisted in the classically-oriented accounting literature, although it was evident rather more by way of implicit assumption than by any extended specific discussion. Amongst the armoury of controls available it was without question the budget to which accountants gave almost all their attention. Indeed some equated financial control with budgeting and many saw the budget primarily as a control tool [Villers, 1969; Lowe, 1970; Dew and Gee, 1973; Searfoss, 1976]. It would appear that the acceptance of the budget as a control tool had become so entrenched that for many accounting writers it did not warrant further discussion. Indeed the notion of the budget as a prime control tool underpinned accountants' continued adherence to exception control.

Exception Control

The accounting literature emphasised the accumulation of costs according to areas of responsibility so that deviations from standard costs and budgets could be identified with the person or group responsible [Ferrara, 1964a; Wallace, 1966]. This was essentially a retrospective view of control where performance evaluation concentrated upon pinpointing responsibility for *poor* performance and focussing management attention upon unfavourable variances from standards [Terry, 1964; Surana, 1969; Gole, 1970]. The weakness-seeking, potentially punitive attitude inherent in this approach, was implied for instance in the following statement:

> "If the facts are to come to light, however, someone must be accountable and take the responsibility on his shoulders. The obvious person is the one whose performance has suffered."
>
> [Taylor and Palmer, 1969:139]

Many accounting writers considered the highlighting of such exceptions in the budget to be an essential trigger device to signal the need for correction. For control purposes, accountants used the phrase 'exception reporting' as their means of highlighting deviations from standard performance [Welsch, 1976; Jarvis and Skidmore, 1978].

Unlike the other component concepts of the classical management COM in the accounting literature, exception control did begin to attract some criticism. Charnes and Stedry [1964] argued that it fostered communication between superiors and subordinates only when something had 'gone wrong'. In this way control efforts might be associated with criticism and punishment in subordinates' perception, and therefore invoke their hostility. McDonough [1971] argued that accountants had adopted an 'ad hoc' approach to investigating exceptions from standard performance and that the emphasis should be shifted from the accountant's exception-based control role of uncovering 'skeletons' and placing blame, to a more neutral role of facilitating interaction between diverse elements in the organisation. Ronen and Livingstone [1975] also criticised exception control as emphasising failure, with only exceptional success attracting higher management attention. As Charnes and Stedry had done they also argued that such an emphasis could lead to subordinate defensiveness, overcaution and other dysfunctional behaviour patterns.

The Model Repeated

Once again a sizeable number of accounting writers chose to continue adhering to the classical management COM just as those in the years before 1960 had done. The only change that had occurred in 1960-1979 was the revision of the concept of co-ordinative control (C_d) to become a concept of congruent control (C_g). As in the classical management COM in Figure 2.3, the classical accounting COM also retained the concepts of total control, authority-based control, exception control, disciplinary control, and 'controls'. By inference, the model was still focussed upon the concept of securing total control with the primary source still considered to be the concept of authority-based control. The intervening concepts which rendered authority-based control operational as a contributor to total control, were the revised concept of congruent control as well as the established concepts of exception and disciplinary control. As before, exception control contributed to total control through the agency of 'controls'.

Sources of Continuity

The continuity of many post-1960 accounting writers' adherence to the classical management COM can be attributed to a number of factors. Much of the accounting literature and many practising accountants still sought principles and prescriptive rules for budgeting [Charnes and Stedry, 1964; Drinkwater, 1973]. Budgeting and standard costs were still being treated with a control emphasis, just as had occurred in earlier decades [Dew and Gee, 1973] and was often still considered in terms of classical management concepts of checking performance, authorising activities, avoiding wastage, co-ordinating operations and encouraging adherence to prescribed top management objectives [Terry, 1964; Sizer, 1975].

> "From the business viewpoint of budgeting is a management accounting technique intended to assist in the process of economising in the use of business resources and assets. More specifically it is a means of co-ordinating and controlling the various activities of a business in order to ensure that the overall objectives of the enterprise are achieved, by the most efficient means."
>
> [Lowe, 1970:764]

Accountants also remained preoccupied with the classical management concern to maximise profits through reduction of costs and optimising control decisions [Stedry, 1960; Lowe, 1970; Matheson, 1970]. The following statement typified this thinking:

> "There is a natural bias among corporate executives in favour of responsibility for profit. Profit is a powerful measurement; it provides a clear objective, is easily understood, and is a good motivator of such men."
>
> [Vancil, 1973:86]

Efficiency too, remained a focus of accountants' attention. Control was stressed as being important for the purpose of securing efficiency of operations throughout the organisation and indeed efficiency was even required of the control process itself [Matheson, 1970; Wilson, 1970].

For instance Shillinglaw [1970] argued that higher management controlled the exercise of authority at lower hierarchical levels by evaluating the performance of subordinate management, secure in the knowledge that misuse or inefficient use of authority would be reflected in lower profits. At times the accounting concern for efficiency regressed to the earlier Taylor concern for securing harder work.

> "'Control' implies a watchfulness, and the standards may be regarded primarily as devices for obtaining more work."
>
> [Batty, 1970:206]

Thus it is evident that just as the pursuit of efficiency and accounting perceptions of budgeting for control had contributed to the predominance of the classical COM in the pre-1960 accounting literature, so they again contributed to its retention in the accounting control literature of the 1960s and 1970s.

ELEMENTS OF STRUCTURALISM

It was not until the 1960s and particularly the 1970s that the accounting literature on control revealed the first signs of any concern for the structural aspect of control. Even then the emergence of structural views was relatively tentative and restricted. A few leading accounting text writers began to stress the need to integrate control with the formal corporate structure of authority and to focus its operation upon the organisation's financial structure [Shillinglaw, 1970; Anthony, 1973; Welsch, 1976]. Beyond that basic assertion however, the discussion ventured little further and very few writers chose to take up the theme or develop it in any specific detail.

With respect to the process-oriented discussion of the relationship between planning and control, the majority of accountants chose to treat them as quite separate functions (planning preceding control). Matheson [1970:549] implied that plans had already been set and would be achieved only if there existed a means for ensuring satisfactory performance,

checking performance against plans and taking executive action. Searfoss
argued that:

> "Once the goals are firmly established and the plans
> are formalized in quantitative terms, the control
> function of the budget comes into play."
>
> [Searfoss, 1976:375]

Hayhurst [1976] argued also that execution of corporate plans demanded
that some form of control be adopted. Burke and Macmullen [1979] also
argued that management functions should follow a cycle where planning
came first, then organising to give effect to plans, then directing
operations, and subsequently controlling performance. Others [Kemp,
1962; Morris, 1974] went even further in treating planning and control as
mutually exclusive functions. They argued for the production of
different and quite separate budgets for different purposes, such as a
planning, a control and a motivational budget. However most of the above
arguments were couched in the form of basic assertions and lacked any
significant substantiating theory or supporting evidence.

Thus the accounting literature on control only exhibited sporadic
examples of structural thinking in the years between 1960 and 1979. No
one concept was explored or developed to the degree that it could be
accorded the description of a structural control concept and hence no
basis existed for a structural accounting COM.

A BEHAVIOURAL MODEL EMERGES

While behavioural factors affecting the exercising of control
received some attention in the accounting literature before the 1960s, it
was not until the 1960s that a sufficient number of accounting writers
adopted a behavioural approach[4] that could support a behavioural COM.
This resulted in the development of several control concepts (self-
control, formal control and expectancy control), all focussed upon the
individual's motivation to perform.

Self-Control

While reference by accounting writers to the concept of self-control occurred more frequently in the 1970s than in the 1960s very few writers referred to it directly. Advocates tended to argue for a control system which focussed upon people, and which supported them in their activities, by allowing them improved control over their own operations rather than policing them in a punitive fashion. The degree to which the control system took this approach, it was felt, would be a significant conditioner of manager attitudes [Anderson, 1963; Buckley, 1973].

> "As management accountants are responsible for the operation of budgetary planning and control systems, they must take account of human behaviour, because the systems are designed to help *people* to control themselves and other people."
>
> [Sizer, 1975:78]

Nevertheless, such references to self-control were fairly sparse, circumspect and brief. One exception was Hopwood's [1974] writing on self-control. He recognised that all forms of control ultimately must be expressed through the actions of individual managers and employees. In his view administrative and social controls had to be both internalised by employees and operate as personal controls over attitude and behaviour before they became operative and effective. The concept of self-control was, for Hopwood, intimately related to the question of human needs.

It can be argued that some accounting writers referred to the concept of self-control indirectly through their discussions of participation. Of course not every accounting reference to participation constituted a reference to self-control. Participation was also examined with respect to a host of other criteria such as motivation, productivity, morale, etc.. When self-control was considered it amounted to observations that control might be more effectively exerted from the bottom of the organisation rather than from the top or that self-control and self-discipline might prove to be a superior motivating force for managers [Brown, 1965; McKenna, 1978]. It is interesting to note that

Boland [1979], while not writing directly on participation, referred to
and used Follett's notion of 'control with' and 'control over' as
operating simultaneously in an organisation.

In a more general sense participation at all levels of management in
the investigation of variances, evaluation and selection of alternatives,
and development of policies was considered by some to enhance overall
control, to motivate people to achieve performance standards, to attain
budgetary objectives and to commit themselves more strongly to cost
controls[5] [Wallace, 1966; Probst, 1971; Welsch, 1971]. Such references
however, were not necessarily oriented towards the concept of self-
control.[6]

The concept of self-control therefore emerged in the post-1960
accounting literature more as a basic statement of recognition rather
than as the product of any detailed conceptual analysis.

Formal Control

While accountants of classical management conviction considered the
usefulness of various mechanisms for excercising formal control through
the organisation's hierarchy of authority, accountants of the behavioural
school were keen to observe the impact of the formal control process upon
manager and subordinate behaviour and the impact of behavioural responses
upon control itself.

Accounting Controls

In beginning to recognise the limitations of accounting data for
management control purposes accountants tended to concentrate upon the
informational inadequacies of the data supplied, the narrow scope of
variables measured, and the lack of quantifiability of some important
control variables [Dew and Gee, 1969]. Furthermore, behavioural
accounting writers no longer assumed that the presence of accounting

controls automatically guaranteed the exercise of effective control [Benninger, 1973]. Hopwood [1974] pointed out that when personnel were evaluated according to their degree of conformity to accounting controls, the controls often became valued as an end in themselves with the possible result that personnel's behaviour could become rigid and defensive. Thus a problem which controls had been designed to overcome could become intensified and if management responded by proliferating the controls, subordinates might take greater pains to avoid or undermine them, or treat them as specifying the maximum limit of required performance.

Controls were also seen as focussing on the consequences of behaviour rather than on a behaviour pattern itself [Hopwood, 1974]. Indeed the elaboration of controls was perceived as a classical management response, via management by exception, to the problem of securing more effective control.

> "Score-Card questions in an organisation patterned after the classical theory have a punitive bias. Or to say almost the same thing, they tend to induce mechanisms of defense and self-protection."
>
> [Golembiewski, 1964:337]

Such concerns, which had also been voiced occasionally in the 1950s, no doubt contributed to behaviourally-oriented accounting writers' interest in the motivational effect of accounting control. In their view a key parameter was the degree of likely attainability of the budget standards. Budgets which offered a reasonable prospect of being attained were observed to be the best performance motivators, the argument being that in satisfying an individual's need for self-fullfillment the budget would become a formalised expression of the latent needs of managers [Weiser, 1968]. It was found that standards which were too tight or too loose would fail to motivate personnel and lead to a decline in performance [Stedry and Kay, 1960] and the degree to which personnel were prepared to internalise standards appeared to be influenced by personality, cultural differences and situational factors such as hierarchical level, age, and time in the job [Hofstede, 1968]. Thus the belief that controls should be set at reasonably attainable levels became embedded in the accounting literature [Welsch, 1971; Buckley, 1973; Ronen and Livingstone, 1975].

Likely attainment of budget standards was also seen to be influenced by an individual's previously experienced success or failure (past failure appeared more likely to predispose an individual to avoid setting a high aspiration level).[7] It also appeared to be adversely affected when an individual was held responsible for items beyond his control, so that some writers favoured including only controllable costs in budget performance reports. The effect of frequency of feedback of performance results against standard was not so clearly determined, with studies producing apparently conflicting results [Buckley, 1963; Cook, 1968; Weiser, 1968; Ronen and Livingstone, 1975; Kenis, 1979].

Dysfunctional Effects

The application of formal control began to be recognised as having, under certain circumstances, potentially dysfunctional effects upon the organisation. Typical of the earlier recognition of potential problems in this regard was the following observation:

> "The application of controls has a long and discouraging history of abuse. Results are concealed with misinformation, staff groups overplay their authority, frustrations run rampant."
>
> [Anderson, 1963:46]

One problem which attracted accountants' attention in this regard was the results of applying pressure for tighter budget standards and improved performance. Argyris' [1957] earlier work on the dysfunctional behaviour patterns that could result from such pressure achieved recognition in the accounting literature [Hofstede, 1968; Welsch, 1971; Hopwood, 1974]. The imposition of harsh, extensive, inflexible pressure to meet standards could push individuals or groups to a critical antagonistic point where the anxieties and resentment induced were observed to produce dysfunctional employee attitudes and behaviour patterns. Confidence and trust in management declined, performance could eventually decline, and absenteeism and employee turnover were likely to increase. Subordinates tended to 'play safe' and pass up the hierarchy the information they thought superiors would like to hear [Likert and Seashore, 1963; Welsch, 1971; Buckley and McKenna, 1972].[8]

Another dysfunctional effect of the exercise of formal control was identified as budgetary slack (also referred to as budget padding or biasing). It was argued that managers padded their budget estimates for self-protection against the current period's performance evaluation and as protection for future budgets. Conservative estimates might thus be thought as increasing the likelihood of attaining budget [Welsch, 1971; Buckley and McKenna, 1972]. Onsi [1973] undertook the most detailed empirical investigation of behavioural variables affecting budgetary slack and observed that the existing literature had already shown that managers bargained for slack by understating revenue and overstating costs, built up slack in 'good years' to reconvert into profit in 'bad years', and that top management was at a disadvantage in trying to determine its magnitude. His study demonstrated the existence of a relationship between budgetary slack and managers' attitude to authoritarian pressure exerted by top management for the attainment of budgeted profit.

The Impact of Evaluation

The effectiveness of formal control in an organisation could also be influenced by the attitudes of both superiors and subordinates to the use of budgetary standards and other controls in evaluating performance. Looking at the situation from top management's point of view, it was argued:

> "Higher management controls the exercise of authority at lower levels by evaluating the performance of subordinate management."

[Shillinglaw, 1970:305]

The budgetee's superior was seen to have a key role to play in the budgetee's motivation to achieve budget standards, particularly through performance appraisals of subordinate conformity to standards [Hofstede, 1968]. On the other hand, attitudes to the budget held by personnel at all hierarchical levels were found to be affected by such variables as personal flexibility, perceived budget characteristics and attitudes towards those characteristics [Collins, 1978]. Indeed Swieringa and Moncur [1972] were able to classify managers' budget-oriented behaviour into four types and related them to various attitude, size and performance variables in the organisations studied. Active participant and unconcerned recipient proved to be the primary budget-oriented behaviour classifications and related most strongly to time spent with other managers, time in present position, time spent with head office personnel and job satisfaction.

Dew and Gee [1973] studied differences between hierarchical levels of management with respect to their views of appropriate success criteria, measurements and related information. Middle managers were found to be less satisfied with the value of control information provided to them than their superiors or the staff who provided the information. This disagreement coincided with their disagreement as to the appropriateness of success criteria. A significant group of managers felt that the principal purpose of budgetary control was to enable higher management to check on their competence as middle managers and that cost information was used to *judge* rather than *help* them. That perception:

> "... led many of these managers to have an enormous inbuilt emotional resistance to the whole idea of the budetary system, which nevertheless they were expected to use for purposes of control."
>
> [Dew and Gree, 1973:23]

This was to a large degree consistent with Hofstede's [1968] finding that subordinates' perception of their superior as only 'cost-conscious' was insufficient for budget motivation, particularly in the light of existing evidence that employee satisfaction and performance were subject to the influence of self and supervisory evaluations. Furthermore Ansari

[1976:208] had found that "the manner of combining variance reports and supervisory styles had an effect on the behaviour of work groups".

Two of the most prominent studies of performance evaluation in the post-1960 accounting literature were conducted by Hopwood [1972, 1973] and Otley [1978]. Hopwood studied the impact upon subordinates' attitudes and behaviour of superiors' style of accounting data use for evaluating subordinate performance. The two significant evaluation styles which emerged were profit conscious and budget constrained, with the profit-conscious style being oriented towards problem solving and as a source of ideas for change and the budget-constrained style placing primary importance upon evaluating performance as the primary source of control, over-shadowing other elements in the managerial process. Both styles of evaluation achieved a concern for costs but only the profit-conscious style achieved it without dysfunctional decision-making and data manipulation. The budget-constrained style appeared to invoke a climate of mistrust and rivalry as well as short-sighted decisions.

Otley argued that the problem was more complex than Hopwood had inferred and tried to isolate evaluation style by studying an organisation with a well designed budgeting system. His results cast doubt upon whether evaluation style was a truly independent, causal variable with respect to subsequent performance, since contrary to Hopwood's results, they suggested that a rigid evaluation style was more likely to lead to better performance than the flexible style. Among possible causes of the different results were differences between Hopwood's interdependent cost centres and Otley's independent profit centres, differences in organisational structure, and differences in industry technology [Otley, 1978; 1980]. While Hopwood did not specifically refer to control in his study, Otley clearly saw a relationship between the exercising of control and the question of evaluation style which they had both studied. At the outset he had argued that it was important to determine whether distortion of accounting information was inevitable and had to be countered by stricter methods of control or whether distortion depended on how accounting information was used in an organisation. By the conclusion of his study

Otely [1978:145] saw budget use as a control problem in which the "mode of operation of the budgetary system is of central importance".

What accounting writers of behavioural orientation appeared to be concluding was that the evaluation activity component of formal control could be either supportive or punitive. Indeed budgetary systems were beginning to be accused of being more often punitive than supportive, particularly in the form of the authoritative feedback of performance information [Buckley and McKenna, 1972; Jarvis and Skidmore, 1978]. These conclusions, at least partially supported by researchers such as Dew and Gee, Hopwood and, to a lesser extent, Otley, had served to confirm similar concerns expressed earlier concerning the impact of cost-conscious managers and excessive emphasis on score-card questions rather than attention-directing and problem-solving questions [Charnes and Stedry, 1964; Golembiewski, 1964; Hofstede, 1968].

An Accounting Focus

From the foregoing analysis of the accounting literature dealing with the concept of formal control it is apparent that behaviourally-oriented researchers devoted the majority of their efforts to the development of this concept. Their writings on the various dimensions of the subject were extensive and attracted more researchers and writers to contribute to the ongoing dialogue. Their focus was upon the use of controls in pursuit of effective control and the problems and pitfalls which this approach involved. What emerged was the identification of a range of factors influencing the perceived attainability of controls, the types of abuse of controls by superiors and subordinates, and associated resulting behaviour. The ultimate concern was with individual motivation to perform but the use of controls to this end was found to be a complex issue yielding results that were not always easy to predict.

Expectancy Control

Accounting researchers' main interest in this theory stemmed from their interest in predicting performance and satisfaction of organisational members. Through expectancy theory these ends were considered in the light of individuals' perceptions of the likelihood of achieving targeted performance, of the likelihood of performance yielding promised rewards and of the value of rewards offered. In examining the expectancy theory of motivation some writers referred to control directly, while any implications for control could only be inferred from other writers indirectly.

Within an empirical framework of budgeting for control, studies by Searfoss [1976] and Rockness [1977] in general revealed a significant positive relationship between perceived attainability (relating to level of difficulty) and motivation to perform in accordance with budget targets, as well as a significant positive relationship between monetary reward structures and motivation to perform in accordance with budget targets. Accountants' concern with the 'tightness' or 'looseness' of controls, in the form of budget standards, therefore appeared to be justified. Studies by Rockness [1977] and Ferris [1977] also found that expectancy theory models were significant predictors of satisfaction, with Rockness finding that satisfaction increased as expected rewards increased and that satisfaction decreased as budget difficulty increased.

Ronen and Livingstone [1975] viewed the expectancy model as underlying the superior-subordindate budget relationship with respect to motivation to perform. They proceeded to identify the expectancy model as accommodating:

1. The assumption that standards should be reasonably attainable (through individual expectancies of performance and reward likelihoods).

2. Participation (through intrinsic and extrinsic values placed by the individual on outcomes).

3.   Management by exception (through the expectancy that goal accomplishment leads to valued extrinsic rewards).

4.   The controlability criterion for evaluation of subordinate performance (through the expectancy that goal-directed behaviour will accomplish the work goal and the intrinsic utility associated with such successful performance).

Thus expectancy theory was proposed as a suitable framework for evaluating the impact of budget variance reports on subsequent subordinate performance. In addition, Birnberg, Frieze and Shields [1977] sought an expanded view of the management control process by examining personnel's cognitive interaction with performance report feedback in making expectancy and variance investigation decisions. These writers argued that internal, intentional attributions[9] (such as effort, diligence or response to incentives), appeared as potentially strong motivators to perform, assuming that individuals would use such attributions to build satisfaction and self-esteem. On the other hand a subordinate making an external attribution (such as difficulty of task, job conflict, tight budget, luck or others' unstable effort) might not respond to failure by greater effort next period, since he or she might see success as beyond his or her own control.

Thus accounting researchers in the 1970s were experimenting with expectancy theory models with a variety of purposes in view. Nevertheless it appears that a small group of writers were moving towards an expectancy control concept even if it was not formally stated. The concept had the potential to expand accountants' understanding of the link between standards attainability/reward structure and motivation to perform. Furthermore, the expectancy model appeared to offer explanations for the impact (both functional and dysfunctional) of classical concepts such as exception control and authority-based control upon motivation to perform. Such an understanding offered the possibility of further development through a closer examination of cognitive processes which underpinned the operation of expectancies.

Residual Classical Proclivity

Accounting writers of behavioural orientation demonstrated a distinct inclination to embrace a number of aspects of the classical management COM even though to all intents and purposes, they were developing quite a different approach to control. Congruent control was still widely supported. Control was said to be required to ensure a congruence between personal and organisational goals. Control efforts were therefore oriented towards creating situations in which each individual, in attempting to satisfy his own personal goals, would be making the maximum contribution to organisational goals and performance standards specified by top management [Wallace, 1966; Weiser, 1968; Dunbar, 1971, 1976; Welsch, 1971; Hopwood, 1972; Buckley, 1973; Searfoss, 1976; Jarvis and Skidmore, 1978; Otley, 1978].

In addition, there were numerous references made by behavioural writers in support of classical control concepts of authority-based control, disciplinary control, and co-ordinative control. Compliance was still sought from subordinates and references to the pursuit of this through direction, restriction and discipline were still being made [Anderson, 1963; Brown, 1965; Dunbar, 1971; Welsch, 1971; Bruns and Waterhouse, 1975]. Indeed Dew and Gee [1973] argued[10] for transferring a military concept of purpose to industrial organisations and sanctioned the use of pressure to force middle management to respond to control information. Exception control still received support from some behavioural writers [Cook, 1968; Ronen and Livingstone, 1975; Kenis, 1979] and the classical orientation of control for efficiency was also very much in evidence. Control was still being argued as a means of assuring subunit efficiency and efficient accomplishment of organisational purposes with budgets representing standards of effectiveness and efficiency [Anderson, 1963; Baumler, 1972; Hopwood, 1972; Dew and Gee, 1973; Otley, 1978; Kenis, 1979].

In view of these numerous classical references, it is clear that behavioural writers in the accounting literature had by no means completely abandoned the foundations laid by their classical management predecessors. While it should be pointed out that many of these classically-oriented statements appeared as preambles or postscripts to behavioural analyses and experiments, nonetheless their frequency of appearance suggests the retention of at least some measure of classical philosophy as a significant backdrop to the behavioural COM in the accounting literature.

A New Accounting Model

It was not until the post-1960s that the accounting literature produced an approach to the conceptualisation of control that represented a viable alternative to the classical management model. It was the behavioural approach which first filled this role. What form did it take? It included some, albeit limited, recognition of situational (S_i) and cognitive (C_o) variables. Self-control (S_e) had finally achieved recognition as a viable concept by a small group of accounting writers. A few writers had also begun to move towards an expectancy control concept (E_x). Most analysis and experimentation by accounting researchers in this field, however, was focussed upon a concept of formal control (F), particularly with reference to the impact of controls and their use on behaviour.

On the basis of these concepts identified from the accounting literature, a behavioural accounting COM emerges as represented in Figure 6.1. The model was founded upon situational and cognitive variables which influenced the three concepts of expectancy control, self-control and formal control. These three concepts in turn jointly appeared to make a direct contribution to motivation to perform. This implied relationship was one in which the exercising of expectancy control, self-control or formal control could influence the strength and direction of the individual's or groups's motivation to perform.

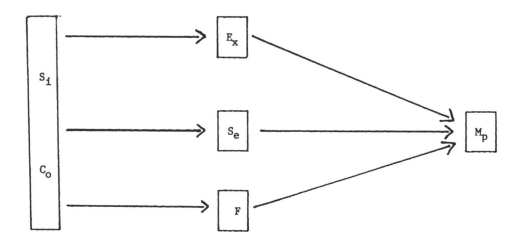

where: S_i = situational variables S_e = self-control

C_o = cognitive variables F = formal control

E_x = expectancy control M_p = motivation to perform

Figure 6.1: A Behavioural Accounting Model of Control

The accounting literature had thus finally provided the basis for a behavioural accounting COM. In some respects, such as formal control, its analysis and conceptual development had attained a considerable degree of sophistication. In other respects, such as self-control and expectancy control, an elementary beginning had only really been made by the close of the 1970s.

A PARTIAL SYSTEMS MODEL

Systems-based approaches to the study of control did not appear in the accounting literature to any significant degree until the 1970s. Early references identified a management control cycle, referred to its systems foundation but still focussed upon static controls with few attempting any flow diagram analysis of control systems [Clay, 1971; Anon, 1973; Itami, 1977]. Others began with references to a systems approach to budgeting but then produced analyses which reflected little by way of systems thinking [Dunbar, 1971]. Hofstede [1968] recognised Von Bertalanffy's general hierarchy of systems, systems-based models of organisations, the importance of feedback loops and first, second and third-order control systems discussed by Eilon [1971] but no clear systems influence became evident in his subsequent analysis. Thus accounting references to systems theory in the late 1960s or early 1970s largely took the form of introductory comments, with little impact upon basic analytical thinking or argument. Often such references would be "tacked on" to classically-oriented discussions of control by regulation, direction, restriction and exception [Surana, 1969; Dunbar, 1971].

It was not until the middle and late 1970s that a serious attempt was made by accounting researchers to apply systems thinking to the subject of control. Even then, the development of thought did not take any clear order of preference and concentrated largely upon contingent control with some attention also being paid to open systems control.

Open Systems Control

The first significant attempts at evolving an open system approach to budgeting and control did not appear in the accounting literature until the late 1970s. Amigoni [1978] proposed a conceptual framework for designing and implementing a management control system. This involved relating independent variables that influence the control process, control system features and controls. Independent variables were the organisation's structural complexity and environmental turbulence. The components of the other factors were:

Control System Features	Control Tools
Detail	Financial Accounting
Relevance	Ratio Analysis
Selectivity	Cost Accounting
Formal responsibility	Responsibility Accounting
Procedural rigidity	Operational Budget
Style of control	Investment Budget
Quickness	
Orientation to Events	

Amigoni found that in a stable environment numerous interrelated business units required more detailed control systems oriented to outputs. Complex organisation structures required more detail at low levels and less at top levels as well as higher degrees of formal responsibility and procedural rigidity and a tighter style of control. A turbulent environment required a future-oriented control system with a high degree of 'quickness'.[11] Thus he argued that control system features were determined by the control tools that comprised them and the manner of employment of such tools in response to structural complexity and high-low environmental turbulence.

Ansari [1979:149] stated that budgets "are one of the most important and pervasive organizational control systems". He then argued that structurally and philosophically the budget was treated as a closed system (in the form of a cybernetic regulator of errors) due to the notion of responsibility accounting being compartmentalised and failing to consider interactions and interdependencies between its component parts. The focus remained on fixing blame through variances rather than managing the whole system. Considerations of internal structure and efficiency of cost centres overshadowed their external and environmental interrelationships. The responsibility accounting system specified controllability in terms of outcomes rather than causes. Competition was rewarded often at the expense of co-operation. Performance evaluation was emphasised at the expense of learning about underlying causes of system-wide variances.

Ansari's open systems approach to budgeting recognised that a cost centre did not exist in isolation but interacted with its environment so that variances should highlight interdependencies and system-wide impacts of disturbances. He defined the manager as a regulator rather than as an authority figure, emphasising his problem solving role rather than just his evaluative role with variances being directed towards global problem-solving rather than local problem-solving. The underlying implication for control was that an open systems framework implied the need to develop systems of joint responsibility where regulation of the whole took precedence over regulation of the parts. Given that control over resources was spread between a number of managers, co-operation should supplant competition, so that problem solving would receive more attention than simply assigning responsibility.

A further adaptation of the open systems approach to control in an accounting context was undertaken in the late 1970s by Itami [1977].[12] He specified a closed-loop control system in order to represent the superior-subordinate operating processes with respect to the control of human control. Since environment was one of the variables built into this closed-loop control system, it also appeared as an open systems concept of control. The management control activities included in this closed-loop open systems concept of control were the influencing of subordinate recognition of criteria for action, subordinates' personal goals, delegated activities and their consequences for subordinates, information about the states of nature and decision-making ability, as well as direct intervention and screening of personnel etc. In constructing this control system, Itami specified its points of emphasis as coping with environmental uncertainty, controlling superiors' control of subordinates (via delegated decision authority), the dynamic and continuous nature of subordinates' operations and the lack of continuous contact between subordinate and superior due to delegated decision-making authority.

The relatively detailed formulations offered by Amigoni and Ansari, as well as the introductory analysis by Itami suggest that the concept of open systems control was in the process of gaining an initial foothold in the accounting literature by the close of the 1970s. The array of control tools available for operation in a management control system had been related in theory to the structure and environment of the organisation, while the focus and manner of use of control information had been broadened to account for the complex interrelationships to be found in both organisational and subunit environments.

Contingent Control

The major thrust of systems-based thinking in the accounting literature took place in the area of contingency theory. Some of the work related to the structuring of working groups in public accounting firms in relation to environment [Watson, 1975], the identification of contingencies affecting organisational subunits and the degree to which management accounting tools such as the budget acted as environmental surrogates [Hayes, 1977]. Other studies considered organisational accounting systems and environment in general but included direct and indirect references to the question of control.

Using Lawrence and Lorsch's [1969] concepts of organisational integration and differentiation, Watson and Baumler [1975] argued that the design of formal control systems should be matched, at least to some extent, to the degree of organisational differentiation present, but that where an existing control system design did not produce such a match, accountants should "not try to impose differentiation through the creation of artificial responsibility centers". Gordon and Miller [1976] elaborated on the design question in advocating that accounting information system design be made contingent upon environment, organisational attributes and management decision-making styles. Some of their arguments had implications for a contingent concept of control. As environmental dynamism and hostility increased and as the need for organisational adaptiveness increased, it was argued that feedback reports on performance and environmental conditions should be supplied to managers more frequently. It was further contended that a heterogeneous environment as well as a decentralised or differentiated organisation could require a more decentralised accounting system with compartmentalised information on the performance of individual subunits or divisions (also relative to each other). This contention was consistent with Watson and Baumler's argument. Frequency and location of control activity was being made contingent upon organisational and environmental characteristics.

A further significant contribution to contingency theory in the
accounting literature was made by Waterhouse and Tiessen [1978]. Having
established that organisational control was contingent upon
organisational environment, technology, and management and operational
functions, they argued that organisations operating in stable
environments with routine technologies could exercise effective control
by means of procedure specification and centralised authority.
Organisations in uncertain environments, using non-routine technologies
could not do this so easily and when employing decentralised decision-
making authority, they could exercise control through the personnel
selection process, through socialisation, planning, internal resource
allocation and performance measurement.

A concept of contingent control had thus arrived in the accounting
literature during the late 1970s. Even then it was not much beyond its
infancy, particularly as few writers chose to address it directly.
Nevertheless it had been clearly argued that both the design and
exercising of control systems should be made contingent upon
organisational structure, environment, technology and *modus operandi*.

The Partial Model

The systems approach to control in the accounting literature
exhibited an abbreviated developmental path and barely facilitated a COM
at all. However, two systems control concepts were sufficiently well
developed by the end of the 1970s that their influence on accounting
thought could not be ignored. Hence they have been incorporated in a
simple, partial systems COM which is represented in Figure 6.2. It
contains only two elements, the concepts of open systems control (C_p) and
contingent control (C_n). In the apparent view of accounting researchers,
one concept did not hinge on the earlier development of the other, since
papers on both appeared almost simultaneously. It could be argued,
however, that the open systems control concept would have contributed to
the formulation of a contingent control concept through the emphasis of
the former upon environmental influences. Similarly, it could be argued

that the contingent control concept improved the potential for practical application of the open systems control concept.

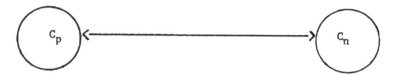

where: C_p = open systems control
         C_n = contingent control

Figure 6.2: A Systems-Based Accounting Model of Control

While systems concepts of control had been somewhat late in developing through the accounting literature, by the close of the 1970s the systems approach had begun to make its presence felt. This occurred largely in an exploratory sense and by the end of the 1970s could not be said to have produced more than a partial systems COM.

PIECEMEAL PROGRESS

From the analysis of progress in accounting research into control between the years 1960-1979, the assertion that it was piecemeal appears justifiable. Accounting writers had paid little attention to the chain of development which had gone before them and therefore lacked any clear perspective of where their contributions stood in terms of schools of thought or of areas of significant conceptual poverty that required attention. Many writers continued to 'mark time' in their continued allegiance to the classical management COM and indeed classical concepts even retained an influence in the accountants' behavioural COM. Some sporadic references to structural aspects of control made an appearance in the accounting literature but did not achieve sufficient support, coherence and complementarity of thinking to produce a distinctive COM. Most writers who may have contributed to such development appear to have been content to remain firmly entrenched in the classical management COM.

Undoubtedly the most significant development in accounting literature on control in the 1960s and 1970s was the emergence of the behavioural COM. In this area a wealth of literature appeared, particularly with respect to the behavioural ramifications of the concept of formal control. While concepts of self-control and expectancy control had also made their appearance, they were still in relative infancy at the end of the 1970s. Indeed other behavioural concepts of control remained untouched by the accounting literature.

Between 1960 and 1979 the systems approach to control in the accounting literature had experienced an even more chequered career than the behavioural model. It arrived somewhat late on the scene, with the majority of published work in this area not appearing until the middle and late 1970s. Even then the number of accounting researchers making a significant contribution was quite small, so that model development had really only just begun by the close of the 1970s. This was reflected in a 'two concept'-based partial model.

Viewed in this light, progress in developing more sophisticated and varied accounting models of control could justifiably be considered to have been piecemeal. Old ideas retained a strong grip in the literature and even impinged upon the new. New approaches in some cases were slow to appear, and when they did either failed to materialise as coherent models or spawned models which were partially complete with respect to their constituent concepts. Even then some concepts were little advanced beyond infancy. Nevertheless, the 1960s and 1970s had witnessed the opening of a number of new doors in the accounting literature on control.

NOTES

1. The quantitative school was seen by Drinkwater to be a new breed of 'Taylorite' and his structural school also appeared to contain systems theory material.

2. Indeed Gole [1970] went so far as to argue that unless areas of responsibility and lines of authority were clearly defined, control became largely a matter of chance.

3. Refer to Figure 2.2.

4. A useful introductory review of behavioural studies relating directly or indirectly to planning and control, has been provided by San Miguel [1977]. It includes reference to both accounting and management writers.

5. Studies revealed a range of conflicting results with respect to such questions [Parker, 1979].

6. Other participative studies related to different subjects such as goal setting, goal congruence, motivation and so on [Dunbar, 1971; Ronen and Livingstone, 1975; Searfoss, 1976].

7. This was based on earlier empirical work by Child and Whiting [1954].

8. One exception to the findings on the effects of pressure to meet standards on subordinates was produced be DeCoster and Fertakis [1968]. They found that supervisors subjected to pressure tended to increase both their directing/organising *and* their human relations improving behaviours towards subordinates. This result was however, qualified by Revsine [1970] as probably resulting from very small or very large degrees of pressure.

9. Attribution theory examines the cognitive processes through which an individual may use data to draw conclusions (attributions) about the cause of a behaviour (causal attributions) and make inferences about the expectancy of a success or failure on a future repetition of the task [Birnberg et al, 1977].

10. Just as Mooney [1947] and Urwick [1937a] had done, decades earlier.

11. Control system quickness was defined by Amigoni [1978:285] as the elapse of time between an environmental event and its communication to managers for their reaction.

12. This analysis of open system control formed the introductory portion of a thesis (published as an American Accounting Association Study No 15) concerned with information analysis for control, in a budget setting.

PART THREE

COMPARATIVE ANALYSIS

CHAPTER 7

MANAGEMENT AND ACCOUNTING MODELS: A LIMITED CORRESPONDENCE

In this chapter the analysis of the conceptual development of control is extended. For each model that has been constructed[1] a comparison is drawn between its appearance in the management literature and in the accounting literature and is oriented towards the conceptual content of each model, the developmental path which it has taken, and the degree of conceptual development attained by the close of the 1970s. The four control models constructed from the management literature are then re-examined to determine the extent to which they may be interrelated. As well as arguments being mounted in support of conceptual links between models, evidence is drawn from some writers whose work, in the sample of literature studied, formed the basis for the models constructed in this thesis. Having identified connections between the control models, a framework of management control models is then constructed and an attempt is made to construct a similar framework for the accounting control models. Finally the chapter provides an overview of coexisting control models in both literature streams by the close of the 1970s including an evaluation of the general progress of model development and an assessment of any particular model's dominance within each stream of literature.

MANAGEMENT AND ACCOUNTING MODEL CONSTITUENTS: A COMPARISON

In considering the comparative conceptual content and developmental path taken by similar models in each stream of literature several questions arise. To what degree were they similar? Did one stream of literature produce more complex models than the other? What was the comparative state of development attained by the end of the 1970s? These questions will be considered on a model-by-model basis.

The Classical Model of Control

In Chapter 2 it was argued that the classical COM, represented in Figure 2.3, was derived from the combination of models which this study constructed on the basis of Taylor's and Fayol's work.[2] After their lifetimes, this model was widely advocated and embellished by the classical management school of writers with no real amendment, even into the 1970s. Accounting writers of the Taylor and Fayol era also appeared to adopt the classical model in its entirety and joined management writers in elaborating and promoting it.

<table>
<tr><td></td><td>1903 - 1959</td><td>1960 - 1979</td></tr>
<tr><td>Management</td><td>T A D C_d E C_n</td><td>T A D C_d E C_n</td></tr>
<tr><td>Accounting</td><td>T A D C_d E C_n</td><td>T A D C_g E C_n
(1960)</td></tr>
</table>

T = total control
A = authority-based control
D = disciplinary control
C_d = co-ordinative control

E = exception control
C_n = 'controls'
C_g = congruent control
(1960) = year of first accounting publication contributing to a concept of congruent control in literature sample studied[3].

TABLE 7.1: Inter-Stream Comparison of Classical Control Model Components

A comparison of classical COM concepts in both streams of literature for the period studied is presented in Table 7.1. From Taylor's seminal work in 1903, the management stream promulgated 6 concepts, without alteration, to the close of the 1970s. The accounting stream appears to have replicated the management stream concepts virtually without any delay at all. Two differences between the streams were, however, apparent. In the 1960s and 1970s the classical model concepts came under increasing criticism in the management literature. Their ambiguities and limitations were subject to scrutiny and discussion to a much greater extent than had occurred in the management literature before the 1960s. Meanwhile, accounting writers continued to reiterate the concepts of the classical model relatively uncritically (through the 1960s and 1970s).

A second difference between the two streams occurred with respect to the concept of co-ordinative control. While the concept remained without alteration in the management model, the accounting stream enlarged its meaning and revised it in the 1960-1979 period, to become a concept of congruent control. Instead of remaining as a control concept aimed at securing co-ordination of effort, the concept was revised by accounting writers so that it became one aimed at aligning personal goals and motivation with formal organisation goals set by top management. This revision represents the only occasion in the period (1900-1979) studied when an accounting COM exhibited a concept not already appearing in its management COM counterpart. Even then, it reflected previous management stream writing. In Chapter 6 it has already been argued that the accounting concept of congruent control was a reversion to the Fayol concept of unity of command-directon-interest.

Overall, by the close of the 1970s, it would appear that the management stream had largely moved on from the classical COM to develop other concepts of control from the perspectives of a number of other schools of thought. In the accounting literature, however, the classical model continued to retain a prominent position.

The Structural Model of Control

From the 1940s onwards another school of management thought, the structural school, began to develop alternative concepts of control to the classical school. This alternative approach, however, still retained elements of both classical management and bureaucratic theory and was distinctive in that it related control concepts to organisation structure and to functions at each level of organisation. A comparison of structural COM concepts in both streams of the literature for the period studied is presented in Table 7.2 and has been assembled on the basis of Figures 3.3 and 5.1. From 1942 the management stream developed 3 control concepts in the first instance. These concepts continued without change until the close of the 1960s when the directive control concept was effectively supplanted by the concept of surveillance or rules-and-records control.

	1942 - 1968	1969 - 1979
Management	CC D AF_1-AF_n	CC S/R AF_1-AF_n (1969)
Accounting	-	-

CC = centralised co-ordinating control

D = directive control

AF_1-AF_n = authority-based functional control

S = surveillance control

R = rules-and-records control

S/R = either S or R depending on organisational size

1942 = year of first management publication contributing to a structural COM in literature sample studied

(1969) = year of first management publication contributing to a concept of surveillance or rules-and-records control in literature sample studied

TABLE 7.2:   Inter-Stream Comparison of Structural Control Model Components

Over the period of the study, for the sample of literature examined, the accounting stream failed to produce sufficient conceptual discussion of the structural approach to control to justify a structural model. Not until the post-1960 period did accounting writers make any reference to structural issues at all, and then their number was very small. Any structurally-oriented discussion in the accounting literature even then tended only to focus upon the process aspect of the planning-control relationship. Nothing material emerged by way of structural accounting control concepts.

The Behavioural Model of Control

Rather than being a derivative of the classical approach (as the structural approach could be said to have been), the behavioural approach to control implied a rejection of the mechanistic and general principles orientation of the classical management approach. Instead, the behaviouralists chose to focus their attention upon the human dimension of control from a situational perspective. The behavioural school made its early appearance in the management literature of the 1930s and still occupied a major place in the management literature on control at the close of the 1970s.

A comparison of behavioural COM concepts in both streams of the literature for the period studied, is presented in Table 7.3. This table has been assembled from Figures 3.4, 5.3 and 6.1. From 1933 the management stream developed five concepts of control focussed upon the concept of motivation to act. Once these concepts had become established in the management literature, they continued unchanged until the late 1950s when the concept of hierarchical control was broadened to become a concept of formal control. This revised concept encompassed the positive and negative aspects of control, the role of controls, and dysfunctional effects of the exercising of formal control. From 1960 two further control concepts were added to the behavioural literature in the management stream. Power-based control gained increasing recognition, and in the 1970s, expectancy control attracted growing attention. This expanded range of control was focussed upon motivation to perform.

	1933 - 1956	1957 - 1979
Management	S_i C_o S_e S_o H M	S_i C_o E_x (1973) S_e S_o F (1957) P (1960) M_p

		1963 - 1979
Accounting	-	S_i C_o E_x S_e F M_p

S_i	= situation variables	F	= formal control
C_o	= cognitive variables	P	= power-based control
S_e	= self-control	E_x	= expectancy control
S_o	= social control	M_p	= motivation to perform
H	= hierarchical control	M	= motivation to act[4]
1933	= year of first management publication contributing to a behavioural COM in literature sample studied		
1963	= year of first accounting publication contributing to a behavioural COM in literature sample studied		
(1957)	= year of first management publication contributing to a concept of formal control in literature sample studied		
(1960)	= year of first management publication contributing to a concept of power-based control in literature sample studied		
(1973)	= year of first management publication contributing to a concept of expectancy control in literature sample studied		

TABLE 7.3: **Inter-Stream Comparison of Behavioural Control Model Components**

During the period to the close of the 1950s some accounting writers had begun to recognise the potential importance of employee reactions to budgets. A number of these expressed concern about the counter-productive reactions in subordinates which the process of budget administration could induce. Of this small group of accounting writers only two[5] went any further than this in trying to consider the implications of such behaviour for control, so that the accounting literature could not be credited with having developed any behavioural concepts of control by the close of the 1950s.

Behavioural concepts of control began to emerge in the accounting literature in the 1960s. The resulting concepts which formed the basis for the behavioural accounting COM differed from their management stream counterparts in a number of respects. The recognition of situational and cognitive variables was somewhat more limited than the managerial stream had given. On the other hand more extensive work was undertaken by accounting writers in developing the concept of formal control, with the impact of accounting controls, dysfunctional effects of exercising formal control, and the impact of performance evaluation receiving considerable attention. Concepts of self-control and expectancy control remained at a much lower level of sophistication in their specification. Missing from the accounting behavioural COM were the management model concepts of social control and power-based control.

The accounting COM differed from the management COM in one other respect. A substantial number of behavioural writers in accounting still retained a marked degree of allegiance to the classical COM.[6] The range of behaviouralist references supporting classical concepts of control lend support to the argument that the advocates of a behavioural approach to control in accounting still looked to the classical school as their foundation. This provided a backdrop to the behavioural accounting COM which was clearly absent from the behavioural management COM.

The above comparative analysis would therefore seem to suggest that at the close of the 1970s the behavioural models in each stream of literature were rather more distanced from each other (in terms of degree of conceptual sophistication and content) than Table 7.3 might at first suggest. The management model was considerably more advanced in terms of number of component control concepts, their detail of specification, and the absence of any allegiance to the classical COM.

The Systems Model of Control

While a number of management writers on control had begun to make references to systems-based approaches in the 1950s, major advances in the development of a systems COM in the management literature were made from the early 1960s. From this viewpoint control emerged as an intrinsic part of organisational activity rather than as an externally imposed constraint and was seen as a means of organisational adaptation to change and disturbance.

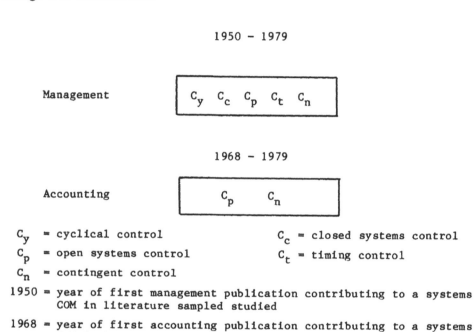

1950 - 1979

Management

C_y C_c C_p C_t C_n

1968 - 1979

Accounting

C_p C_n

C_y = cyclical control C_c = closed systems control
C_p = open systems control C_t = timing control
C_n = contingent control
1950 = year of first management publication contributing to a systems COM in literature sampled studied
1968 = year of first accounting publication contributing to a systems COM in literature sample studied

TABLE 7.4: Inter-Stream Comparison of Systems
Control Model Components

A comparison of systems COM concepts in both streams of literature for the period studied is presented in Table 7.4. This table has been assembled from Figures 5.8 and 6.2. Mainly from the management literature of the 1960s and 1970s five systems control concepts emerged. Of the four management models of control constructed in this thesis the systems model experienced the shortest period of conceptual development. Nevertheless it had achieved a detailed degree of specification in a relatively short span of time.

Contributions to any systems concepts of control did not appear in the accounting literature until the late 1960s. As might be expected from such a limited number of contributions, the accounting stream only managed to generate what might best be described as a partial systems COM. It included only two control concepts: open system control and contingent control. Both were developed simultaneously, whereas in the management literature the concept of open systems control had acted in part as a logical foundation for the concept of contingent control. Even then the open systems control concept rested on few contributions and stood in need of further attention by accounting writers. The contingent control concept, too, had only been addressed indirectly by some of its accounting contributors, so that it could be said to be still in its infancy at the end of the 1970s. Thus the best that could be said of the development of a systems approach to control in accounting by the end of the 1970s was that a beginning had been made, and that at best only a partial model was in existence.

In comparison with the management model at the close of the 1970s, the accounting model was very much inferior. Its open systems and contingent concepts were not as well specified, it had paid very little attention to closed systems control, and had not considered cyclical or timing control.

THE MANAGEMENT MODEL FRAMEWORK

By the end of the 1970s, control concepts identified in the management literature had contributed to four major control models: classical, structural, behavioural and systems. They did not, however, sit apart from one another as isolated models but were to varying degrees interrelated. The links between them were often forged through relationships between their component concepts. While some models were more strongly interconnected than others they appear to have been related in a framework as represented in Figure 7.1. It must be emphasised that the connections represented in Figure 7.1 are conceptual and do not imply any chronological order of precedence. It is to the nature of these connections, however, that some consideration must be given.

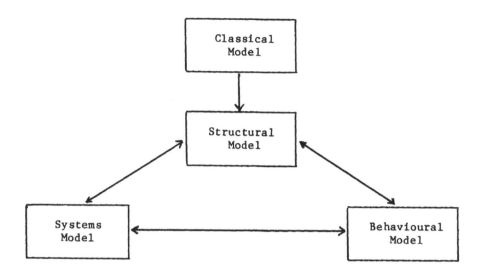

FIGURE 7.1: The Management Control Model Framework

Classical-Structural Links

As argued earlier in this study the structural COM had its foundations in the classical school. Indeed the two models shared some key constituent concepts. Consistent with the classical concept of authority-based control, the structural COM contained the concepts of authority-based functional control and surveillance control. Just as the classicists expounded a concept of co-ordinative control, so the structuralists pursued centralised-co-ordinative control. Similarly the classical 'controls' concept of control was matched by the structural 'rules and records' concept of control. The two models were clearly interrelated to a significant degree. This was to be expected when it is remembered that the structural school drew on the thinking of writers on scientific management, classical management and bureaucracy [Duncan, 1975]. Indeed structuralists looked to Fayol [Duncan, 1975; Hodgetts, 1979; Wren, 1979] and Weber [Huse and Bowditch, 1973; Pugh, Mansfield and Warner, 1975] as founders of their tradition. The classical-structural link within the management model framework was therefore a particularly strong one.

Structural-Behavioural Links

On the surface the structural and behavioural models of control would not appear to be so clearly interrelated. Some common ground did exist between the two although each treated it from a different perspective. While the structural COM had encompassed control by surveillance or rules and records and authority-based functional control, the behavioural COM encompassed these in a concept of formal control but then proceeded to adopt a critical approach to its use. Similarly, while the structural COM incorporated the concepts of centralised-co-ordinative and authority-based functional control, the behavioural COM recognised the existence of power-based control but saw it as accruing not just from the exercise of formal control but also from the exercise of self-control and social control. Connections between the structural and behavioural schools were also alluded to by other writers. Etzioni [1965] for example, concluded that the organisation structure was one of control and that the hierarchy of control was the most central element of organisational structure. However in order to examine this structure he classified the means of control distributed among various organisational positions in terms of coercive power (physical means of control), utilitarian power (material means of control) and identitive power (people identifying, as a form of control). In this way aspects of the structural and behavioural models of control were both utilised.

In a systems-oriented paper Ansari [1977] attempted to integrate what he termed the structural and behavioural approaches to control system design. According to his perspective the structural view of control was a highly mechanistic, closed systems view which defined control as a problem of designing optimal information networks. He saw the behavioural approach as emphasising the human and social processes inherent in organisational control. Pugh, Mansfield and Warner [1975] pointed to another link between the structural and behavioural schools in referring to Porter and Lawler's studies [1968] which linked attitudes and job satisfaction firmly to the formal organisation structure. Salaman [1979:146] argued that "the final, demonstrated structure" of an organisation was not the result of members' obedient execution of senior executives' directions as represented in rules, regulations, payment systems, budgetary limits, work design, supervision etc., but was the result of members' reactions and resistance to, and interpretation and avoidance of these formal limitations and restrictions. Once again structural and behavioural approaches to control were interrelated.

Thus while at first sight the structural and behavioural models of control may have appeared to be rather distant from each other, they focussed on some common concepts, albeit from differing perspectives. Further, there were those management writers who sought to integrate, at least partially, the two approaches to control or who detected relationships between the models' component concepts.

Behavioural-Systems Links

When the behavioural and systems models of control at the end of the 1970s are reviewed, connections between their component concepts do not emerge as clearly as in the previous comparisons. Nevertheless, links between the general approaches are still discernible. Bertalanffy [1972], a founder of general systems theory, pointed to its humanistic concern with relations between man and his world, with symbols, values, social entities and with cultures. Yet, some of its critics pointed to the differing motivations, attitudes and values which could render social organisation subsystem behaviour less predictable than that of biological systems [Silverman, 1970]. Overall however, a number of writers were discerning an underlying link between systems and behavioural approaches by arguing that systems and contingency thinking underpinned such schools as the behaviouralists [Kast and Rosenzweig, 1979]. Management theorists, psychologists and indeed economists could be observed to have shared an open systems view of the organisation as they grappled with the impact of technology, human behaviour, economy and so on [Eldridge and Crombie, 1974].

On a more specific level, Reeves and Woodward's [1970] classification of two intersecting scales of control revealed a combined behavioural-systems approach to control, with one scale representing personal and mechanical control at its extremes (essentially behavioural) and the other scale representing unitary and fragmented control at its extremes (essentially systems-based). Further specific links appeared with respect to the systems model concept of contingent control. Studies were made of organisational effectiveness being contingent upon the total amount of existing organisational control. Thus McMahon and Perritt's [1973] and Todd's [1977] systems-based studies supported Tannenbaum's essentially behavioural theory of total amount of control. In their theory of organisational integration and differentiation, again systems-based, Lorsch and Lawrence [1972] stressed the importance of interpersonal skills for achieving integration in organisations operating in dynamic and diverse environments. Allen and Gabarro [1972:22] pointed to the major strength of the Tavistock school's socio-technical approach (a foundation of contingency theory) as their "systematic treatment of the complex realities of organizational life, thereby allowing us to identify the diverse causes of behaviour in organizations". Kast and Rosenzweig [1979] drew the same conclusion in observing that a number of important studies undertaken by the Tavistock school had demonstrated the complex interrelationship between the technical and psychosocial systems. With respect to the contingency theory approach to organisational analysis that grew out of the Tavistock school's work, both Bowey [1976] and Dessler [1977] argued that contingency theory placed such schools as classical and behavioural "in their proper perspective" (rather than usurping them) and that indeed contingency theorists had demonstrated an increasing concern for the part played by individuals' motivations and interactions in generating organisational structure.

Both researchers and observers in the 1970s appear to have recognised linkages between the behavioural and systems schools of thought. These linkages largely took the form of combined behavioural-systems approaches to research questions or of behavioural factors being advocated or incorporated in the systems approach not only to organisational activity in general but also with particular reference to control. The relationship between the behavioural and systems models of control appeared to be potentially stronger in the sphere of contingent control, which allowed much greater scope for incorporating behavioural control variables within any conceptual design. Thus while the linkage between the behavioural and systems models was of a somewhat different character to the classical-structural and structural-behavioural links, the weight of argument had established a clear behavioural-systems model linkage nonetheless.

Systems-Structural Links

Just as systems thinking was seen as capable of incorporating the behavioural approach to organisations and control, so it was also argued by some that the systems approach also embodied the process approach of the structural school [Hodgetts, 1979]. However, the clearest link between the systems and structural models of control lay in their mutual attention to organisation structure. The structural school, as its name implied, placed great importance upon relating control to the hierarchical organisation structure. Systems theorists, and particularly contingency theorists, went further and examined the relationship between the design of organisation structure and its environment. Comparative studies attempted to determine the way in which aspects of structure were affected by contextual variables such as size, technology and ownership [Pugh, Mansfield and Warner, 1975].

The systems concern with structural issues was most noticeably manifest in the open systems control concept. The open systems view of organisations argued for their adaptation to environment by changing the structure and processes of their internal components. Since the organisation was seen to depend upon its interaction with the environment for survival and efficiency, organisation structure was studied in relation to variables such as technology, markets etc. [Silverman, 1970; Kast and Rosenzweig, 1972]. Indeed in the face of environmental uncertainty, it was argued that the systems approach to design of organisation structures was most appropriate since it accounted for environmental influences and did not propose 'one best way' of structuring organisations but allowed for more flexible and appropriate structures with less resort to the traditional hierarchy and with more provision for dynamic interaction between organisational subunits [Coleman and Palmer, 1973; Hellriegel and Slocum Jr, 1973].

The contingency theorists' concern with structural issues was best demonstated by Lawrence and Lorsch's [1969] analysis of the relationship between the uncertainty of an organisation's environment and its internal structure. They identified three organisational subsystems, marketing, economic-technical, and scientific, and hypothesised that the structure of each subsystem would depend upon the predictability of its environment. They also hypothesised that since environments of departments differed, departmental structure and management might also differ.[7] Their findings revealed that organisational subsystems did develop structures related to the degree of certainty in their particular environment.

It is clear then, that primarily through the agency of open systems theory and contingency theory, the systems and structural models of control were underpinned by a mutual concern with structural aspects of organisations. The approaches of the two schools to this question differed quite markedly, but they were nevertheless focussing upon common ground.

The Fabric of Control

By the close of the 1970s the management literature had produced more than just sophisticated versions of early classical control concepts, or an array of independent and unrelated new concepts of control. Over time, a number of major schools of thought had achieved prominence and had addressed the question of control from their own perspectives with the result that each contributed something new, added dimensions, or revised conceptual approaches to the ongoing development. In time this had allowed a fabric of control to emerge in the form of concepts welded into four major models. Yet not only were

concepts integrated within each model but also the models were found to
be interrelated as in the management model framework shown in Figure
7.1. The links between the framework's constituent models were of
differing nature in some cases. Such variations occurred as the linking
of models through common control concepts, shared concerns about general
organisational functioning, and mutual interest in particular
organisational and environmental variables. Nevertheless these
interrelationships were clearly discernible to researchers and
commentators alike. This does not imply that the end of control's
conceptual development had been reached in the 1970s, but the
identification of such a model framework does testify to the growing
mutual awareness of the writers responsible for each model's continuing
development.

MANAGEMENT AND ACCOUNTING FRAMEWORKS: THE CONTRAST

While the management literature on control between 1900 and 1979
sponsored four management models of control, the accounting literature on
control during the same period facilitated rather less than that. By the
close of the 1970s the classical accounting COM exhibited the same degree
of sophistication in its conceptual specification as the classical
management COM. The behavioural accounting COM however, fell some
distance short of the conceptual specifications of its management
counterpart. It contained fewer control concepts and most of its control
concepts were more primitive than their management counterparts.
Furthermore a considerable number of behavioural accounting writers still
maintained an allegiance to at least some aspects of the classical COM
(whereas such continued allegiance was not in evidence amongst management
writers studied). The systems-based COM constructed from concepts
identified in the accounting literature contained only two concepts by
the close of the 1970s. Not only was this fewer than the five control
concepts which made up the management literature's systems COM, but the
specifications of the two accounting concepts had not been developed to
the degree attained by the comparable concepts within the management
model. At best, the systems control concepts in accounting could only be

assembled into a partially developed systems COM.

Such findings inevitably pose the question of whether a viable framework of accounting models can be constructed at the close of the 1970s. Several major difficulties arise in this respect. The accounting literature had facilitated the construction of only two developed control models (and one partial model in its infancy). One of these models (the behavioural model) fell some distance short of its management counterpart and therefore could not be regarded as a well-developed model. In addition, contributions to behavioural and systems concepts of control in the accounting literature occurred relatively recently in the period studied, so that accounting writers did not appear to have considered the possible interrelationships between classical, behavioural and systems approaches to the study of control.

Given these impediments it was considered that the accounting literature on control at the close of the 1970s did not justify the construction of a model framework. This conclusion stands in stark contrast to the framework of management models of control. While both streams of control-related literature showed every sign of continuing their conceptual development beyond the 1970s, the management stream appeared to be considerably in advance of the accounting system.

MODELS AT THE CLOSE OF THE 1970S: A QUESTION OF DOMINANCE

At the beginning of the 20th century, both the management and accounting streams of literature shared one common conceptual approach to control, the classical COM. By the close of the 1970s the position had changed. The management literature had supported the construction of four control models, while the accounting literature had supported the construction of two developed control models and a partially developed model. In each stream of literature these models appear to have been coexisting, rather than new arrivals on the scene usurping the roles of previously existing models.

Some observations can be made about a difference in predominance of

particular models between each stream of literature. In the management
literature the classical COM was the foundation model and indeed spawned
the structural COM as a partial offshoot. Nevertheless as early as the
1930s, classical dominance was being challenged by a developing
behavioural approach to the conceptualisation of control. By the 1970s
the classical COM was one of four well developed control models and
appears to have been the model subject to most criticism. Accordingly it
could be argued that by the close of the 1970s the classical COM was no
longer dominant in the management literature. Other models (such as
behavioural and systems) which largely rejected its mechanistic,
principles-based approach, offered themselves as viable alternative
approaches to control and appeared to be assuming positions of equal, if
not greater, importance.

The same could not be said of the accounting literature. The
classical COM remained as the only developed COM into the 1960s. While
by the end of the 1970s an alternative behavioural COM had been
developed, it had still some distance to go (in comparison with the
management behavioural COM) before it could be regarded as having matured
into a well developed model. Furthermore the continued allegiance of a
sizeable number of behavioural accounting writers to classical control
concepts might suggest that amongst some of the accounting fraternity,
the behavioural COM might be considered to be partially derived from the
classical COM. The only other approach to control to have commenced
development in the accounting literature was the systems approach which,
however, was still in its infancy at the close of the 1970s. Meanwhile
the classical COM continued to attract relatively uncritical attention
during the 1960s and 1970s. These observations would appear to justify
the conclusion that in the accounting literature at the close of the
1970s, the classical COM retained its predominance.

The question of model dominance therefore appears to meet with a
different answer from each of the two streams of literature examined in
this study. By the end of the 1970s it did not appear that any one COM
could lay claim to dominance in the management literature. In the
accounting literature, on the other hand, the classical COM continued to
assert its authority.

NOTES

1. Classical, structural, behavioural and systems.

2. Refer to Figures 2.1 and 2.2.

3. Tables 7.1 to 7.3 provide such dates for new or revised control concepts appearing from the late 1950s onwards.

4. M and M_p do not appear to have been different concepts but represent different terms for the same concept.

5. Dent [1931] and Peirce [1954], in the sample of literature studied.

6. Refer to Chapter 6, subsection entitled **Residual Classical Proclivity.**

7. This was termed 'differentiation'.

CHAPTER 8

THE TIMING OF MANAGEMENT AND ACCOUNTING MODEL DEVELOPMENT

The management and accounting literature between 1900 and 1979 produced control concepts which differed in number and in degree of development and resulted in significant differences between the management and accounting COMs. A further question concerns the comparative timing of the development of accounting and management control models. Did the management and accounting models develop concurrently or did one stream of literature lag behind the other to a significant degree at some point in time?

This chapter compares the relative timing of publication dates between the sample of management and accounting publications used as the basis for identifying control concepts and constructing control models in this study. This comparison is undertaken with respect to corresponding management and accounting models and the period of any time-lags is then identified. After identifying material time-lags between the management and accounting control-related literature, the type of factors which may have contributed to such a lag are considered.

This study has been based on an extensive sample of published texts and papers relating to control, identified in both the management and accounting literature between 1900 and 1979. For the purpose of studying the relative timing of models that have been identified, the period 1900- 1979 was divided into equal 5-year time period blocks. In each block the number of publications already referred to as having contributed to a particular model were then counted for each of the management and accounting streams.[1] The results of this frequency analysis appear in Table 8.1 which outlines frequency of control-related publications over time classified by both control model type and stream of literature. In the first instance the implications of these results will be considered model-by-model.

Years	Classical		Structural		Behavioural		Systems	
	Management (n)	Accounting (n)	Management (n)	Accounting (n)	Management (n)	Accounting (n)	Management (n)	Accounting (n)
1900-04	1	1						
1905-09	0	0						
1910-14	2	1						
1915-19	1	2						
1920-24	5	1						
1925-29	0	3				1*		
1930-34	2	6			1	2*		
1935-39	6	8			4	3*		
1940-44	0	5	1		3	1*		
1945-49	9	7	9		2	2*		
1950-54	1	4	4		1	2*	4	
1955-59	1	1	2		6	1*	6	
1960-64	2	5	1	1	14	4	6	
1965-69	7	8	6	0	11	6	18	2
1970-74	5	15	4	4	10	12	15	2
1975-79	0	6	2	4	16	13	11	9
Total Publications	42	73	29	9	68	47	60	13

* Papers concerned with behavioural problems in budgeting (not directly referring to control).

n = number of publications (for each 5 year period)

TABLE 8.1

Comparative Timing of Control-Related
Publications by Model and Stream

SIGNIFICANT ACCOUNTING TIME-LAGS

As indicated in Chapter 2 the classical model had its beginnngs in the work of Taylor and Fayol, with Taylor's major publications appearing in 1903 and 1911[2] and Fayol's appearing in 1916 and 1923. By the end of the 1920s the accounting literature appeared to have taken up the pursuit of a classical management model of control quite quickly, with 8 accounting publications having appeared on the topic by that time in comparison with 9 management publications. Thus from the early 1900s the two streams of literature essentially pursued their development of a classical model of control concurrently.

The timing of the development of the structural model of control in the two streams was a different story altogether. From the sample of publications considered in this study the management stream first began to exhibit a structuralist approach in the 1940-44 period.[3] A considerable increase in attention was evident between 1945 and 1954, with 16 management publications appearing before any accounting publications. Even then only one accounting publication appeared in the accounting literature before 1970. Accordingly it is arguable that no significant interest in a structural approach to control was evident in the accounting literature until 28 years after the first sign of management interest in the subject. This represents a considerable lag in accounting control model development.

The development of a behavioural model of control in the management and accounting streams also exhibited a difference in timing. While a first inspection of Table 8.1 might convey the impression that the two streams developed behavioural models concurrently, in fact this was not the case. Accounting publications shown in the table during the period 1925-1959 referred only to behavioural problems which had been observed in the operation of corporate budgeting systems and did not directly refer to control at all.[4] In contrast, management literature in the behavioural area during that period (and subsequently) was very much concerned with the question of control and its effects on people. Contributors included Mayo [1933, 1946], Barnard [1938], Roethlisberger and Dickson [1939], Emch [1954], Davis [1957], Argyris [1957] and Vickers [1958]. It was not until the 1960s that the accounting literature produced evidence of behavioural approaches to the study of control. Before 1960 however, the sample of management literature in this study had produced 17 publications exhibiting behaviourally-based approaches to control. Even when accounting interest picked up after 1960 it did not match the degree of management attention until the 1970s. Effectively then, it could be argued that serious accounting attempts to develop a behavioural model of control did not commence until 30 years after the management literature's first efforts, with comparable levels of interest not being matched until even later.

The systems model of control was the latest to develop in the management literature, but once again, accounting lagged behind. Management interest appeared to commence in the early 1950s whereas the first glimmer of accounting interest did not appear until the late 1960s and even then was completely overshadowed[5] by management interest until the early 1970s. Thus while it is arguable that the accounting literature lagged 18 years (1950 to 1968) behind management's first attempts at developing a systems model of control, it could be argued that serious accounting attempts at model development lagged yet another 10 years behind management.[6]

A summary view of the comparative control model development between accounting and management literature is provided in Table 8.2. The column entitled 'Basic Accounting Lag' measures the number of years by which the first sign of accounting interest[7] in a particular model's development lagged behind the first sign of interest exhibited by the management literature.[8] The column entitled 'Effective Accounting Lag' measures the number of years after the first sign of management interest that the level of accounting interest approximately matched the level of management interest in a particular model's development.[9] With the exception of the classical management model, material time-lags, both basic and effective, in accounting model development were detected with respect to structural, behavioural and systems models. Indeed in only one instance (basic accounting lag in systems control model development) was the accounting lag less than 20 years.

Model	Basic Accounting Lag (Years)	Effective Accounting Lag (Years)
Classical	Nil	Nil
Structural	(M1942-A1962) 20	(M1942-A1970) 28
Behavioural	(M1933-A1963) 30	(M1933-A1970) 37
Systems	(M1950-A1968) 18	(M1950-A1975) 25

M = management literature commencement year
A = accounting literature commencement year

TABLE 8.2: The Accounting Model Time-Lag

CONCURRENT CLASSICAL DEVELOPMENT

The development of a classical management COM appears to have taken place almost concurrently in the management and accounting streams of literature.[10]   The conceptual sophistication and detail of argument contained in Taylor and Fayol's writings, however, suggest that management and accounting development of the classical control model can be argued as having proceeded concurrently, once their seminal work had been published.   This pattern of development was in marked contrast to the significant lags in accounting attention to structural, behavioural and systems models of control.   A number of factors may have influenced this concurrent development.

In the first instance the classical management COM appears to have represented the only available approach to control until at least 1930 and probably into the late 1930s or early 1940s.   The rapidity of accounting adoption of classical management concepts could also be partly explained by the publicity which the Taylor formulation in particular received.   Taylor sought publicity for his ideas by publishing and making speeches under the auspices of the American Society of Mechanical Engineering, by his attempts to install his system of scientific management in organisations, by the promotion of his ideas by close colleagues, by the public interest in the investigations of the Committee of the House of Representatives, and by the formal promotion of the Taylor Society.   Thus it is likely that accountants were more rapidly and frequently exposed to elements of the classical COM than appears to have been the case with later management models.

The relative simplicity of classical management prescriptions may also have attracted a following in the accounting literature rather more quickly than later management models of control.   The prescriptive, principles-based approach appeared to be time-saving and easily applied in practice, so that this would have increased its attractiveness for accountants.   The air of certainty surrounding it may also have enhanced its appeal.[11]

The budget which concerned accountants so much also lent itself to the relatively simplistic approach of the classical COM. Its governmental origins had emphasised its use as a limiting and restricting form of control which was later transferred into corporate use.[12] Such an emphasis was consistent with the classical approach to control and rendered the budget eminently suitable as a vehicle for classical management thinking. The budget would therefore have been well placed to speed the impact of the classical COM upon the accounting literature.

Finally, the shared concerns of both management and accounting writers for scientific management and work practices and for efficiency of production, offered fertile ground for their sharing of classical principles as well.[13] Accounting writers' demonstrable concern to pursue these ideals may have caused them to quickly emulate the classical management approach to control as the most apparently logical path to fulfillment of such ideals.

While the above factors may not have comprised the total sum of influences for a speedy accounting adoption of the classical management COM, they appear to have been an important influence. The relative strengths of their individual impact remains an unknown, but when envisaged in some combination, their presence undoubtedly made a significant contribution to the exceptional speed (never subsequently replicated) with which the accounting literature adopted a management model of control.

DIFFERENTIAL FREQUENCIES

In addition to the general lag in accounting adoption of most management control models, for the sample studied, management and accounting literature publication frequencies differed over time with respect to particular models.[14] The structural COM attracted considerable interest in the management stream during the years 1945-49, after which interest declined but then revived in the years 1965-69 before declining again. Yet before 1970 the sample studied included 23 management publications and only one accounting publication. As management interest declined in the 1970s, accounting interest finally became apparent.

The development of the behavioural COM saw a steady, albeit moderate, level of management interest between the years 1930 and 1954, with a substantial growth in interest occurring from 1955 to 1964 and continuing at quite high levels subsequently. In contrast, the first effective accounting interest in developing a behavioural COM appeared after 1960 and continued to grow at a somewhat slower pace than management interest. For example, in the years 1955 to 1969, the sample studied included 31 control-related management publications and 10 control-related accounting publications.

In the development of a systems model of control, management interest completely outweighed accounting interest. Between the years 1950 and 1974 the sample of literature studied included 49 management publications and only 4 accounting publications.

Once again the development of the classical management model appears to have been the exception. During the period 1900-1979 accounting interest overtook management interest. Indeed, after 1960, there was a marked surge of accounting interest when compared with management interest, with accounting publications peaking at 15 in the years 1970-1974 (compared with 5 for management).

In addition to considering relative frequencies of interest by management and accounting writers over time, the total of publications for the period 1900-1979 deserves consideration. Table 8.1 reveals a marked discrepancy between the two streams. Structural publications in management totalled 29 compared with only 9 for accounting. Behavioural publications in management totalled 68 compared with 47 or effectively[15] 35 in accounting. Systems-oriented publications in management totalled 60 compared with 13 for accounting. Only in respect of the classical approach did accounting overtake management, with 73 publications to management's 42.

What might be concluded from this analysis of relative levels of interest between the management and accounting streams over time? In a sense it serves to amplify the significance of the accounting literature's general lag behind the management literature in control model development. Higher levels of accounting interest in a particular school was generally preceded by a high level of interest by management writers in an earlier period. Indeed with respect to 3 models of control, management publications far outweighed accounting publications for the sample and period studied. The one exception with respect to both developmental time-lag and differential frequency of interest was the classical model of control. While Taylor and Fayol's work must be regarded as the model's foundation, in later years accounting interest overtook management's interest and indeed exceeded it in total for the 1900-1979 period. While possible reasons for the accounting lag in general will be considered later in this chpater, the results from Tables 8.1 and 8.2 give the accounting stream the appearance of having persisted with the classical control model at the expense of developing alternative models (to a degree), while management stream attention had in large measure moved on to develop other models of control.

IN THE MANAGEMENT WAKE

In both timing and level of interest in the 4 models of control identified in this study, the accounting literature followed in the wake of the management literature. In the case of the structural, behavioural and systems models both the time-lag and difference in periodic interest levels were particularly marked. These lags and differences were not of the same order of magnitude however in the classical model of control. Nevertheless the balance of evidence would suggest that the timing of management and accounting control model development corresponded only to a very limited degree between 1900 and 1979. In general, accounting development lagged well behind that of management.

THE ACCOUNTING LAG: CONTRIBUTING FACTORS

Having established the occurrence of a significant accounting lag in timing, degree of attention and conceptual sophistication of control model development between 1900 and 1979, the question then arises as to the possible factors which may have contributed to this situation. While it is not possible to identify all such likely factors, or even to identify some factors with absolute certainty, factors considered by this study were those which had an arguably reasonable probability of influence and those for which some related evidence was available.

A Preoccupation with 'Control Tools'

It could be argued that in its professed role of assisting management decision-making, management accounting has pursued its task of collecting, recording, measuring and assessing performance through a pronounced concentration on the design and operation of control tools. Such a preoccupation would be conducive to the overlooking of conceptual aspects of control and would have increased the probability that accounting writers would lag behind management writers in control model development.

Sample	Control Tools			General			
	Costing	Budgeting	Divisional Performance	Responsibility Accounting	Human Behaviour	Planning and Control	Organisational/ Management Control
21	5	18	8	8	5	1	4
100%	24%	86%	38%	38%	24%	5%	19%
texts with "general" chapters 15=100%				53%	33%	7%	27%

TABLE 8.3

Identity of Control-Related Chapters in
Management Accounting Texts

In order to test this proposition a sample of 21 management accounting texts of post-1970 dates of publication were selected for analysis.[16] As the texts were published towards the end of the period covered by this study they are assumed to represent recent generally accepted thought in management accounting and provide the severest test of the proposition. Control-related chapters and chapters in control-related sections were selected from chapter indexes and analysed as in Table 8.3.[17] Of the 21 texts, 6 (29%) included no general chapter relating to control at all, while in the remainder, chapters relating to control tools clearly outweighed general control chapters by a significant margin. As Table 8.3 reveals, 86% of texts covered budgeting in sections on control, 24% covered costing and 38% covered divisional performance measurement. All texts that covered divisional performance in sections on control, also covered budgeting at the same time. Those texts including 'general' chapters in sections related to control tended to concentrate on responsibility accounting (53%) while only 27% included a chapter relating to organisational or management control. When all 21 texts are considered, that percentage falls to 19%. The above evidence tends to suggest that the management accounting literature considered control mainly in terms of control tools (budgeting in the majority of cases) and allowed much less attention to the more general, conceptually-oriented aspects of control.

A further test of the proposition was undertaken by analysing conceptual definitions and discussions of control appearing in the same sample of 21 management accounting texts. The data are summarised in Table 8.4. Of the 21 texts, 48% included control tools within their conceptual discussions of control. When 3 texts containing no conceptual coverage of control are excluded, the percentage of texts referring to control concepts that included control tools in their definition rose to 56%. Thus even when management accounting texts attempted a conceptual discussion of control, approximately half still couched their definitions in terms of control tools, at least to a degree. A similar result emerged from an analysis of 11 budgeting texts as shown in Table 8.5.[18] Of texts sampled, 45% included the budget as a 'control' within conceptual definitions or discussions of control. When 4 texts providing no conceptual discussion at all are excluded, that percentage rises to 71%.[19] This provides further confirmation of the results obtained from analysis of management accounting texts.

Authors	Page References	Classical Management	Control Tools	Structural	Behavioural	Systems
		Reference Classification				
Amey & Egginton [1973]	380-398, 445-447, 551-566		X	X		X
Anthony & Reece [1975]	5, 452-464, 531-533	X		X	X	
Anthony & Welsch [1977]	443-448, 708	X	X	X		
Batty [1975]	4, 353, 367	X	X	X		
Bierman & Dyckman [1976]						
Burke & Smyth [1972]	10, 12-13, 15-18, 607-612	X		X		
Crowningshield & Gorman [1974]						
Davidson et al [1978]	194-197, glossary 500	X		X		
De Coster & Schafer [1979]	14-15, 301-302, glossary 734	X		X		
Dopuch et al [1974]	291-318	X	X	X	X	
Drabin & Bierman Jr [1978]						
Gray & Johnston [1977]	51, 53, 476-477, 492-496	X			X	
Heitger & Matulich [1980]	246, glossary 799	X	X			
Horngren [1977]	6, 164-165, 192-193, 236	X			X	
Louderback & Dominiak [1975]	2	X				
Lynch & Williamson [1976]	5, 7, 134, 242-251	X	X		X	
Matz & Usry [1976]	4, 43-44	X	X			
Moore & Jaedicke [1980]	3, 8, 42-43, 303	X	X			
Shillinglaw [1977]	5-10	X	X			
Sizer [1979]	21-22, 330			X		
Thornton [1978]	9, 148-153	X		X	X	
Total Number of References		15	10	10	6	1
Number of References as % of Sample (21)		71%	48%	48%	29%	5%
Number of References as % of texts with conceptual discussion (18)		83%	56%	56%	33%	6%

TABLE 8.4

Conceptual References to Control in a
Sample of Management Accounting Texts

While the above evidence is restricted and only considers the issue in terms of textual content and length as a representation of accounting attitudes and concerns, it does provide at least a partial indication of the likelihood of the proposition's validity. Three sets of evidence have been evaluated:

1.   Management accounting text sections and chapters.

2.   Management accounting text conceptual control discussions and definitions.

3.   Budgeting text conceptual control discussions and definitions.

All three lend support to the proposition that the accounting literature tended to be preoccupied with control tools in its treatment of control.

Authors	Page References	Classical	Budget Tool	Structural	Systems
Batty [1970]	28-30, 65-66, 205-207		X	X	X
Bunge [1968]					
Edey [1960]	19-21	X	X		
Heckert & Willson [1967]	11-12, 19	X	X		
Houck (Jr) [1979]	3-22, 211-212, 216	X	X	X	
Jones & Trentin [1971]	27, 53, 101	X	X	X	
Matthews [1977]					
Rautenstrauch & Villers [1968]					
Sweeney & Wisner [1975]					
Vatter [1969]	4-6	X		X	
Walsch [1976]	5-6, 16-19, 35-37, 46	X		X	X
	Total number of references	6	5	5	2
	Number of references as % of sample (11)	55%	45%	45%	18%
	Number of references as % of texts with conceptual discussion (7)	86%	71%	71%	29%

TABLE 8.5

Conceptual References to Control in a
Sample of Budgeting Texts

Such a preoccupation is not difficult to understand given the traditional role of accounting as a measurement-oriented discipline. Since the accounting role has consistently been one of designing financial measures as well as collecting, recording and measuring results, a preoccupation with control tools would be a logical outcome of accounting writers' focus upon measurement systems and practices. That focus could have constrained the degree of attention paid by accounting writers to conceptual aspects of control. It also apears to have been a product of accountants' continued allegiance to the classical model of control being an elaboration of its concept of 'controls'-based control.

In contrast, the management discipline has been concerned with a wide range of variables in organisational functioning, of which measurement has been only one. Having a much broader focus than accounting, management writers may therefore have been less constrained in their interests and more likely to pay more attention to issues such as the conceptual aspects of control.

A Neglect of Conceptual Aspects of Control

A related question to that of control tool preoccupation is whether this accounting preoccupation appears to have led to a neglect of conceptual aspects of control in the accounting literature. This neglect, if it did occur, would seem to be at odds with the management accounting emphasis upon the facilitation of management planning and control. Nevertheless such neglect would also have predisposed accounting control models to lag behind management model development.

The proposition that there has been a comparative neglect of conceptual aspects of control in the management accounting literature was therefore tested in several ways. The management accounting and budgeting texts sampled for Tables 8.4 and 8.5 were analysed for type of concepts considered. Both budgeting and management accounting texts concentrated heavily upon classical management approaches to control, consistent with observations in Table 8.1. Structural aspects of control also received considerable emphasis, with much less attention being accorded to behavioural approaches to control and only a minor degree of attention being paid to systems approaches to control. Low emphasis results cannot be discounted due to early publication dates, given the post-1969 dating of most texts sampled. Thus all control model developments should be capable of reflection in the sample studied.

The high degree of attention to the classical management approach appears to be consistent with a well developed classical accounting COM. The minimal attention to the systems approach also appears to be consistent with a partially developed accounting systems model still in its infancy. The moderate degree of attention to behavioural approaches appears to be consistent with the behavioural accounting model developed by the close of the 1970s, although behavioural approaches in budgeting texts were notable by their absence. The marked degree of attention to structural approaches in both management accounting and budgeting texts however, is surprising given the accounting writers' failure to develop a coherent structural model of control by the close of the 1970s. From the above evidence and the perspective which it represents, the proposition appears to be moderately well supported.

Authors	Page References	(a) Length of Conceptual Discussion (pages)	(b) Text Length (pages)	a/b (%)
Amey & Egginton [1973]	380-398, 445-447, 551-566	36.0	655	5.5
Anthony & Reece [1975]	5, 452-464, 531-533	14.5	532	2.7
Anthony & Welsch [1977]	443-448, 708	4.5	722	0.6
Batty [1975]	4, 353, 367	1.5	882	0.2
Bierman & Dyckman [1976]	Nil	0	545	0
Burke & Smith [1972]	10, 12-13, 15-18, 607-612	9.5	649	1.5
Crowningshield & Gorman [1974]	Nil	0	720	0
Davidson et al [1978]	194-197, glossary 500	2.0	536	0.4
De Coster & Schafer [1979]	14-15, 301-302, glossary 734	2.0	751	0.3
Dopuch et al [1974]	291-318	28.0	684	4.1
Drebin & Bierman [1978]	Nil	0	363	0
Gray & Johnston [1977]	51, 53, 476-477, 492-496	5.5	737	0.7
Heitger & Matulich [1980]	246, glossary 799	1.5	796	0.2
Horngren [1977]	6, 164-165, 192-193, 236	3.0	900	0.3
Louderback & Dominiak [1975]	2	0.5	427	0.1
Lynch & Williamson [1976]	5, 7, 134, 242-251	6.5	464	1.4
Matz & Usry [1976]	4, 43-44	1.5	940	0.2
Moore & Jaedicke [1980]	3, 8, 42-43, 303	1.5	552	0.3
Shillinglaw [1977]	5-10	6.0	955	0.6
Sizer [1979]	21-22, 330	2.0	501	0.4
Thornton [1978]	9, 148-153	6.0	551	1.1
	Totals	132	13862	1.0

TABLE 8.6

Space allocated in Management Accounting Texts
to Conceptual Discussion of Control

A further test of the proposition was undertaken on the basis of the percentage of text length devoted to conceptual discussions of control. The same management accounting and budgeting texts were studied and the analysis appears in Tables 8.6 and 8.7. The average percentage of textual length devoted to conceptual control discussion for management accounting texts was 1.0% and for budgeting texts was 1.1%. Thus the two samples yielded relatively consistent total averages. Only 14% (3 texts) of the sample of management accounting texts and 9% (1 text) of the sample of budgeting texts recorded a percentage of text length devoted to conceptual discussion greater than 2%. Given the manifest emphasis given to management planning and control as objective functions of management accounting, a subjective evaluation of the above percentages would suggest that the attention paid to conceptual aspects of control by the accounting literature was uniformly rather low. This observation would therefore tend to support the proposition.

Authors	Page References	(a) Length of Conceptual Discussion (pages)	(b) Text Length (pages)	a/b (%)
Batty [1970]	28-30, 65-66, 205-207	4.5	416	1.1
Burge [1968]	Nil	0	221	0
Edey [1960]	19-21	2.0	158	1.3
Hecker & Willson [1967]	11-12, 19	1.0	573	0.2
Houck Jr [1979]	3-22, 211-212, 216	22.0	231	9.5
Jones & Trentin [1971]	27, 53, 101	0.5	304	0.2
Matthews [1977]	Nil	0	234	0
Rautenstrauch & Villers [1968]	Nil	0	337	0
Sweeney & Wisner [1975]	Nil	0	132	0
Vatter [1969]	4-6	1.5	159	0.9
Welsch [1976]	5-6, 16-19, 35-37, 46	6.0	594	1.0
Totals		37.5	3359	1.1

TABLE 8.7

Space Allocated in Budgeting Texts
to Conceptual Discussion of Control

One further test of the proposition was undertaken by assessing the frequency of appearance of control-related articles appearing in accounting journals. Two journals selected were *Journal of Accounting Research* and *Management Accounting* (N.A.A. - New York). The basis of selection was one accounting research journal (*Journal of Accounting Research*) and one professional management accounting journal (*Management Accounting*). These two journals had attained the highest in perceived quality rankings for their respective categories in a study by Weber and Stevenson [1981:606]. The period sampled from both journals was 1970-79 inclusive and the main theoretical articles were analysed for those which included some reference relating to management or organisational control in their title. This would include non-conceptual as well as conceptual discussions of control. The analysis is summarised in Tables 8.8 and 8.9.

Vol. No.	Year	(a) Control-Related Articles	(b) Main Theoretical Articles	$(^a/_b)$ %
8	1970	1	16	6
9	1971	2	15	13
10	1972	1	18	6
11	1973		15	0
12	1974		14	0
13	1975	1	12	8
	Supplement		6	0
14	1976	2	12	17
	Supplement		5	0
15	1977		12	0
	Supplement		5	0
16	1978	1	17	6
	Supplement		6	0
17	1979		21	0
	Supplement		6	0
Total	1970-1979	8	180	4%

TABLE 8.8

Frequency of Control-Related Articles Appearing in
Journal of Accounting Research

Vol. No.	Year	(a) Control-Related Articles	(b) Main Theoretical Articles	$(^a/_b)$ %
	1970	10	137	7
	1971	7	138	5
	1972	3	142	2
	1973	7	141	5
	1974	2	114	2
	1975	11	141	8
	1976	6	145	4
	1977	6	127	5
	1978	1	109	1
	1979	2	110	2
Total	1970-1979	55	1304	4%

TABLE 8.9

Frequency of Control-Related Articles Appearing in
Management Accounting (NAA - New York)

The *Journal of Accounting Research* contained an overall average of control-related to main theoretical articles 1970-79 of 4%. This included 4 years' issues where no control-related articles appeared at all (of a sample of 10 years). *Management Accounting* also contained an overall average of control-related to main theoretical articles 1970-79 of 4%. The overall average of 4% for both journals was remarkably consistent since it might have been expected that a higher percentage would have been achieved in *Management Accounting* as it would cover a much more restricted and relevant (to control) subject area than the *Journal of Accounting Research*. A closer examination of the 55 articles identified in *Management Accounting* as control-related revealed that only 2 (i.e. 4% of control-related articles and 0.2% of main theoretical articles) were primarily focussed upon organisational/management/ conceptual aspects of control. The vast majority, on the other hand, were concerned with control tools.[20] Thus, once again, the level of attention paid to conceptual aspects of control in both research and professional accounting journals was not material.

In summary, the proposition that there has been a comparative neglect of the conceptual aspects of control in the accounting literature was tested by reference to three sets of evidence:

1. Types of conceptual approaches to control considered in a sample of management accounting and budgeting texts.

2. Percentage of above texts' length devoted to conceptual discussions of control.

3. Frequency of appearance of control-related articles in a sample of research and professional accounting journal issues.

Moderate support for the proposition was received from 1, with stronger support for the proposition coming from the results of 2 and 3. Once again it must be emphasised that such tests do not examine the proposition from all possible perspectives and necessarily involve subjective judgement. Nevertheless in combination they strengthen the case for arguing that there was at least some degree of neglect of conceptual aspects of control in the accounting literature. On this basis it could be argued that such neglect would in all probability have contributed to the accounting lag in control model development when compared with the management literature.

The Relative Extent of Management Accounting Research

In attempting to detect and confirm the probability of influence on the accounting development lag of various factors, the question arose as to whether research in management accounting had occupied a minor proportion of the accounting literature compared to other accounting subject areas. If this should prove to be the case it might further account for some of the accounting lag in control model development. Accordingly the proposition was mounted that management accounting research had been neglected relative to other major subject areas in the accounting literature.

Vol. No.	Year	Management Accounting (n)	Financial Accounting (n)	Finance (n)	Auditing (n)	Information and Decision-Making Theory (n)	Other (n)	Total (n)
1	1963	2	5				3	10
2	1964	2	8		1		2	13
3	1965	1	6	1			3	11
4	1966	1	7				3	11
5	1967	1	9					10
6	1968	2	9	2				13
7	1969	2	6					8
Subtotal	Number	11	50	3	1	0	11	76
1963-1969	% (of 16)	14%	66%	4%	1%	0%	14%	100%
8	1970	4	4	4		3	1	16
9	1971	6	4	1	1	3		15
10	1972	1	5	2		6	4	18
11	1973	2	2	6	3		2	15
12	1974	2	5	4		2	1	14
13	1975	1	2	5	1	2	1	12
	Supplement				6			6
14	1976	3	3	4		1	1	12
	Supplement					5		5
15	1977		3	3	3	2	1	12
	Supplement						5	5
16	1978	4	4	3	1	3	2	17
	Supplement		1	4			1	6
17	1979	3	4	6	3	5		21
	Supplement				6			6
Subtotal	Number	26	37	42	24	32	19	180
1970-1979	% (of 180)	14%	21%	23%	13%	18%	11%	100%
Total	Number	37	87	45	25	32	30	256
1963-1979	% (of 256)	14%	34%	18%	10%	13%	12%	100%

n = number of main articles published.

TABLE 8.10

Classification of Main Articles by Major Subject in *Journal of Accounting Research*

To test this proposition the *Journal of Accounting Research* was examined for type of articles published from its inception Vol. 1 in 1963 to Vol. 17 in 1979 (and supplement) inclusive. Main theoretical articles (excluding research reports) were classified according to major subject area, with the proportion of total articles produced in each category shown in percentage figures for 1963-69, 1970-79 and 1963-79. The results are set out in Table 8.10.

For all three groups of periods management accounting articles comprised a constant 14% of total number of articles. Since 6 categories (including 'other') were identified, an equal share of total articles by each for any period would produce a figure of 17% for each category. Accordingly it would not appear that the management accounting area suffered a significant degree of neglect. Some qualifications to this conclusion should, however, be made. Financial accounting publications always outweighed management accounting publications by a significant margin, with the difference being most pronounced in the 1963-69 period (14% management accounting versus 66% financial accounting). Furthermore the 1970-79 period saw a marked rise in prominence of finance, auditing and information/decision-making theory articles, with management accounting being outranked in publishing frequency by finance (23%) and information/decision-making theory (18%). Thus while the management accounting percentage of total articles remained constant it continually received less attention relative to financial accounting and in the 1970s moved from being the second identifiable area of importance in accounting research (though producing less than a quarter of the financial accounting article total) to the fourth identifiable area of importance, closely followed by another category (auditing).[21] A further qualification to the results in Table 8.10 would be that the percentages attributed to each subject category might be a reflection of the journal's editorial policy. If the policy had become one of achieving approximate parity between subject groups over time, this might explain to some extent the constant percentage of management accounting publications over time.

What can be concluded from this evidence? It would appear that for the 1963-79 period, management accounting had maintained a constant percentage of total accounting research publications and that 14% has not been an immaterial proportion. On the other hand it would appear that in earlier years it was of minor importance relative to financial accounting, and subsequently slipped down the publishing frequency rankings as it was overtaken by other emerging subject areas.

The proposition that management accounting research was neglected relative to other areas of accounting research can therefore be only weakly supported by the above evidence at best. The results are inconclusive and cast some doubt about the likely influence on the accounting model development lag by the relative extent of management accounting research.

A Lack of Management Accounting Standards

Another factor which could have influenced the development of control models in the accounting literature was professional accounting standards issued as a guide to accounting practice. An argument can be mounted for the potentially beneficial influence of accounting standards upon the development of accounting concepts on the basis that standards usually require the inclusion of conceptual definitions, thus promoting a consideration of concepts by standard setters. Further, the usual practice of issuing exposure drafts or discussion documents for general comment by accountants, academics, corporations, government agencies, etc, before producing a standard, promotes further discussion of both concepts and technical procedures. Standards themselves can be the subject of familiarisation seminars when first issued or mooted, and once established, often become the subject of critical academic teaching in the training of accountants. Hence the creation of accounting standards has the capacity to promote increased attention among accountants to conceptual issues involved.

Accordingly a lack of management accounting standards would probably have inhibited to some degree the extent of accounting discussion of conceptual aspects of control. Therefore the proposition that the number of management accounting standards produced by leading accounting professional bodies has been relatively few, was considered. In order to test this proposition, the accounting standards issued by the accounting professions of four leading Western countries and by the International Accounting Standards Committee were examined for the proportion of management accounting standards issued as at 31 December 1979 and, to extend the test, as at 31 December 1981. The results are outlined in Table 8.11.

Country	Issuing Body	Series No.	Total Issued as at 31/12/79	Total Issued as at 31/12/81	Number of Standards Containing Management Accounting Emphasis
Australia	A.S.A. & I.C.A.	AAS1-AAS10	9	10	0
Canada	C.I.C.A.	Recommendation Nos. 1500-1800 3000-3840 4000	43	44	0
Great Britain	A.S.C.	SSAP1-18	15	18	0
United States of America	F.A.S.B.	Statement of Financial Accounting Standards Nos. 1-53	33	53	0
International Accounting Standards	I.A.S.C.	IAS1-16	8	13	0
			108	138	0

A.S.A. & I.C.A.   Australian Society of Accountants and Institute of Chartered Accountants
C.I.C.A.   Canadian Institute of Chartered Accountants
A.S.C.   Accounting Standards Committee
F.A.S.B.   Financial Accounting Standards Board
I.A.S.C.   International Accounting Standards Committee

TABLE 8.11

Accounting Standards and Management Accounting Coverage

The results of this analysis in Table 8.11 clearly demonstrate a complete neglect of the management accounting area by standard setters. The vast majority of accounting standards promulgated by the end of 1979 and 1981 related to financial accounting. In only two subject areas was there a possibility of standards carryng some implication for management accounting. These were inventories and segment reporting. In relation to inventories, ISA2, SSAP9, CICA Recommendation 3030 and AAS2 all concentrated upon valuation and presentation of inventory in the balance sheet, for presentation to shareholders. In relation to segment reporting, FASB Statements 17, 21 and 24, CICA General Accounting Section 1700, and IAS14 all treated the subject in terms of external reporting of segmented performance to shareholders and the public. Thus the only two subject areas covered in the results shown in Table 8.11 that may have been management accounting-related, proved not to be. These results clearly confirm the proposition under test.

The proposition was subject to further testing in relation to Securities and Exchange Commission Accounting Series Releases in the USA and Accounting Research Studies issued by the American Institute of Certified Public Accountants. From 1 April 1937 to August 1968, Accounting Series Releases Nos 1 to 112 were issued by the SEC. None of these were found to be cost or management accounting related. Similarly Accounting Research Studies Nos. 1 to 15 were examined and only one, No. 13 (inventories), bore any relationship to management accounting. These results added further confirmation to the proposition.

It would appear that the only significant accounting standards related to management accounting were promulgated by the United States Federal Government's Cost Accounting Standards Board set up by Congress in 1970 but disbanded in 1980. Their standards, rules and regulations included subchapters on administration, procurement practices, disclosure statement and cost accounting standards. However it was clearly stated that the cost accounting standards were designed to achieve uniformity and consistency in cost accounting principles followed by defence contractors and subcontractors under United States Federal Government contracts, with particular reference to the pricing, administration and settlement of contracts. The scope of these standards was therefore very limited indeed and applied to only one sector of economic activity in one country with very little apparent effect on the management accounting literature in general. It would not appear therefore, that this restricted group of standards modifies the support for the proposition being tested, to any significant degree.

One further observation can be made regarding the contribution of management accountants to the profession as a whole. In June 1979 the International Federation of Accountants (IFAC) Management Accounting Committee conducted a questionnaire survey of 72 accounting bodies of IFAC and received 49 replies [Anon, 1981:568-569]. It was found that of the total governing council members of the 49 respondents, approximately 68% of councillors were from public practice, so that non-public (management) accountants appeared to be under-represented.[22] This under-representation was also evident in the committee structure of these bodies. Of the 37 bodies who had issued accounting standards, 22 involved non-public (management) accountants in some part of the committee stage while 15 bodies did not appear to involve them at all. On this basis it could be argued that management accounting has been neglected to some degree by a considerable number of professional accounting bodies, including those involved in accounting standard setting.

The evidence examined above has taken serveral forms:

1. Selected accounting standards promulgated by professional accounting bodies.

2. Sundry research bulletins and practice regulations issued by professional accounting bodies and government agencies.

3. A survey of management accountants' involvement in professional accounting bodies.

The results have demonstrated a questionable level of management accountants' involvement in standard setting and a virtual absence of management accounting standards. Hence the proposition that the number of management accounting standards produced by leading accounting professional bodies has been relatively few is supported. It is therefore argued that such a pronounced lack of management accounting standards (relative to financial accounting in particular) could well have inhibited the attention paid to conceptual aspects of control in the accounting literature.

The Recency of an Academic Accounting Tradition

Yet another variable which may have contributed towards the lag in development of accounting models of control is the time-span over which an academic tradition in accounting developed. It is arguable that if the academic tradition in accounting had been of relatively short duration up to 1979, the development and maturity of control models could be expected to have been somewhat restricted. Thus a lag or comparative recency in development of accounting models of control might in part be a reflection of a comparative recency in the academic accounting tradition. The proposition to support this contention is that the history of academic accounting education is a comparatively recent one. This proposition was subject to testing by means of a brief review of the history of academic accounting education in the USA and in the UK.

Accounting Education in the United States

It could be argued that academic accounting education began as a subset of management education with the rise of university business schools in the USA. While in 1897 only one university had recognised accounting in its catalogue,[23] compared with 12 or more institutions in 1907 [Carey, 1969][24], some early experiments with the teaching of accounting did take place in American universities. In 1851 a school of commerce was incorporated in the University of Louisiana but was discontinued in 1857. The University of Illinois established a School of Commerce in 1868 (named as such in 1870) including a subject of bookkeeping. The Wharton School of Finance and Economy was founded in 1881. Still, by the end of 1900 only 7 such institutions existed in the US [Lockwood, 1938].

Allen [1927] examined 2200 university catalogues from 1900 to 1926 and found that in 1910 there were 52 universities and colleges giving accounting courses (of which 29 offered advanced courses). By 1916, this number had risen to 116 (though only 35 schools offered cost accounting courses) and in 1926 he identified 335 universities and colleges which offered accounting courses[25] (with 147 teaching cost accounting). These courses appear to have been for the most part technically and practically oriented as for instance evidenced by 48 schools in 1916 giving a course in accounting problems, in some cases called 'C.P.A. Problems'. An early American leader in academic accounting education was the School of Commerce, Accounts and Finance of New York University which in 1900 provided courses in Theory of Accounts, Practice in Auditing and Auditing, using a largely practical approach [Lockwood, 1938; Slocum and Roberts, 1980]. In 1916 Columbia University was using 'laboratory' teaching via model sets of books and records of business [Carey, 1969]. This represented an innovation in accounting teaching, but of a practical orientation nonetheless.

While American universities generally embraced accounting courses relatively early in the 20th century, the world's first academic accounting journal, *The Accounting Review*, did not commence publication until 1926, and by 1946 was still the world's only academic accounting journal [Parker, 1980:308]. Indeed the prestigious [Weber and Stevenson, 1981:606] American academic accounting journal, *Journal of Accounting Research*, did not commence publication until 1963.

Although study of accounting was quite well established in American universities and colleges by the 1930s, they did not provide the monopoly source of entrants to the accounting profession. A survey by the committee on research and statistics of the Texas Society of Certified Public Accountants found that of 226 CPA's who replied to a questionnaire, only 60 percent were college graduates and of those who received their CPA certificates in the years 1941-1945, still only 66.8 percent held college degrees. In October 1949 it was reported that New York was the only state requiring successful completion of a 4-year college course as a prerequisite for the CPA certificate [Carey,

1949a,b]. In fact while the number of college graduates entering the accounting profession were increasing less than half were accounting majors [Carey, 1970].

The teaching of accounting in American universities had begun with a highly practical and technical approach. This continued into the 1960s. In 1959 however, the Gordon and Howell (financed by the Ford Foundation) and the Pierson (financed by the Carnegie Corporation) reports on the current standards of business education criticised many accounting courses for containing too much descriptive material of vocational training type. In 1967 the results of a 5-year study of the common body of knowledge required for American CPA's by a 12 man commission of the American Institute of Certified Public Accountants were published in a 354 page report entitled 'Horizons for a Profession'. Descriptive, vocational training courses were again not recommended [Carey, 1970] and academic breadth was advocated as a replacement for the stringent specialisation common in accounting courses. The study supported a conceptual rather than a technical approach to accounting education and emphasised the importance of research [Buckley, 1972]. After the report's publication representatives of 668 universities and colleges particpated in seminars to discuss it and almost universally endorsed the conceptual rather than procedural approach to formal accounting education [Carey, 1970]. To encourage this change of emphasis the Board of Examiners for the Uniform CPA examinations embarked on a policy of progressively broadening the base of examination, thus requiring changes in accounting curricula as well as "deeper excursions into supporting fields of study" [Buckley, 1972:8].

What can be concluded from this review of American accounting education? While it shared almost as long a history as university business schools, its early development up to the 1920s involved relatively few universities and even by the late 1940s university graduates with accounting majors did not form the majority of entrants to the American accounting profession. More importantly, accounting was for many years taught as a practical, technically-oriented subject with little attention to theoretical or conceptual approaches until the

1960s. The tradition of research in accounting was comparatively recent, with *The Accounting Review* moving progressively towards becoming a research journal [Buckley, 1972] and the *Journal of Accounting Research* only commencing publication in the 1960s. Thus while the American evidence would not appear to support the proposition that an academic accounting tradition has been a particularly recent phenomenon it has suggested a qualifying argument that its conceptual content was limited until the 1960s. Such a late conceptual development would most likely have contributed to a lag in the accounting development of models of control.

Accounting Education in the United Kingdom

Academic accounting education in the United Kingdom has a much more recent history than the United States. University teaching of accounting was minimal until after World War II [Stacey, 1954]. Some early beginnings were represented by the establishment of chairs of accounting at the Universities of Edinburgh and Glasgow in 1919 and 1925 respectively. Even earlier (1902) the first faculty of commerce in England was created at the University of Birmingham with Lawrence Dicksee appointed to the professorship. In 1919 he took the Chair of Accounting and Business Organisation at the University of London and was then succeeded in 1926 by F.R.M. de Paula[26] [Anon, 1966:84]. That chair lapsed in 1930 and the Birmingham chair also remained vacant for years before and after 1944. No professor of accounting worked again in London until 1947 and with one exception (Bristol, 1955), no further new chairs were established in England and Wales until 1962 [Solomons and Berridge, 1974].

Up to the 1960s accounting was not alone with regard to a paucity of attention in UK universities who were also slow to concede that business or management studies were suitable components of a university education and such studies "were slow to penetrate either at undergraduate or graduate level" [Wheatcroft, 1970:3]. However Stacey [1954] contended that the record of accountancy as a university subject was even more dismal than business administration.[27]

From 1962 onwards, however, growth in UK chairs of accounting was quite vigorous. By the end of 1974 there were 28 professors of accounting plus 2 vacant chairs. Three of these professors had no first degree and only 9 held higher degrees,[28] but all were members of professional accounting bodies, with 19 being Chartered Accountants. The balance, representing largely management accounting bodies, thus constituted only 32% of the UK accounting professoriate [Parker, 1975].

Management studies also grew very quickly in UK universities from the early 1960s onwards. By 1968-69, 30 universities offered postgraduate management courses and between 1966-67 and 1969-70, 30 more specialist or generalist courses were introduced. By 1969 31 universities also offered undergraduate courses in management, business or commerce as part of the syllabus for a first degree [Wheatcroft, 1970].

Before World War II the main educational route to professional accounting body membership was via articles served by the clerk under a Chartered Accountants practitioner [Green, 1970]. The 'Universities Scheme' inaugurated in 1945 allowed an articled clerk to obtain both a degree and membership of the Institute of Chartered Accountants in England and Wales in 5.75 to 6 years, with a minimum of 3 years being spent on practical work under the supervision of his principal. Entries to universities under this scheme did not exceed 200 per annum until 1956-57 [Anon, 1966:191]. Indeed by the mid-1950s only a small minority of recruits to the accounting profession had been previously educated at a university [Stacey, 1954]. Until that time professional bodies of accountants did not appear to have encouraged the teaching of accounting at universities [Stacey, 1954].[29] In 1965-66 graduate entry to the accounting profession in Scotland was only 9% of the total and was still only 36% of the total in 1969-70.[30] In England 'relevant' accounting-oriented degree graduates of universities only constituted 16% of total graduate entry and 5% of total entry to the Institute of Chartered Accountants in England and Wales in 1972 [Solomons and Berridge, 1974].

Stacey [1954] has argued that the responsibility for not encouraging the development of accounting as an academic study could be attributed to the attitude of professional accounting bodies.   In 1927 F.R.M de Paula[31] wrote:

> "so far as I am aware, the Institute and the Society have not directly concerned themselves with the academic study of accountancy or research work, and, ... have not concerned themselves directly with the educational methods in force within the profession itself."

Decades later, in 1961, The Report of the Committee on Education and Training of the Institute of Chartered Accountants in England and Wales, pronounced that it preferred correspondence courses to university tuition [Parker, 1980:309].   Attitudes in the profession, it would appear, had not changed perceptibly.

The first academic accounting journal to appear outside the USA was *Accounting Research*, a quarterly journal sponsored by the Society of Incorporated Accountants in 1948 [Solomons and Berridge, 1974].   This was intended to provide a scholarly medium for publication of theoretical and practical contributions to the state of accounting knowledge.   Following the integration of the Society and the Chartered Institute in 1957, however, the journal was discontinued.   This decision was attributed to the scant regard for professors and academic journals held by Institute Council members and to their belief that most of the articles were abstruse and of no practical value [Parker, 1980].   The successor to *Accounting Research*, called *Accounting and Business Research* and again sponsored by the Institute of Chartered Accountants in England and Wales, did not reappear until the beginning of the 1970s.

Accounting education in British universities has proved to be a comparatively recent phenomenon and did not emerge as a major sector in either university teaching or entrance to the profession until the 1960s. The attitude of the accounting profession to accounting education remained apathetic for decades. Even when university accounting graduates began to emerge in material numbers in the early 1970s, they still constituted a minority of entrants to the accounting profession. When accounting in universities did come to be recognised by the accounting profession it was sponsored as part of professional training contracts. Given the pronounced practical and indeed anti-theoretical stance of professional accounting bodies at least until the 1960s it may be arguable that approved courses would have been largely practical and technical in orientation. Certainly until the 1970s British conceptual and theoretical accounting research would have suffered through a lack of accounting academics and a lack of British research journal venues for publication of results. Such evidence would support the proposition that the British academic accounting tradition has been a comparatively recent phenomenon, although only marginally more recent than the academic management education tradition. However the considerable degree of professional apathy (and indeed, antipathy) towards university education, the paucity of academic leaders, and the minority proportion of graduate entry to the accounting profession may all have contributed to a further lag in the conceptual development of accounting models of control.

The Academic Accounting Tradition

Returning to the proposition being tested, it was proposed that the history of academic accounting education is a comparatively recent one. In terms of an absolute time-frame, the evidence supports the proposition. In both the USA and the UK the time span to 1979 was less

than 100 years. Indeed a significant tradition of university teaching of
accounting would only number 60 years in the USA and 30 years in the
UK. Such support for the proposition must be qualified however by the
observation that in both countries, the history of management education
in universities was not very much longer than accounting. Thus the
proposition is only weakly supported by the evidence.

The evidence does however suggest a further proposition concerning
factors influencing the lag in development of accounting models of
control. It would appear likely that in both countries university
accounting education was largely practical and technically oriented.
Forces for an upgrading of conceptual and theoretical content did not
emerge until the mid-1960s. Venues for publication of academic research
in accounting were restricted and the accounting profession still
consisted of a majority of accountants who were not university graduates
(with accounting majors). This justifies mounting the proposition that
the theoretical and conceptual tradition in academic accounting education
is a relatively recent phenomenon.[32] Given the likelihood of this
proposition being confirmed, it could be argued that the lack of a
significant period of theoretical and conceptual tradition in academic
accounting may have contributed to the lag in accounting control model
development.

Factors Reviewed

A number of factors have been suggested as potential contributors to
a lag in the timing, degree of attention to and conceptual sophistication
of accounting models of control. A review of the arguments for their
influence and the results of evidence tested will serve to place the
above analyses in an overall perspective.

It was argued that an accounting preoccupation with control tools would be conducive to the overlooking of the conceptual dimensions of control. Accounting writers might therefore continue to develop control tools without considering their supporting conceptual framework, purposes and conceptual rationale. The associated proposition that accounting writers had been preoccupied with control tools was strongly supported by the evidence examined. Hence it could be argued with justification that this preoccupation may have helped create conditions conducive to a lag in accounting control model development.

A related argument was that conceptual aspects of control may have simply been neglected. This would clearly predispose accounting model development to be lagged in both timing and conceptual sophistication. The associated proposition that conceptual aspects of control had been neglected in the accounting literature was tested by recourse to three sources of evidence. One source of evidence yielded results which lent moderate support to the proposition while results from two other sources provided strong support for the proposition. Again, therefore, it could be argued with justification that a neglect of conceptual aspects of control did occur in the accounting literature and very probably contributed to the lag in accounting control model development.

A neglect of management accounting—oriented research relative to research in other subject areas within accounting was argued to be a potential influence conducive to the accounting control model development lag. This was based on the premise that the majority of analyses of the conceptual nature of control in the accounting literature would tend to occur in a management accounting context, particularly as management accounting writers emphasised their concern to assist management to plan and control organisational activities. Thus a neglect of management accounting—oriented research might presage a neglect of conceptual

control model development. The associated proposition that management
accounting research was neglected relative to other subject areas of
accounting was tested but results lent only weak support at best to the
proposition. It would therefore appear that the argument that management
accounting research was neglected and thus retarded accounting control
model development, fails.

It was also argued that a paucity of management accounting standards
would have accounted in part for a retarded development of accounting
control models. Accounting standards issued by professional accounting
or government regulatory bodies often undertake conceptual definition of
component concepts, promote academic and professional discussion at
exposure-draft stage and even after final confirmation evoke further
critical academic research and teaching. Hence if it were found that few
management accounting standards existed, another potential impetus for
control model development in the accounting literature would be absent.
Testing of standards and pronouncements in several leading accounting
nations revealed a virtual absence of management accounting standards and
thus provided strong support for the proposition that up to 1979 there
was a paucity of management accounting standards. Accordingly it can be
argued with justification that the virtual absence of management
accounting standards left vacant a potentially important forum for the
further development of conceptual models of control in the accounting
literature.

One further argument was put. It was argued that a recency of
academic accounting tradition would have played a significant part in the
accounting model development lag. The expiration of only a short period
of academic contribution to professional accounting education might imply
that due to earlier likely neglect of theoretical and conceptual aspects
of accounting by practitioner-educators in the professional body part-

time education system, conceptual aspects of control would only have been highlighted by the more recent academic accounting educators. Accordingly the associated proposition that the academic accounting tradition was a comparatively recent one was tested by recourse to a review of accounting education history in the USA and the UK. The results obtained yielded only weak support for the proposition and hence the argument that a recency of academic accounting tradition played a significant part in the accounting model development lag, fails.

The educational history evidence analysed above did however suggest an alternative proposition. It was that the theoretical and conceptual tradition in academic accounting education has been relatively recent. Available evidence suggested the existence of considerable justification for this proposition. Accordingly an argument can be mounted for the reasonable probability that the apparent recency of a theoretic/ conceptual tradition in academic accounting education may have been a factor contributing to the retarded development of conceptual accounting models of control.

MATERIAL TIMING DIFFERENCES

The management and accounting streams had taken developmental paths of markedly differing timing. In all control models the management stream had taken the initiative in commencing a model's development and indeed in all but the classical model of control had predated accounting interest by periods of 20 to 30 years.[33] In terms of number of publications during the 1900-1979 period too, in all but the classical model, management publications outweighed accounting publications to a significant degree.[34] Thus the developmental processes leading to both management and accounting models only corresponded to a limited extent. The longer span of time and greater number of contributions in the

management model development process (than in accounting) laid the
foundation for a management control model framework which at the close of
the 1970s the accounting literature had failed to match.

A number of factors have been advanced as probable contributors
towards the retarded timing of accounting control model development.
These were an accounting preoccupation with control tools, a related
neglect of conceptual aspects of control, the virtual absence of
management accounting standards, and the recency of a theoretic/
conceptual tradition in academic accounting education. While these
factors may not necessarily have constituted the sum total of influences
upon the timing of accounting control model development, it appears
likely that, acting in concert, they made a significant contribution to
the accounting lag.

NOTES

1. The count included multiple publications by any one particular author as well as 'one-off' publications by the majority of authors. The count for each stream also included some authors who produced publications on control from a management perspective as well as from an accounting perspective, although these were in a minority.

2. Taylor's testimony before the Special Committee of the House of Representatives was published in 1912.

3. This is represented by Urwick's contribution in 1942.

4. The accounting references to behavioural problems in budgeting that did occur before 1960, were mainly in the nature of a brief aside or comment on the aspect as part of a larger work on budgeting in general.

5. In 1965-69 management publications sampled, totalled 18, to accounting publications' total of 2, and in 1970-74 totalled 15 to accounting's 2.

6. A total effective time-lag from management to accounting, of 28 years.

7. Measured by the first related accounting publication from the sample studied.

8. Measured by the first related management publication from the sample studied.

9. The first period of structural model development in which accounting interest (4 publications) matched management interest (4 publications) was 1970-74. The first such period in behavioural model development (10 management compared with 12

accounting publications) was 1970-74. The first such period in systems model development (11 management compared with 9 accounting publications) was 1975-79.

10.   Refer again to Table 8.1

11.   Such arguments were also mounted by Stephenson [1968] to explain why classical thinking had persisted so long in management practice.

12.   Refer to section entitled **Aspects of Budget Development** in Chapter 4.

13.   Refer to section entitled **Scientific and Efficiency Concerns** in Chapter 4.

14.   Refer to Table 8.1.

15.   Discounting accounting publications in the years 1925-1959.

16.   These texts were selected from the holdings of Monash University Humanities and Social Sciences Library via that library's subject catalogue.

- 265 -

17.   Refer to supporting Appendix A.

18.   These texts were selected from the holdings of Monash University
      Humanities and Social Sciences Library via that library's subject
      catalogue.

19.   One exception to this trend, not included in the table, was a text
      by Amey [1979] which provided conceptual discussions throughout
      the length of the text.   This was the only text found to have
      taken such an approach and represented such a significant
      exception that it was excluded from arithmetic percentages to
      obviate its potentially distorting effects on results.
      Nevertheless its achievement deserves recognition here.

20.   This adds further confirmation to the proposition that the
      accounting literature was preoccupied with control tools.

21.   This relies on the 1970-79 percentages and draws on the following
      ranking of importance:

      1.   finance 23%
      2.   financial accounting 21%
      3.   information and decision-making theory 18%
      4.   management accounting 14%
      5.   auditing 13%.

22.   For example governing councillors of the following bodies were:

             American Institute of Certified Public Accountants
                             - 88 % public practitioners

             The Institute of Chartered Accountants in England and Wales
                             - 66% public practitioners

             The Canadian Institute of Chartered Accountants
                             - 74% public practitioners

23.   The Wharton School of Finance at the University of Pennsylvania.

24.   These included New York University in 1900, and the Universities
       of Wisconsin, Illinois, California, Chicago, Michigan, Vermont,
       Kansas, Harvard and the Cincinnati School of Commerce and
       Accounts.

25.   An editorial [Anonymous, 1925:293] in *The Journal of Accountancy*,
       noted the involvement of American university schools in accounting
       education and similar developments in Canada, especially at McGill
       University in Montreal.

26.   Appointed from a readership in accounting (since 1924) at the
       London School of Economics.

27.   In comparison with other more established UK university
       disciplines, accounting appeared even more impoverished, as
       revealed by Solomons' and Berridge's [1974] survey of size of
       full-time academic staff in departments of law, engineering and
       accountancy as at July 1972, for the Universities of Birmingham,
       Bristol, Exeter, Lancaster, Leeds, Liverpool, Manchester,
       Southhampton, Wales (Cardiff), Edinburgh, Glasgow, Strathclyde.
       In total, the results were:

	Professors	Others
Engineering	124	1005
Law	35	163
Accountancy	13	66

28.   These included the 3 who had no first degree.

29.   In 1951, the number of university students majoring in accountancy
       under the English accountancy scheme was just under 350 relative
       to a total university population of approximately 85,000 (0.4%)
       [Stacey, 1954].

30.   In Scotland however, part-time attendance at university classes in
       law, economics and accountancy was required of articled clerks in
       the accounting profession until the institution of the 'academic
       year' in 1960-61. This allowed the clerk to spend a full academic
       year at university attending prescribed classes and studying for
       the Institute of Chartered Accountants of Scotland final

examinations. This year would normally be the third in a 5 year apprenticeship [Solomons and Berridge, 1974].

31. In a Letter to the Editor, *The Accountant*, 1 January 1927:31.

32. Since the proposition has been generated from the data itself, it is not possible to subject it to immediate test using the same data.

33. Refer to Table 8.2.

34. Refer to Table 8.1.

CHAPTER 9
SUMMARY AND CONCLUSIONS

In this historical study of management and accounting approaches to
the conceptual specification of control, the development of the
management stream of thought and then the accounting stream of thought
were studied as two distinct progessions over time, both covering the
period 1900 to 1979. Numerous control concepts were identified and
assembled into models based on the schools of thought which they
represented. Such a model—based historical analysis of control concept
development has not been available to date in the literature of
management or accounting. These models have revealed the conceptual
nature and structure of control to be rather more complex than simple
definitional statements have hitherto implied.

For each literature stream[1] the changes in component structure of
each model were analysed. In considering the progress of models in each
stream, further attention was paid to these socio-economic factors to
whose likely influence over a model's emergence or development, some
reasonable degree of probability could be attributed.[2] From the
comparison of the relative progress of model development over time
between the two streams of literature it has been concluded that
accounting lagged behind and mirrored management control model
development, though with increasing imperfection in later decades of the
period studied.

A FOUNDATION FOR CONTROL MODELLING

For the period 1900 to 1979 the classical management school of thought served as a foundation for the development of both management and accounting models of control. The classical COM was essentially generated by the scientific management literature. This approach to control was undoubtedly best represented by the writings of Taylor and Fayol. From their work the most direct and detailed classical analyses of the nature of control and its conceptual elements could be distilled to a degree not possible from the writings of other classical management writers. Even so the Taylor-Fayol models were not articulated by them as such but were constructed from the summation of their major writings. What resulted, however, were models whose component concepts were considerably more complex in total structuring than the basic definitions of control that they promulgated would at first imply.

In attempting to reach an understanding of the factors that were likely to have exercised an influence over the development of the Taylor and Fayol models of control, the socio-economic environment within which they worked as well as their personal histories were examined. Consequently, while recognising the exceptional nature of their contributions to management thought, it was concluded that both authors were 'men of their time' and accordingly produced control concepts reflective of their period and their backgrounds. The degree of commonality between their environments and personal backgrounds were found to be such that the models constructed from their conceptual writings were held to be predisposed towards the mutual conceptual compatibility that was evident. Thus the classical management COM was constructed from their models' combination and appeared to be reiterated and embellished in both the management and accounting streams of literature for many subsequent decades.

THE EVOLUTION OF MANAGEMENT MODELS

While the classical management COM was found to hold almost total sway in the management literature until the 1930s, two further models of control had commenced development in the management literature by the end of the 1940s. The structural COM emerged as an adaptation of the classical model, emphasising the relating of control to organisational structure as embodied in the hierarchy of authority and emphasising the functional or process aspects of exercising control. Key elements of the classical COM were incorporated in the structural COM virtually intact, with further conceptual dimensions added on.

At almost the same time a behavioural COM was developing in the management literature. This represented a pronounced departure from classical management thought. It had moved away from the formal, authority-based approach to control characteristic of the classical control model, to take account of individual and group-based control as well as dysfunctional aspects of formal control. The focal point of this model became one of 'motivation to act'. Inherent in the behavioural model was a rejection of the classical model's preoccupation with formal, mechanistic aspects of control and a substitution of an orientation towards human behaviour aspects of control.

By the late 1970s the classical COM had come in for increasing criticism in the management literature. The structural COM had been further refined and the behavioural model had been expanded with the addition of further component concepts. In addition, a considerable degree of attention was paid to the development of a systems COM. While some elementary work had been published on this subject in the management literature of the 1950s, the 1960s and 1970s saw a marked upsurge of interest and quite rapid development of systems control concepts.

Thus by the close of the 1970s the management stream of literature had facilitated the construction of four models of control. Subsequent analysis revealed that these were interrelated either through common control concepts, through mutual interest in particular organisational and environmental variables, or through shared concerns about aspects of organisational functioning. Such relationships were identified from time to time by various researchers and commentators in the management literature. On the basis of this set of observed interrelationships, it was argued that the management literature, while continuing the process of conceptual control development, had by the close of the 1970s produced an interwoven conceptual fabric of control (in the form of a framework of control models).

THE ACCOUNTING MIRROR: DERIVATIVE BUT DEFECTIVE

The accounting literature at first followed hard on the heels of the management literature in adopting the classical management COM. It then mirrored the classical management COM in virtually every conceptual detail. Several factors were advanced as possibly creating conditions conducive to an accounting reflection of the classical management COM. These were the historic nature of the budget, the accounting pursuit of scientific practices and efficiency, and the perception of the budget as being primarily oriented towards control. Indeed by the close of the 1950s the accounting control literature had done little more than reiterate the classical management COM. The accounting literature's persistence with the classical COM continued relatively uncritically through the 1960s and 1970s. In the early 1970s interest in some quarters actually appears to have increased.

The 1970s did see some faltering steps towards a structural approach to control among some accounting writers, but the level[3] of discussion and analysis did not lay sufficient foundation for a viable model by the end of the 1970s. On the other hand, a behavioural COM attracted considerable interest in the accounting literature of the 1960s and 1970s. The growth of literature in this area, particularly in the 1970s, produced three concepts of control which mirrored concepts in the behavioural control model of the management stream. Nevertheless by the end of the 1970s, while the accounting literature had produced a coherent COM, it still lacked some concepts already established in the corresponding management COM and some of its existing concepts were not well developed. At the same time it was apparent that a considerable number of contributors to the behavioural accounting COM continued to expound elements of the classical COM. Thus while the behavioural model in the management literature had represented a break with the classical tradition, the behavioural model in the accounting literature still clung to its classical predecessor in certain aspects.

In the late 1970s in particular, accounting researchers began to exhibit an interest in the systems approach to control. However, by the end of the 1970s only limited development had taken place with attention being predominantly paid to only two concepts.[4] As a result it could only be said that the accounting literature at best had spawned a partial COM which again appeared to be attempting to mirror the systems COM in the management literature.

From evidence examined in this study it appears highly probable that during the 1970-79 period the accounting literature on control followed the lead of the management literature on control. With the exception of the classical model of control, accounting model development lagged behind management model progress to a significant degree, both in terms of time and conceptual content. Yet in every respect the accounting literature attempted to adopt identical control concepts to those contained in the management models. No instance was found where accounting writers produced a new or different control concept before it had appeared in the management literature.[5] Indeed each model with the exception of the classical model, lagged behind its management model counterpart by approximately 20 years or more.

The accounting mirror was therefore derivative but defective. Accounting model development consistently lagged behind that of management models while attempting to replicate their conceptual content. This derivation of accounting models of control was, however, imperfect. The accounting models, by the close of the 1970s had fallen well short of matching their management counterparts, with one model still lacking two concepts,[6] one in its infancy[7] and another model missing altogether.[8] Furthermore it was evident that in some conceptual accounting approaches to control, old ideas maintained a grip and at times impinged upon the new.[9]

Could the albeit imperfect mirroring of management concepts of control in the accounting literature have been a mere case of coincidence? This study concludes that far from being mere coincidence, the reflection of management concepts of control in the accounting literature was the result of a conscious or unconscious replication of management concepts by accounting writers. This conclusion is based upon two major findings of this study. First, it has become clear that in all but the classical model of control, management models of control preceded accounting models of control by a minimum period of approximately 20 years. Second, the accounting literature between 1900 and 1979 did not produce one control concept which did not replicate a control concept already established in the management literature.

Furthermore quite a number of accounting control concepts were inferior (in terms of theoretical specification) to their management counterparts. Even in terms of the number of well developed control models at the close of the 1970s, the management literature was clearly continuing to take the lead. These observations further support the conclusion that the accounting attempt at replication of management control models was not a mere case of coincidence.

CONTRIBUTIONS TO A LIMITED CORRESPONDENCE

The limited correspondence between the framework of management models of control constructed in this thesis, and the models constructed from the accounting literature by the close of the 1970s appears to have been largely attributable to two factors. From the literature sample studied, with the exception of the classical control model, the first signs of accounting interest in behavioural, structural and systems approaches to control lagged behind the first signs of interest in the management literature between 18 and 30 years.[10]

Furthermore, a related observation has been made[11] with respect to total number of publications supporting the construction of each model in the period 1900-1979. The number of management publications outweighed the number of accounting publications on structural, behavioural, and systems approaches to control to a pronounced degree. Management writers' structural publications totalled 29 relative to an accounting total of 9 publications, their behavioural publications totalled 68 relative to an accounting total of 47 publications, and their systems publications totalled 60 relative to an accounting total of 13 publications. Therefore the limited correspondence between management and accounting models of control at the close of the 1970s appears to be attributable in large degree to two interrelated factors:

1. A pronounced time-lag in accounting interest in the conceptual specification of control relative to management interest.

2. A decidedly lower total level of accounting interest in the conceptual specification of control over the period of the study.[12]

Furthermore the limited correspondence between structural, behavioural and systems models of control in accounting and management may also be partly attributed to the marked preference shown by many accounting writers (relative to management writers) for retaining the classical COM.[13]

CONTRIBUTIONS TO THE TIME-LAG

The question then arises as to why accounting writers' interest fell behind that of management writers in terms of timing and total publishing frequency. The attempt to identify contributing factors has been focussed upon the accounting time-lag since it can be argued that time-lag and publishing frequency are interrelated. Table 8.1 shows that with respect to the structural, behavioural and systems model of control, the time-lag between first management and accounting publications accounts for a sizeable portion of the difference between total management and accounting publishing frequency. Furthermore, the factors identified as probably contributing to the accounting time-lag, could be viewed as equally applicable contributors to the differences in total publishing frequency between the literature of management and accounting.

In attempting to identify factors which may have contributed to the time-lag between management and accounting model development, a number of accounting-related influences were investigated. Arguments were raised as to the likely effect of such factors and associated evidence-based propositions were tested in order to determine the degree of existing support for them. Four factors emerged as having potentially made some contribution to the accounting literature's conceptual development lag with respect to control. First it would appear that accountants may have been preoccupied with control tools at the possible expense of their attention to the conceptual nature of control itself. Second, available evidence would seem to suggest that the accounting literature did tend to neglect or pay inadequate attention to conceptual aspects of control. Both of these interrelated factors could have been conducive to a lag in control model development through depressed levels of attention being given to such research while concentrating attention upon formal measurement, reporting and decision-making techniques. Third, investigations revealed an almost complete absence of management accounting-oriented professional or public body practice standards. This supported the contention that such a lack could have restricted motivation and opportunities for exploring the conceptual nature of control among both practising and academic accountants. Fourth, investigations yielded what appears to be a justifiable proposition that the tradition of conceptual and theoretical research and teaching in academic accounting education has been a relatively recent phenomenon both in the USA and in the UK. This suggested the argument that the development of conceptual models of control in the accounting literature may have been hindered to some extent by an earlier lack of concern and familiarity with conceptual approaches to control by accounting writers.

The above influences do not exclusively represent all the possible factors which may have exerted an influence. Nor is it possible to detect the relative importance of these identified factors. What is contended, however, is that there is a reasonable probability that acting in some combination, these four factors contributed in part to a time-lag between management and accounting models of control.

BEYOND DEFINITION

The conceptual development of control in management and accounting theory has proved to be a much more complex process than the mere progressive revision of definitions. Even at the outset, while Taylor and Fayol provided formal definitions of control, the summation of their writings disclosed a much more complex and detailed specification of control concepts. Indeed their views of control could not be simply encapsulated in one concept but each contained a number of interrelated concepts.

While subsequent schools of thought revised or broke away from the classical model of Taylor and Fayol, all consistently approached the question of control with a view to specifying multiple concepts. Similarly, while individual writers attempted at various points to produce neat all-purpse definitions of control, the majority of the literature on control belied the implied simplicity and certainty of such efforts. Yet in this study it has been possible to ascertain a conceptual form and progression from the sizeable array of concepts revealed in the history of both the management and accounting literature. Through focussing upon model development, patterns of change have been traced in both steams of literature together with likely conditioning factors. From this basis it has been possible to compare developmental paths and to enquire into differences.

What can be said with certainty is that the conceptual approach to control in both the management and accounting literatures has moved well beyond mere definition. Indeed this occurred at a much earlier point in time than the casual observer may have presumed. Both streams of literature have conclusively demonstrated that the conceptual complexity of control is poorly served by simple definitional statements. Rather, control has come to be represented, however imperfectly, as a multi-model framework. The attempts of management and accounting theory to portray that framework is a continuing process.

NOTES

1. Management or accounting.

2. Socio-economic conditions were primarily related to the development of management models, given the finding that accounting models appear to have been largely derived from the former.

3. Both in terms of number and frequency of contributions and in terms of depth and detail of analysis.

4. Open systems control and contingent control.

5. Even the appearance of the concept of congruent control in the post-1960 classical accounting COM represented a virtual reversion to the earlier Fayol control concept of unity of command-direction-interest.

6. The behavioural accounting COM.

7. The systems COM in accounting.

8. The non-existent structural model of control in accounting.

9. This has been argued with respect to the classical and behavioural COMs in the accounting literature on control.

10. Refer to Table 8.2.

11. In Chapter 8.

12. As evidenced by number of publications studied.

13. Given that Table 8.1 shows 73 accounting compared to 42 management publications relating to the classical model of control.

APPENDIX A

CONTROL-RELATED SECTIONS IN 21 MANAGEMENT ACCOUNTING TEXTS

Amey and Egginton [1973]

PART 3	CONTROL SYSTEMS
Chapter 13:	Enterprise Control
Chapter 14:	Cost Accumulation
Chapter 15:	Control Through Standards
Chapter 16:	Control Through Internal Resource Allocation
Chapter 17:	Control Through Profitability Measures
Chapter 18:	A Critique of Accounting Controls

Anthony and Reece [1975]

No control related section headings
Only chapter mentioning control
Chapter 20:   Responsibility Accounting: The Management
Control Process

Anthony and Welsch [1977]

PART 3	RESPONSIBILITY ACCOUNTING
Chapter 10:	The Management Control Structure
Chapter 11:	The Management Control Process
Chapter 12:	Programming and Budget Preparation
Chapter 13:	Standard Costs
Chapter 14:	Analysis of Variances
Chapter 15:	Control Reports and Their Use
Chapter 16:	Information Processing
Chapter 17:	Summary: The Total Picture

Batty [1975]

No section headings
Chapters mentioning control
Chapter 3:   Budgetary Control
Chapter 15:   Control and Communication
Chapter 20:   Control of Capital Expenditure
Chapter 21:   Internal Control and Internal Audit
Chapter 25:   Credit Control

Bierman and Dyckman [1976]

PART 1   AN INTRODUCTION TO COST CLASSIFICATION,
              ACCUMULATION AND CONTROL

Chapter 1:   The Accountants' Role
Chapter 2:   Cost Classification
Chapter 3:   Accounting for Overhead Costs
Chapter 4:   Cost Accounting Systems
Chapter 5:   Cost Control and Variances

Burke and Smyth [1972]

PART 1   PLANNING AND CONTROL

Chapter 1:   The Relationship Between Accounting and
              Management
Chapter 2:   The Budget as a Planning Device
Chapter 3:   The Budget as a Control Device
Chapter 4:   Standard Costs for Planning and Control
Chapter 5:   Performance Reporting
Chapter 6:   Rate of Return as a Measure of Performance

Crowningsheild and Gorman [1974]

No section headings
Chapters mentioning control
Chapter 5:   Materials and Labour: Costing and Control
Chapter 24:   Statistical Quality Control

Davidson et al [1978]

PART 3   PLANNING AND CONTROL

Chapter 8:   The Planning and Control Process
Chapter 9:   Period Budgeting: Establishing Plans for Action
              and Standards for Control
Chapter 10:   Measuring and Interpreting Variances from
              Standards
Chapter 11:   Divisional Performance Measurement and Control

De Coster and Schafer [1979]

PART 3	**PLANNING AND CONTROL SYSTEMS FOR DECISION IMPLEMENTATION**
Chapter 8:	Budgeting: A Systematic Approach to Planning
Chapter 9:	Budgetary Control, Responsibility Accounting, and Their Behavioural Implications
Chapter 10:	Measurement of Divisional Performance

Dopuch et al [1978]

PART 3	**STANDARDS AND CONTROL**
Chapter 8:	Management Control Systems
Chapter 9:	The Use of Standards and Budgets in Organisational Control
Chapter 10:	The Master Budget
Chapter 11:	Comparison of Standards with Actual Performance: Variance Analysis
Chapter 12:	Assessing the Significance of Standard Costs Variances

Drebin and Bierman [1978]

No section headings
Only chapter mentioning control
Chapter 9:   Control of Inventory

Gray and Johnston [1977]

No section headings
Chapters mentioning control

Chapter 12:	Choosing a Management Control Strategy
Chapter 13:	Responsibility Reporting and Control
Chapter 14:	Reporting for Control of Expense Centres: Standard Cost Systems
Chapter 15:	Reporting for Control of Expense Centres: Flexible Budgets; Managed Expenses
Chapter 16:	Report for Control of Revenue Centres
Chapter 17:	Reporting for Control of Profit Centres and Investment Centres

Heitger and Matulich [1980]

PART 3		**PLANNING, CONTROL AND RESPONSIBILITY REPORTING**

Chapter 7:   Basic Budgeting Concepts
Chapter 8:   Standard Costs
Chapter 9:   Flexible Budgeting and Manufacturing Overhead
              Variance Analysis
Chapter 10:   Costing Non-Manufacturing Activities and the Use
              of the Contribution Approach in Costing
Chapter 11:   Decentralised Operations and Responsibility
              Accounting
Chapter 12:   Accounting Data and Pricing Decisions
Chapter 13:   Capital Budgeting
Chapter 14:   The Public Sector and Not-For-Profit Budgeting

Horngren [1977]

SECTION 2   MULTIPLE PURPOSE SYSTEMS FOR MANAGEMENT CONTROL

Chapter 5:   Budgeting in General: Profit Planning
Chapter 6:   Systems Design, Responsibility Accounting, and
              Motivation
Chapter 7:   Standard Costs: Direct Material and Direct
              Labour
Chapter 8:   Flexible Budgets and Overhead Control
Chapter 9:   Standard Absorption Costing: Overhead Variances
Chapter 10:   Income Effects of Alternative Product-Costing
              Methods
Chapter 11:   Relevant Costs and the Contribution Approach to
              Decisions

Louderback and Dominiak [1975]

PART 4   CONTROL AND PERFORMANCE EVALUATION

Chapter 9:   Responsibility Accounting
Chapter 10:   Control and Evaluation of Cost Centres
Chapter 11:   Divisional Performance Measurement

Lynch and Williamson [1976]

SECTION 3   CONTROL

Chapter 6:   Materials and Labour
Chapter 7:   Flexible Budgeting and Overhead Variance Analysis
Chapter 8:   Human Relations and Responsibility Accounting

Matz and Usry [1976]

Moore and Jaedicke [1980]

Shillinglaw [1977]

    PART 3   **FURTHER TOPICS IN PERIODIC PLANNING AND CONTROL**

    Chapter 19:   Behavioural Aspects of Responsibility Accounting
    Chapter 20:   Standard Costing on the Comprehensive Plan
    Chapter 21:   Analysis of Factory Cost Variances
    Chapter 22:   Cost Variances in Financial Reporting
    Chapter 23:   Control of Project Costs
    Chapter 24:   Divisional Profit Reporting
    Chapter 25:   Profit Analysis
    Chapter 26:   Interdivisional Transfer Pricing

Sizer [1979]

    No section headings
    Only chapter mentioning control
    Chapter 9:   Budgetary Planning and Control Systems

Thornton [1978]

    SECTION HEADING   **ACCOUNTING AND BUSINESS CONTROL**

    Chapter 12:   The Acquisition of Long Term Resources
    Chapter 13:   Use of Resources (1) - Material Control
    Chapter 14:   Use of Resources (2) - Labour Control
    Chapter 15:   Use of Resources (3) - Expense Control and
                Depreciation Methods
    Chapter 16:   Investment Results
    Chapter 17:   Standard Costing (1) - Basic Procedure and
                Primary Variance Analysis
    Chapter 18:   Standard Costing (2) - Further Variance Analysis

BIBLIOGRAPHY

Aitken, H.G.J., Taylorism at Watertown Arsenal: Scientific Management in Action 1908-1915, Cambridge, Massachusetts, Harvard University Press, 1960.

Aldcroft, D.H. and Richardson, H.W., The British Economy 1870-1939, London, Macmillan, 1969.

Alford, B.W.E., Depression and Recovery: British Economic Growth, 1918-39, London, Macmillan, 1972.

Allen, C.E., "The Growth of Accounting Instruction Since 1900", The Accounting Review, Vol.II, No.2, June 1927, pp.150-166.

Allen, F.L., The Big Change: America Transforms Itself 1900-1950, New York, Bantam Books, 1952.

Allen, S.A. III and Gabarro, J.J., "The Sociotechnical and Cognitive Models" in Lorsch, J.W. and Lawrence, P.R. (eds.), Organization Planning: Cases and Concepts, Homewood, Illinois, Richard D. Irwin, 1972, pp.17-27.

Amey, L.R. and Egginton, D.A., Management Accounting: A Conceptual Approach, London, Longman Group Ltd., 1973.

Amey, L.R., Budget Planning and Control Systems, London, Pitman Publishing Ltd., 1979

Amigoni, F., "Planning Management Control Systems", Journal of Business Finance and Accounting, Vol.5, No.3, Autumn 1978, pp.279-291.

Anderson, C.M., "Motivation - The Essential in Budgeting", NAA Bulletin, Vol.44, June, 1963, p.46.

Anonymous, "The Size of Works and the Efficiency of Control", Engineering, Vol.109, No.1, January 30th, 1920, pp.135-136.

Anonymous, "Standard Factory Organisation", Engineering, Vol.104, No.10, October 12th, 1917, pp.377-378.

Anonymous, "Editorial", The Journal of Accountancy, Vol.40, No.4, October 1925, p.293.

Anonymous, "Control in the Management Process", The Accountant, Vol.169, No.5164, December 6th, 1973, pp.755-756.

Anonymous, The History of the Institute of Chartered Accountants in England and Wales 1880-1965, and of its Founder Accountancy Bodies 1870-1880: the Growth of a Profession and its Influence on Legislation and Public Affairs, London, Heinemann, 1966.

Anonymous, "The Role of Management Accountants", The Australian Accountant, Vol.51, No.8, September 1981, pp.568-569.

Ansari, S.L., "Behavioral Factors in Variance Control: Report on a Laboratory Experiment", Journal of Accounting Research, Vol.14, No.2, Autumn 1976, pp.189-211.

Ansari, S.L., "An Integrated Approach to Control System Design", Accounting, Organizations and Society, Vol.2, No.2, 1977, pp.101-112.

Ansari, S.L., "Towards an Open Systems Approach to Budgeting", Accounting, Organizations and Society, Vol.4, No.3, 1979, pp.149-161.

Anthony, R.N., Planning and Control Systems: A Framework for Analysis, Austin, Graduate School of Business Administration, Harvard University, 1965.

Anthony, R.N., "Characteristics of Management Control Systems", in Thomas, W.E. Jr. (ed.), Readings in Cost Accounting, Budgeting and Control, Cincinnati, South Western Publishing Co., 1973, pp.27-42.

Anthony, R.N. and Reece, J.S., Management Accounting Principles, 3rd ed., Homewood, Illinois, Richard D. Irwin, 1975.

Anthony, R.N. and Welsch, G.A., Fundamentals of Management Accounting, Homewood, Illinois, Richard D. Irwin, 1977.

Argyris, C., Personality and Organisation, the Conflict Between System and the Individual, New York, Harper and Row, 1957.

Ashworth, R., "What British Business Expects of Budgetary Control", The Accountant, Vol.XCII, No.3155, 25th May, 1935, pp.747-748.

Atkinson, J.W., An Introduction to Motivation, Princeton, Van Nostrand, 1964.

Argyris, C., Personality and the Organization, New York, Harper and Row, 1957.

Argyris, C., <u>Understanding Organizational Behaviour</u>, Homewood, Dorsey Press, 1960.

Argyris, C., <u>Interpersonal Competence and Organisational Effectiveness</u>, London, Tavistock, 1962.

Argyris, C., <u>Integrating the Individual and the Organisation</u>, New York, J. Wiley, 1964.

Bagwell, P.S. and Mingay, G.E., <u>Britain and America 1850-1939: A Study of Economic Change</u>, London, Routledge and Kegan Paul, 1970.

Baker, E.A., The Control of Manufacturing Costs, <u>The Americas</u>, Vol.4, January, 1918, pp.16-18.

Banks, E.H., <i>"Control Exercised Through the Medium of the Budget"</i>, <u>The Canadian Chartered Accountant</u>, Vol.30, No.4, Issue 165, April 1937, pp.285-294.

Barnard, C.I., <u>The Functions of the Executive</u>, Cambridge, Massachusetts, Harvard University Press, Copyright 1938. 16th and 17th printings, 1964 and 1966.

Barrett, T.J., <i>"Control Through Accounting"</i>, <u>The Accountants Journal</u> (U.K.), March 1959, pp.105-107.

Barzun, J. and Graff, H.F., <u>The Modern Researcher</u>, New York, Harcourt, Brace and World, 1970.

Batty, J., <u>Management Accountancy: Including Financial Management and Control</u>, 4th ed., London, MacDonald and Evans Ltd., 1975.

Batty, J., <u>Corporate Planning and Budgetary Control</u>, London, MacDonald and Evans, 1970.

Baumler, J.V., <i>"Defined Criteria of Performance in Organizational Control"</i>, <u>Administrative Science Quarterly</u>, Vol.16, September, 1971, pp.340-349.

Baumler, J.V., <i>"Description and Investigation of Sub-Goal Oriented Approaches to Organizational Control"</i>, in Burns, T.J. (ed.), <u>Behavioral Experiments in Accounting</u>, Columbus, Ohio, College of Administrative Science, Ohio State University, 1972, pp.73-109.

Bell, G.B., <i>"The Influence of Technological Components of Work on Management Control"</i>, in Litterer, J.A. (ed.), <u>Organizations: Structure and Behavior</u>, Vol.1, Second Edition, New York, John Wiley and Sons, 1969, pp.441-445.

Benninger, L.J., "Standard Costs for Income Determination, Control, and Special Studies", The Accounting Review, Vol.25, No.4, October 1950, pp.378-383.

Benninger, L.J., "Accounting Controls: A Tool for Modern Management", Cost and Management, Vol.47, No.4, July-August, 1973, pp.20-25.

Bentley, F.R., "Effective Management Control", The Accountants Journal (U.K.), April 1959, pp.173-174.

Berlo, D.K., "Morality or Ethics? Two Approaches to Organizational Control', The Personnel Administrator, Vol.20, No.2, April 1975, pp.16-19.

Bertalanffy, L.V., "The Theory of Open Systems in Physics and Biology", Science, January 13, 1950, pp.23-29.

Bertalanffy, L.V., Problems of Life, New York, John Wiley and Sons, 1952.

Bertalanffy, L.V., General Systems Theory, New York, George Braziller Inc., 1968.

Bertalanffy, L.V., The History and Status of General Systems Theory", Academy of Management Journal, Vol.15, No.4, December 1972, pp.407-424.

Bhattacharyya, S.K., "Management Control Systems and Conflicts - A Framework for Analysis and Resolution", The Chartered Accountant (India), Vol.XVII Part XII, June 1969, pp.643-654.

Bierman, H. Jr. and Dyckman, T.R., Managerial Cost Accounting, New York, Macmillan, 1971.

Bierman, H. Jr. and Dyckman, T.R., Managerial Cost Accounting, 2nd ed., New York, Macmillan Publishing Co., 1976.

Birnberg, J.G., Frieze, I.H. and Shields, M.D., "The Role of Attribution Theory in Control Systems", Accounting, Organizations and Society, Vol.2, No.3, 1977, pp.189-200.

Bliss, C.A. and McNeill, R.B., "Management Control in Uniform", Harvard Business Review, Vol.XXII, No.2, Winter 1944, pp.227-238.

Boland, R.J. Jr., *"Control, Causality and Information System Requirements"*, Accounting, Organizations and Society, Vol.4, No.4, 1979, pp.259-272.

Bonini, C.P., *"Simulation of Organizational Behavior"* in Bonini, C.P., Jaedicke, R.K. and Wagner, H.M. (eds.), Management Controls: New Directions in Basic Research, New York, McGraw-Hill, 1964, pp.91-101.

Bonini, C.P., Jaedicke, R.K., Wagner, H.M., (eds.), Management Controls: New Directions in Basic Research, New York, McGraw-Hill, Inc., 1964.

Bowey, A.M., *"Approaches to Organisation Theory"*, Social Science Information, Vol.11, No.6, December 1972, pp.109-128.

Bowey, A.M., The Sociology of Organisations, London, Hodder and Stoughton, 1976.

Braverman, H., Labor and Monopoly Capital: The Degradation of Work in the 20th Century, New York, Monthly Review Press, 1974.

Brech, E.F.L. (a), *"Summary and Review"*, British Management Review, Vol.VII, No.3, 1948, pp.87-103.

Brech, E.F.L. (b), *"The Principles of Management - A Commentary on Mr. Wilfred Brown's 'Principles of Organisation'"*, British Management Review, Vol.VII, No.1, 1948, pp.41-67.

Brech, E.F.L., The Principles and Practice of Management, London, Longmans, Green and Co., 1953.

Brodie, M.B., Fayol on Administration, London, Lyon Grant and Green, 1967.

Brody, D., Labor in Crisis: The Steel Strike of 1919, Philadelphia, J.B. Lippincott Co., 1965.

Brody, D., Steelworkers in America: The Nonunion Era, New York, Russell and Russell, 1970. (Copyright 1960, by the President and Fellows of Harvard College.)

Bronner, S.Z., *"Cost Controls for the Road Ahead"*, N.A.C.A. Bulletin, Vol.34, No.5, January 1953, pp.607-615.

Brown, C.L., *"The Out Thing, or Oh, What a Dirty Word is Control"*, Managerial Planning, May-June, 1972, pp.29-32.

Brown, R.O., *"Who Controls Whom?"*, NAA Bulletin, Vol.46, April 1965, pp.17-18.

Brown, W.B.D., *"Principles of Organisation"*, British Management Review, Vol.6, No.1, 1947, pp.41-50.

Brown, W., and Jaques, E., Glacier Project Papers, New York, Heinemann Press, 1965.

Brownlee, W.E., Dynamics of Ascent: A History of the American Economy, New York, Alfred A. Knopf, 1974.

Bruns, W.J. Jr. and Waterhouse, J.H., *"Budgetary Control and Organization Structure"*, Journal of Accounting Research, Vol.13, No.2, Autumn 1975, pp.177-203.

Buckley, A., *"Accounting in Organisations"*, Accountancy, Vol.83, No.959, July 1973, pp.62-67.

Buckley, A. and McKenna, E., *"Budgetary Control and Business Behaviour"*, Accounting and Business Research, Vol.2, No.6, Spring 1972, pp.137-149.

Buckley, J.W., In Search of Identity: An Inquiry into Identity Issues in Accounting, Los Angeles, The California Certified Public Accountants Foundation for Education and Research, 1972.

Bunge, W.R., *"Management Control: Postwar Model"*, The Controller, Vol.14, No.9, September 1946, pp.500-502.

Bunge, W.R., Managerial Budgeting for Profit Improvement, New York, McGraw-Hill Book Co., 1968.

Burke, W.L. and Macmullen, J.S., *"An Overall Structure for Management Planning and Control"*, Accounting and Finance, Vol.19, No.1, May 1979, pp.20-51.

Burke, W.L. and Smyth, E.B., Accounting for Management; Cost Analysis, Planning, Control and Decision Making, 2nd ed., Sydney, The Law Book Co. Ltd., 1972.

Burns, T. and Stalker, G.M., The Management of Innovation, London, Tavistock, 1961.

Burns, T. and Stalker, G.M., *"Mechanistic and Organic Systems"* in Litterer, J.A. (ed.), Organizations: Systems, Control and Adaptation, Vol.II, 2nd edition, New York, John Wiley & Sons, 1969, pp.345-348. (Reprinted from "The Management of Innovation", London, Tavistock Publications Ltd., 1961, pp.119-125.)

Burns, T.J. (ed.), Behavioral Experiments in Accounting: Papers, Critiques, and Proceedings of the Accounting Symposium held on October 1 and 2, 1971, College of Administrative Science Monograph No.AA-7, Columbus, Ohio, College of Administrative Science, The Ohio State University, 1972.

Cammann, C., *"Effects of the Use of Control Systems"*, Accounting, Organizations and Society, Vol.1, No.4, 1976, pp.301-313.

Carey, J. (a), *"Editorial: What Should be the Educational Requirements for the Accounting Profession?"*, The Journal of Accountancy, Vol.88, No.4, October 1949, pp.275-276.

Carey, J. (b), *"Editorial: Educational Background of Certified Public Accountants"*, The Journal of Accountancy, Vol.88, No.1, July 1949, pp.4-5.

Carey, J.L., The Rise of the Accounting Profession: From Technician to Professional 1896-1936, New York, American Institute of Certified Public Accountants, 1969.

Carey, J.L., The Rise of the Accounting Profession: To Responsibility and Authority 1937-1969, New York, American Institute of Certified Public Accountants, 1970.

Caron, F., An Economic History of Modern France, translated by Bray, B., New York, Columbia University Press, 1979.

Carr, E.H., What is History?, Harmondsworth, Middlesex, Penguin Books, 1964.

Cartwright, D., *"Influence, Leadership, Control"* in March, J.G. (ed.), Handbook of Organizations, Chicago, Rand McNally & Co., 1965, pp.1-47.

Chandler, A.D. Jr., Strategy and Structure: Chapters in the History of the Industrial Enterprise, Garden City, New York, Anchor Books, Doubleday & Co. Inc., 1966. (First published by Massachusetts Institute of Technology, 1962.)

Chandler, A.D. Jr., *"The Development of Modern Management Structure in the U.S. and U.K."* in Hannah, L. (ed.), Management Strategy and Business Development, London, Macmillan, 1976.

Charnes, A. and Stedry, A., *"Exploratory Models in the Theory of Budget Control"* in Cooper, W.W., Leavitt, H.J. and Shelly, M.W. II (eds.), New Perspectives in Organization Research, New York, John Wiley and Sons, 1964, pp.212-249.

Charns, M.P., *"The Theories of Joan Woodward and James Thompson"* in Lorsch, J.W. and Lawrence, P.R. (eds.), Organization Planning: Cases and Concepts, Homewood, Illinois, Richard D. Irwin and the Dorsey Press, 1972, pp.28-37.

Child, J., British Management Thought: A Critical Analysis, London, George Allen & Unwin Ltd., 1969.

Child, J., *"Organization Structure and Strategies of Control: A Replication of the Aston Study"*, Administrative Science Quarterly, Vol.17, June 1972, pp.163-177.

Child, J., *"Strategies of Control and Organizational Behavior"*, Administrative Science Quarterly, Vol.18, March 1973, pp.1-17.

Child, J., Organization: A Guide to Problems and Practice, London, Harper and Row, 1977.

Child, J. and Whiting, J.W.M., *"Determinants of Level of Aspiration: Evidence From Everyday Life"* in Brand, H. (ed.), The Study of Personality, New York, John Wiley, 1954, pp.145-158.

Cipolla, C.M. (ed.), The Fontana Economic History of Europe: Contemporary Economies - 1, Glasgow, Collins/Fontana, 1976.

Clapham, J.H., The Economic Development of France and Germany 1815-1914, 4th Edition, London, Cambridge University Press, 1966.

Clark, G.K., The Critical Historian, London, Heinemann, 1967.

Clark, G.K., Guide for Research Students Working on Historical Subjects, 2nd edition, Cambridge, Cambridge University Press, 1972.

Clay, M., *"Management Control Systems"*, The Accountant, Vol.164, No.5031, May 20th, 1971, pp.669-672.

Coburn, F.G., *"The Work of Management"*, Industrial Management, July 1917, pp.515-520.

Coleman, C.J. and Palmer, D.D., *"Organizational Applications of System Theory"*, Business Horizons, Vol.16, December 1973, pp.77-84.

Colgan, C.Y., *"Understanding Budget Preparation and Control"*, The Journal of Accountancy, Vol.46, No.2, August 1928, pp.106-112.

Collins, F., *"The Interaction of Budget Characteristics and Personality Variables with Budgetary Response Attitudes"*, The Accounting Review, Vol.LIII, No.2, April 1978, pp.324-335.

Collis, A.G.D., *"Organisation Concepts"*, British Management Review, Vol.VIII, No.2, July 1949, pp.5-19.

Committee on Historiography, The Social Sciences in Historical Study, U.S.A., Social Science Research Council, 1954. (A Report.)

Committee to Prepare a Statement of Basic Accounting Theory, A Statement of Basic Accounting Theory, Evanston, Illinois, American Accounting Association, 1966.

Commons, J.R., *"A Cross Section of Industrial Control"*, Administration, Vol.1, No.2, February 1921, pp.145-150.

Cook, D.M., *"The Psychological Impact of Certain Aspects of Performance Reports"*, Management Accounting (New York), Vol.49, No.1, July 1968, pp.26-34.

Coonley, H., *"The Control of an Industry in the Business Cycle"*, Harvard Business Review, Vol.1, No.4, July 1923, pp.385-397.

Coonley, H., *"The Development of Industrial Budgeting"*, The Annals, The American Academy of Political and Social Science, Vol.CXIX, May 1925, pp.64-79.

Coonley, H., *"Control and Size in Management: What are the Controllable and Uncontrollable Factors in Management"*, Bulletin of The Taylor Society Vol.XV, No.1, February 15th, 1930, pp.18-31.

Copley, F.B., Frederick W. Taylor: Father of Scientific Management, Volumes 1 and 3, first edition, New York, Harper and Brothers, 1923 (reprinted New York, Augustus M. Kelley 1969).

Crossman, P., *"The Genesis of Cost Control"*, The Accounting Review, Vol.XXVIII, No.4, October 1953, pp.522-527.

Crowningshield, G.R. and Gorman, K.A., Cost Accounting: Principles and Managerial Applications, 3rd ed., Boston, Houghton, Mifflin Co., 1974.

Cruft, A.G., *"Scientific Management or Sterile Authority"*, British Management Review, Vol.8, No.3, 1949, pp.72-86.

Cumming, J.G., *"Some Leading Principles of Administration"*, The Calcutta Review, No.285, July 1916, pp.229-230, 237.

Cyert, R.M., and March, J.G., A Behavioral Theory of the Firm, Englewood Cliffs, New Jersey, Prentice-Hall, 1963.

Dale, E., *"New Perspectives in Managerial Decision-Making"*, The Journal of Business of the University of Chicago, Vol.XXVI, No.1, January 1953, pp.1-8.

Davidson, S., Schindler, J.S., Stickney, C.P. and Weil, R.L., Managerial Accounting: An Introduction to Concepts, Methods and their Uses, Hinsdale, Illinois, The Dryden Press, 1978.

Davis, B.N., *"Trends of Managerial Control"*, Journal of Business, University Hall, Iowa City, May 1940, p.13.

Davis, K., Human Relations in Business, New York, McGraw-Hill Book Co., 1957.

Davis, K., Human Relations at Work, (2nd edition of "Human Relations in Business", 1957), New York, McGraw-Hill Book Co., 1962.

Davis, K., Frederick, W.C. and Blomstrom, R.L., Business and Society: Concepts and Policy Issues, 4th edition, New York, McGraw-Hill Book Co., 1980.

Davis, R.J., *"Administrative Control: As Illustrated by the Hills Brothers Company"*, Bulletin of The Taylor Society, Vol.XVII, No.1, February 1932, pp.6-17.

Dawson, R.I. and Carew, D.P., *"Why Do Control Systems Fall Apart?"*, Personnel, Vol.46, No.3, May 1969, pp.8-16.

DeCoster, D.T. and Fertakis, J.P., *"Budget-Induced Pressure and Its Relationship to Supervisory Behaviour"*, Journal of Accounting Research, Vol.6, No.2, Autumn 1968, pp.237-246.

DeCoster, D.T. and Schafer, E.L., Management Accounting: A Decision Emphasis, New York, John Wiley and Sons, 1979.

Dent, A.G.H., *"Budgetary Business Control in Practice"*, The Manchester Guardian Commercial, December 24th, 1931, p.549.

Dessler, G., Management Fundamentals: A Framework, Preston, Virginia, Preston Publishing Co. (A Prentice-Hall Co.), 1977.

Dessler, G., Organization and Management: A Contingency Approach, Englewood Cliffs, New Jersey, Prentice-Hall, 1978.

Dessler, G., Organization Theory: Integrating Structure and Behavior, Englewood Cliffs, New Jersey, Prentice-Hall Inc., 1980.

Dew, R.B. and Gee, K.P., "A New Framework for Management Control", Management Accounting, (U.K.), Vol.47, May 1969, pp.203-208.

Dew, R.B. and Gee, K.P., Management Control and Information, New York, John Wiley and Sons, 1973.

Dew, R.B. and Gee, K.P., "The Choice of Management Control Information - Further Findings", Management International Review, Vol.13, No.1, 1973, pp.47-52.

Donald, W.C., "Higher Management Controls", British Management Review, Vol.6, No.1, 1947, pp.51-70.

Dopuch, N., Birnberg, J.G., and Demski, J., Cost Accounting: Accounting Data for Management's Decisions, 2nd ed., New York, Harcourt Brace Jovanovich, 1974.

Drebin, A.R. and Bierman, H. Jr., Managerial Accounting: An Introduction, 3rd ed., Philadelphia, W.B. Saunders Company, 1978.

Drinkwater, D.A., "Management Theory and the Budgeting Process", Management Accounting, (N.A.A.), Vol.54, No.12, June 1973, pp.15-17.

Drucker, A.P.R., "Factory Production Under Budgetary Control", The Accounting Review, Vol.5, No.4, December 1930, pp.301-304.

Drucker, P.F., "Controls, Control and Management" in Bonini, C.P., Jaedicke, R.K. and Wagner, H.M. (eds.), Management Controls: New Directions in Basic Research, New York, McGraw-Hill, 1964, pp.286-296.

Drury, H.B., Scientific Management: A History and Criticism, 3rd Edition, New York, Columbia University, Studies in the Social Sciences, 1922.

Dubin, R., *"Control Evasion at the Managerial Level"* in Dubin, R., <u>Human Relations in Administration: With Readings</u>, 4th ed., Englewood Cliffs, New Jersey, Prentice Hall, Inc., 1974, pp.498-502. (Reprinted from Argyris, C. et al., Social Science Approaches to Business Behavior, Homewood, Illinois, The Dorsey Press, 1962, pp.42-47.)

Dugdale, H., *"Management-Control Accounting: Standard Costs and Budgets"*, <u>The Accountant</u>, Vol.CXXV, No.3995, July 14th, 1951, pp.28-30.

Dugdale, H., *"Management Accounting: Aspects of Control Measures Afforded"*, <u>The Accountants Journal</u> (U.K.), December 1953, pp.347-348.

Dunbar, R.L.M., *"Budgeting for Control"*, <u>Administrative Science Quarterly</u>, Vol.16, March 1971, pp.88-96.

Duncan, W.J., <u>Essentials of Management</u>, Hinsdale, Illinois, Dryden Press, 1975.

Dunkerley, R., *"Budgetary Control - A Review"*, <u>International Management Conference Proceedings</u>, 6th Congress, Manufacturing Section, 1935, pp.26-30.

Dutton, H.P., *"A History of Scientific Management in the United States of America"*, <u>Advanced Management</u>, Vol.18, October 1953, pp.9-12.

Edey, H.C., <u>Business Budgets and Accounts</u>, London, Hutchinson, 1959.

Edey, H.C., <u>Business Budgets and Accounts</u>, 2nd ed., London, Hutchinson University Library, 1960.

Eilon, S., <u>Management Control</u>, London, Macmillan and Co. Ltd., 1971.

Eldridge, J.E.T. and Crombie, A.D, <u>A Sociology of Organisations</u>, London, George Allen and Unwin, 1974.

Emch, A.F., *"Control Means Action"*, <u>Harvard Business Review</u>, Vol.32, No.4, July-August, 1954, pp.92-98.

Emerson, H., <u>The Twelve Principles of Efficiency</u>, New York, The Engineering Magazine Company, 1913.

Emery, F.E. and Trist, E.L., *"Sociotechnical System"* in <u>Management Science, Models and Techniques</u>, Vol. 2, Churchman, C.W. and Verhulst, M., New York, Pergamon Press, 1960.

Emery, F.E. and Trist, E.L., *"The Causal Texture of Organizational Environments"* in Litterer, J.A. (ed.), <u>Organizations: System, Control and Adaptation</u>, Vol.2, 2nd edition, New York, John Wiley and Sons, 1969, pp.220-228. (Reprinted from <u>Human Relations</u>, Vol.18, August 1963, pp.20-26).

Emery, J.C., <u>Organisational Planning and Control Systems: Theory and Technology</u>, London, Macmillan, 1969.

Etzioni, A., *"Compliance as a Comparative Base"* in Litterer, J.A. (ed.), <u>Organizations: Structure and Behavior</u>, Vol.1, Second Edition, New York, John Wiley and Sons, 1969, pp.121-132.

Etzioni, A., *"Organizational Control Structure"* in March, J.G. (ed.), <u>Handbook of Organizations</u>, Chicago, Rand McNally & Co., 1965, pp.650-677.

Etzioni, A., <u>Modern Organizations</u>, Englewood Cliffs, New Jersey, Prentice-Hall, 1964.

Fayol, H., *"The Administrative Theory in the State"*, reprinted in Gulick, L. and Urwick, L. (eds.), <u>Papers on the Science of Administration</u>, New York, Institute of Public Administration, 1937, pp.99-114. An address given before the Second International Congress of Administrative Science at Brussels, September 13th, 1923, translated from the French by Sarah Greer, Institute of Public Administration.

Fayol, H., <u>General and Industrial Management</u>, London, Sir Isaac Pitman & Sons, 1949. (First published in French as "Administration Industrielle et Generale-Prevoyance, Organisation, Commandement, Co-ordination, Controle", Bulletin de la Societe de l'Industrie Minerale, 1916.)

Ferrara, W.L. (a), *"Responsibility Accounting - A Basic Control Concept"*, <u>NAA Bulletin</u>, Vol.46, September 1964, pp.11-19.

Ferrara, W.L. (b), *"What Managerial Functions Does Accounting Serve?"*, <u>Financial Executive</u>, Vol.32, No.7, July 1964, pp.27-33.

Ferris, K.R., *"A Test of the Expectancy Theory of Motivation in an Accounting Environment"*, <u>The Accounting Review</u>, Vol.LII, No.3, July 1977, pp.605-615.

Fiske, W.P., *"Developments in Cost Control"*, <u>N.A.C.A. Bulletin</u>, Vol.29, No.2, September 15th, 1947, pp.65-73.

Fleming, J.E., *"The Spectrum of Management Control"*, <u>S.A.M. Advanced Management Journal</u>, Vol.37, No.2, April 1972, pp.54-61.

Fletcher, F.R., *"Standards as a Means of Reducing Costs"*, <u>National Association of Cost Accountants Yearbook</u>, 1922, pp.157-191.

Follett, M.P., <u>The New State: Group Organization The Solution of Popular Government</u>, New York, Longmans Green & Co., 1918.

Follett, M.P., <u>Creative Experience</u>, New York, Peter Smith, reprinted 1951 by permission of Longmans Green & Co., copyright 1924.

Follett, M.P. (a), *"How Must Business Management Develop in Order to Possess the Essentials of a Profession"* in Metcalf, H.C. and Urwick, L. (eds.), <u>Dynamic Administration: The Collected Papers of Mary Parker Follett</u>, London, Sir Isaac Pitman & Sons Ltd., 1941, pp.117-145. This paper was presented on October 29th, 1925.

Follett, M.P. (b), *"Individualism in a Planned Society"* in Metcalf, H.C. and Urwick, L. (eds.), <u>Dynamic Administration: The Collected Papers of Mary Parker Follett</u>, London, Sir Isaac Pitman & Sons Ltd., 1941, pp.295-314. This paper was the last prepared by Miss Follett for the Bureau of Personal Administration Annual Conferences, and was presented in a series entitled "Economic and Social Planning" on April 14th, 1932.

Follett, M.P. (c), *"The Meaning of Responsibility in Business Management"* in Metcalf, H.C. and Urwick, L. (eds.), <u>Dynamic Administration: The Collected Papers of Mary Parker Follett</u>, London, Sir Isaac Pitman & Sons Ltd., 1941, pp.146-166. This paper was presented on April 29th, 1926.

Follett, M.P. (d), *"Power"* in Metcalf, H.C. and Urwick, L. (eds.), <u>Dynamic Administration: The Collected Papers of Mary Parker Follett</u>, London, Sir Isaac Pitman & Sons Ltd., 1941, pp.95-116. This paper was presented in January 1925.

Follett, M.P. (e), *"Business as an Integrative Unity"* in Metcalf, H.C. and Urwick, L. (eds.), <u>Dynamic Administration: The Collected Papers of Mary Parker Follett</u>, London, Sir Isaac Pitman & Sons Ltd., 1941, pp.71-94. This paper was first presented before a Bureau of Personal Administration conference group in January 1925.

Follett, M.P., *"The Process of Control"*, (presented 1932), in Gulick, L. and Urwick, L. (eds.), <u>Papers on the Science of Administration</u>, New York, Institute of Public Administration, 1937, pp.161-169.

Follett, M.P. (a), *"The Illusion of Final Authority"* in Fox, E.M. and Urwick, L (eds.), <u>Dynamic Administration: The Collected Papers of Mary Parker Follett</u>, 2nd Edition, London, Pitman Publishing, 1973, pp.117-131. This paper was first presented on December 10th, 1926 at a meeting of the Taylor Society, New York.

Follett, M.P. (b), *"The Psychology of Control"* in Fox, E.M. and Urwick, L. (eds.), <u>Dynamic Administration: The Collected Papers of Mary Parker Follett</u>, 2nd Edition, London, Pitman Publishing, 1973, pp.148-174. This paper was first presented in March 1927.

Fox, A., <u>A Sociology of Work in Industry</u>, London, Collier Macmillan, 1971.

Fox, E.M. and Urwick, L. (eds.), <u>Dynamic Administration: The Collected Papers of Mary Parker Follett</u>, 2nd Edition, London, Pitman Publishing, 1973.

Franklin, B.A. (a), *"Cost Methods That Give the Executive Control of His Business: I. The Philosophy of Costs"*, <u>The Engineering Magazine</u>, January 1912, pp.577-585.

Franklin, B.A. (b), *"Cost Methods That Give the Executive Control of His Business: V. Labour from the Cost Viewpoint"*, <u>The Engineering Magazine</u>, May 1912, pp.192-197.

Franklin, B.A. (c), *"Cost Methods That Give the Executive Control of His Business: IV. The Economic Consideration of Material by Costs"*, <u>The Engineering Magazine</u>, April 1912, pp.48-56.

Franklin, B.A. (d), *"Cost Methods That Give the Executive Control of His Business: VI. The Vexing Question of Expense"*, <u>The Engineering Magazine</u>, June 12, pp.421-433.

Franklin, B.A. (e), *"Cost Methods That Give the Executive Control of His Business: VIII. Cost System - The Basic Improvement"*, <u>The Engineering Magazine</u>, August 1912, pp.703-709.

Frazer, G.E., *"Budgetary Control Over Costs"*, <u>National Association of Accountants Proceedings of International Cost Conference</u>, 1922, pp.226-236.

French, J.R.P. and Raven, B., *"The Bases of Social Power"* in Cartwright, D. and Zander, A. (eds.), <u>Group Dynamics: Research and Theory</u>, New York, Harper and Row, 1960, pp.607-623.

Friedlaender, H.E. and Oser, J., <u>Economic History of Modern Europe</u>, New York, Prentice-Hall, 1953.

Furukawa, E., *"Budgetary Control in Decentralized Management"*, Hitotsubashi Journal of Commerce and Management, Vol.1, No.1, March 1961, pp.11-20.

Gairns, A.J., Planning and Controlling, Sydney, Rydges Business Journal, 1949.

Gantt, H.L., *"Production and Sales"*, The Engineering Magazine, January 1916, pp.593-600.

George, C.S. Jr., The History of Management Thought, 2nd Edition, Englewood Cliffs, New Jersey, Prentice-Hall, 1972.

Gessner, E.J., *"Managerial Accounting Control"*, The Certified Public Accountant, Vol.XVI, No.5, May 1936, pp.261-273.

Gillett, S.H., *"Management and the Accountant"*, The Accountant, Vol.CXX, No.3884, May 28th, 1949, pp.435-440.

Gilman, G., *"An Inquiry into the Nature and Use of Authority"* in Haire, M. (ed.), Organization Theory in Industrial Practice, New York, Wiley, 1962, pp.105-142.

Gole, V.L., *"Managerial Control"*, The Chartered Accountant in Australia, Vol.44, No.1, July 1970, pp.22-28.

Golembiewski, R.T., *"Accountancy as a Function of Organization Theory"*, The Accounting Review, Vol.39, No.2, April 1964, pp.333-341.

Gordon, L.A. and Miller, D., *"A Contingency Framework for the Design of Accounting Information Systems"*, Accounting, Organizations and Society, Vol.1, No.1, 1976, pp.59-69.

Gray, J. and Johnston, K.S., Accounting and Management Action, 2nd ed., New York, McGraw-Hill, 1977.

Green, W.L., History and Survey of Accountancy, Brooklyn, New York, Standard Text Press, 1930.

Gregg, P., A Social and Economic History of Britain 1760-1963, 4th Edition revised, London, George G. Harrap & Co., 1964.

Gross, B.M., Organizations and Their Managing, London, Collier Macmillan, 1968. (First published in New York by the Free Press, 1964.)

- 302 -

Gulick, L., *"Notes on the Theory of Organization"*, (presented 1936), in Gulick, L. and Urwick, L. (eds.), Papers on the Science of Administration, New York, Institute of Public Administration, 1937, pp.3-45.

Haber, S., Efficiency and Uplift: Scientific Management in the Progressive Era, 1890-1920, Chicago, The University of Chicago Press, 1964.

Haberstroh, C.J., *"Control as an Organizational Process"* in Litterer, J.A. (ed)., Organizations: Systems, Control and Adaptation, Vol.2, 2nd edition, New York, John Wiley and Sons, 1969, pp.308-312. (Reprinted in Management Science, Vol.6, January 1960, pp.165-171.)

Handlin, O. and M.F., The Wealth of the American People: A History of American Affluence, New York, McGraw-Hill, 1975.

Harrison, G.C., Cost Accounting to Aid Production: A Practical Study of Scientific Cost Accounting, 2nd ed., New York, Engineering Magazine Co., 1924.

Hawkins, J., *"Budgeting in Industry"*, The Cost Accountant, Vol.14, No.8, January 1935, pp.271-277.

Hayes, D., *"The Contingency Theory of Managerial Accounting"*, The Accounting Review, Vol.LII, No.1, January 1977, pp.22-39.

Hayhurst, G., *"A Proposal for a Corporate Control System"*, Management International Review, Vol.16, No.2, 1976, pp.93-103.

Hecox, F.S., *"Phases of Budgetary Control"*, The Journal of Accountancy, Vol.48, No.3, September 1929, pp.187-190.

Heckert, J.B. and Willson, J.D., Business Budgeting and Control, 3rd ed., New York, The Ronald Press Co., 1967.

Heitger, L.E. and Matulich, S., Managerial Accounting, New York, McGraw-Hill Book Co., 1980.

Hellriegel, D. and Slocum, J.W. Jr., *"Organizational Design: A Contingency Approach"*, Business Horizons, Vol.16, April 1973, pp.59-68.

Helm, W.P., *"Budget System is Powerful Stabilizing Force"*, American Bankers Association Journal, Vol.23, August 1930, pp.104, 148-150.

Hendricksen, E.S., Capital Expenditures in the Steel Industry 1900 to 1953, New York, Arno Press, 1978. (Originally presented as the author's thesis for the degree of Doctor of Philosophy in Economics, University of California, 1956.)

Hensel, P.H., "Advantages and Uses of Budgets", The Canadian Chartered Accountant, Vol.30, No.1, Issue No.162, January 1937, pp.11-18.

Herzberg, F., Mausner, B. and Snyderman, B.B., The Motivation to Work, 2nd edition, New York, John Wiley and Sons, 1959.

Hill, M.F., "Some Essentials of Control Accounting", N.A.C.A. Bulletin, Vol.26, No.24, August 15th, 1945, pp.1105-1119.

Hodgetts, R.M., Management: Theory, Process and Practice, Second Edition, Philadelphia, W.B. Saunders Company, 1979.

Hodgkinson, C., Towards a Philosophy of Administration, Oxford, Basil Blackwell, 1978.

Hofstede, G.H., The Game of Budget Control, London, Tavistock Publications, 1968.

Hogan, W.T., Economic History of the Iron and Steel Industry in the United States, Vols. 1, 2 and 3, Lexington, Massachusetts, Lexington Books, D.C. Heath and Company, 1971, pp.1-1435.

Hohenberg, P., A Primer on the Economic History of Europe, New York, Random House, 1968.

Holden, P.E., Fish, L.S. and Smith, H.L., Top-Management Organization and Control, New York, McGraw-Hill, 1951. Copyright 1941 and 1948, Stanford University.

Holstrum, G.L., "The Effect of Budget Adaptiveness and Tightness on Managerial Decision Behaviour", Journal of Accounting Research, Vol.9, No.2, Autumn 1971, pp.268-277.

Homans, G.C., The Human Group, Harcourt, Brace and World, 1950.

Hopwood, A.G., "An Empirical Study of the Role of Accounting Data in Performance Evaluation", Journal of Accounting Research, Empirical Research in Accounting: Selected Studies, 1972, pp.156-182.

Hopwood, A.G., An Accounting System and Managerial Behaviour, Westmead, Farnborough, England, Saxon House/Lexington Books, 1973.

Hopwood, A.G., <u>Accounting and Human Behaviour</u>, London, Accountancy Age Books, Haymarket Publishing, 1974.

Hopwood, A.G., *"Towards an Organizational Perspective for the Study of Accounting and Information Systems"*, <u>Accounting, Organizations and Society</u>, Vol.3, No.1, 1978, pp.3-13.

Horngren, C.T., *"Motivation and Coordination in Management Control Systems"*, <u>Management Accounting</u>, Vol.XLVIII, No.9, May 1967, pp.3-7.

Horngren, C.T., <u>Cost Accounting: A Managerial Emphasis</u>, 4th ed., London, Prentice Hall International, 1977.

Hoxie, R.F., <u>Scientific Management and Labour</u>, New York, D. Appleton & Co., 1916.

Houck, L.D. Jr., <u>A Practical Guide to Budgetary and Management Control Systems: A Functional and Performance Evaluation Approach</u>, Lexington, Massachusetts, Lexington Books, 1979.

Hoverland, H.A. and Stricklin, W.D., *"Management and Accounting Concepts of Control"*, <u>Management Accounting</u> (N.A.A.), Vol.48, No.12, June 1967, pp.33-37.

Hovey, F.F., *"Cost Accounting and Budget Making"*, <u>Bulletin of The Taylor Society</u>, Vol.XVI, No.3, June 1931, pp.97-107.

Huse, E.F. and Bowditch, J.L., <u>Behaviour in Organizations: A Systems Approach to Managing</u>, Reading, Massachusetts, Addison-Wesley Publishing Company, 1973.

Imdieke, L.F. and Smith, C.H., *"International Financial Control Problems and the Accounting Control System"*, <u>Management International Review</u>, Vol.15, No.4-5, 1975, pp.13-28.

Ishikawa, A. and Smith, C.H., *"A Feedforward Control System for Organizational Planning and Control"*, <u>International Studies of Management and Organization</u>, Vol.III, No.4, Winter 1973-74, pp.5-29.

Itami, H., <u>Adaptive Behavior: Management Control and Information Analysis</u>, Studies in Accounting Research No.15, U.S.A., American Accounting Association, 1977.

Ivancevich, J.M., *"An Analysis of Control, Bases of Control, and Satisfaction in an Organizational Setting"*, <u>Academy of Management Journal</u>, Vol.13, No.4, December 1970, pp.427-436.

Jackson, J.H. and Morgan, C.P., Organization Theory: A Macro Perspective for Management, Englewood Cliffs, New Jersey, Prentice-Hall, 1978.

Jaedicke, R.K., "Accounting Data for Purposes of Control", The Accounting Review, Vol.37, No.2, April 1962, pp.181-188.

Jarvis, B. and Skidmore, D., "The Accountant and The Control Process in Business", Accountancy, Vol.89, No.1021, September 1978, pp.99-100.

Johnson, R.A., Kast, F.E. and Rosenzweig, J.E., The Theory and Management of Systems, New York, McGraw-Hill, 1963. (Revised 1967).

Jolders, J.W., "Organization for Corporate Control", The Controller, Vol.13, No.1, January 1945, pp.10-12, 23.

Jones, R.L. and Trentin, H.G., Budgeting: Key to Planning and Control: Practical Guidelines for Managers, 2nd ed., U.S.A., American Management Association, 1971.

Kakar, S., Frederick Taylor: A Study in Personality and Innovation, Cambridge, Massachusetts, MIT Press, 1970.

Kassander, A.R., "Standard Costs and Budgets - How Do They Control?", L.R.B. and M. Journal, Vol.23, No.3, May 1942, pp.1-8.

Kast, F.E. and Rosenzweig, J.E., Organization and Management: A Systems Approach, New York, McGraw-Hill, 1970.

Kast, F.E. and Rosenzweig, J.E., Contingency Views of Organization and Management, Chicago, Science Research Associates, 1973.

Kast, F.E. and Rosenzweig, J.E., Organization and Management: A Systems and Contingency Approach, 3rd edition, New York, McGraw-Hill, 1979.

Kast, F.E. and Rosenzweig, J.E., "The Modern View: A Systems Approach" in Beishon, J. and Peters, G. (eds.), Systems Behaviour, London, Harper and Row, 1972, pp.15-26.

Katz, D. and Kahn, R., The Social Psychology of Organisations, New York, Wiley, 1966.

Kemp, P.S., "Accounting Data for Planning, Motivation, and Control", The Accounting Review, Vol.37, No.1, January 1962, pp.44-50.

Kemp, T., The French Economy 1913-1939: The History of a Decline, London, Longman, 1972.

Kennis, I., *"Effects of Budgetary Goal Characteristics on Managerial Attitudes and Performance"*, The Accounting Review, Vol.LIV, No.4, October 1979, pp.707-721.

Klein, F., *"Essentials for Effective Budgetary Control"*, The Controller, Vol.7, No.11, November 1939, pp.400-403.

Klein, F., *"Maintaining Expense Control Under Current Conditions"* in Stafford, N.D., Klein, F., Fountain, H.A. and Nickerson, C.B. (eds.), Present Day Administrative and Financial Controls, Financial Management Series Number 71, New York, American Management Association, 1942, pp.11-19.

Knoeppel, C.E., *"Laws of Industrial Organization - I"*, Industrial Management: The Engineering Magazine, Vol.LVIII, No.4, October 1919, pp.265-268.

Knoeppel, C.E., *"Laws of Industrial Organization - IV"*, Industrial Management: The Engineering Magazine, Vol.LIX, No.1, January 1920, pp.43-47.

Koch, E.G., *"Three Approaches to Organization"*, Harvard Business Review, Vol.39, No.2, March-April 1961, pp.33-34, 36, 40, 43, 160, 162.

Koenig, C.J., *"Control During Action"*, Advanced Management, Vol.16, June 1951, pp.9-11.

Koontz, H., *"A Preliminary Statement of Principles of Planning and Control"*, Academy of Management Journal, Vol.1, No.1, April 1958, pp.45-61.

Koontz, H. and O'Donnell, C. (eds.), Management: A Book of Readings, New York, McGraw Hill, Inc., 1964.

Koontz, H. and O'Donnell, C., Management: A Systems and Contingency Analysis of Managerial Functions, 6th edition, New York, McGraw-Hill, 1976.

Kopelman, R.E., *"Organizational Control System Responsiveness, Expectancy Theory Constructs, and Work Motivation: Some Interrelations and Causal Connections"*, Personnel Psychology, Vol.29, 1976, pp.205-220.

Krupp,S., Pattern in Organization Analysis: A Critical Examination, New York, Holt Rinehart and Winston, Inc., 1961.

Lawler, E.E. III, *"Control Systems in Organizations"* in Dunnette, M.D. (ed.), Handbook of Industrial and Organizational Psychology, Chicago, Illinois, Rand-McNally Inc., 1976, pp.1247-1291.

Lawrence, P.R. and Lorsch, J.W., Organisation and Environment: Managing Differentiation and Integration, Boston, Harvard Graduate School of Business Administration, 1967.

Lawrence, P.R. and Lorsch, J.W., *"Differentiation and Integration in Complex Organizations"* in Litterer, J.A. (ed.), Organizations: Systems, Control and Adaptation, Vol.2, 2nd edition, New York, John Wiley and Sons, 1969, pp.229-253. (Reprinted from Administrative Science Quarterly, Vol.12, No.1, June 1967, pp.1-47).

Lazarus, A., *"The Budget in Business"*, The Annals, The American Academy of Political and Social Science, Vol.CXIII, May 1924, pp.56-68.

Lewis, N.R., Parker, L.D. and Sutcliffe, P., *"Financial Reporting to Employees: The Pattern of Development 1919 to 1979"*, Accounting, Organizations and Society, Vol. 9, No. 3/4, 1984, pp.275-289.

Likert, R., The Human Organization: Its Management and Value, New York, McGraw-Hill, 1967.

Likert, R. and Seashore, S.E., *"Making Cost Control Work"*, Harvard Business Review, Vol.41, No.6, Nov-Dec. 1963, pp.96-108.

Lindberg, R.A., *"The Unfamiliar Art of Controlling"* in Skousen, K.F. and Needles, B.E. Jr., (eds.), Contemporary Thought in Accounting and Organizational Control, Encino & Belmont, California, Dickenson Publishing Co., 1973, pp.142-149. (Reprinted from Management Services, May-June 1969, pp.15-20.)

Litterer, J.A., Organizations: Structure and Behaviour, Vol.1, Second Edition, New York, John Wiley and Sons, 1969.

Litterer, J.A., Organizations: System, Control and Adaptation, Vol.2, Second Edition, New York, John Wiley and Sons, 1969.

Litterer, J.A., The Analysis of Organizations, New York, John Wiley & Sons, 1965.

Litterer, J.A., The Analysis of Organizations, 2nd edition, New York, John Wiley and Sons, 1973.

Livingstone, J.L., *"Management Controls and Organizational Performance"*, Personnel Administration, Vol.28, No.1, January-February 1965, pp.37-43.

Lockwood, J., *"Early University Education in Accountancy"*, The Accounting Review, Vol.XIII, No.2, June 1938, pp.131-144.

Loncar, F.E., *"Budgetary Planning - Yesterday and Today"*, N.A.C.A. Bulletin, Vol.37, April 1956, pp.949-955.

Longmuir, P., *"Recording and Interpreting Foundry Costs"*, The Engineering Magazine, September 1902, pp.887-894.

Loomba, N.P., Management - A Quantitative Perspective, New York, Macmillan Publishing Co., 1978.

Lorange, P. and Scott Morton, M.S., *"A Framework for Management Control Systems"*, Sloan Management Review, Vol.16, No.1, Fall 1974, pp.41-56.

Lorsch, J.W. and Lawrence, P.R. (eds.), Organization Planning: Cases and Concepts, Homewood, Illinois, Richard D. Urwin and the Dorsey Press, 1972.

Lorsch, J.W., *"Product Innovation and Organisation"* in Litterer, J.A. (ed.), Organizations: Structure and Behavior, Vol.1, Second Edition, John Wiley and Sons, New York, 1969, pp.325-335.

Lorsch, J.W. and Lawrence, P.R., *"Environmental Factors and Organizational Integration"* in Lorsch, J.W. and Lawrence, P.R. (eds.), Organization Planning: Cases and Concepts, Homewood, Illinois, Richard D. Irwin and the Dorsey Press, 1972, pp.38-48.

Louderback, J.G. III and Dominiak, G.S., Managerial Accounting, Belmont, California, Wadsworth Publishing Co., 1975.

Lowe, E.A., *"Budgetary Control - An Evaluation in a Wider Managerial Perspective"*, Accountancy, Vol.LXXXI, No.927, November 1970, pp.764-769.

Lowe, E.A. and McInnes, J.M., *"Control in Socio-Economic Organizations: A Rationale for the Design of Management Control Systems, (Section 1)"*, The Journal of Management Studies, Vol.VIII, May 1971, pp.213-227.

Lukens, W.P., *"The Partnership Between Accounting and Management"*, N.A.C.A. Bulletin, Vol.13, No.18, May 15th, 1932, pp.1227-1238.

Luneski, C., *"Some Aspects of the Meaning of Control"*, The Accounting Review, Vol.39, No.3, July 1964, pp.591-597.

Luthans, F., Organizational Behavior: A Modern Behavioral Approach to Management, New York, McGraw-Hill, 1973.

Luthans, F., Organizational Behavior, Second Edition, New York, McGraw-Hill Book Company, 1977.

Luthans, F. and Kreitner, R., Organizational Behavior Modification, Glenview, Illinois, Scott Foresman & Co., 1975.

Lynch, R.M. and Williamson, R.W., Accounting for Management: Planning and Control, 2nd ed., New York, McGraw-Hill Book Co., 1976.

Machin, J., "Measuring the Effectiveness of an Organisation's Management Control Systems", Management Decision, Vol.11, No.5, Winter 1973, pp.260-279.

Machin, J.L.J., "A Contingent Methodology for Management Control", The Journal of Management Studies, Vol.16, No.1, February 1979, pp.1-29.

Maddock, J., "Organisation for Control: The Influence of Control Procedures on Organisation Structure", British Management Review, Vol.8, No.2, July 1949, pp.63-83.

Makin, F.B. (a), "Budgetary Control - I", The Accountant, Vol.CII, No.3404, 2nd March 1940, pp.227-288.

Makin, F.B. (b), "Budgetary Control - II", The Accountant, Vol.CII, No.3406, 16th March 1940, pp.288-290.

Mantell, L.H., "Objectives, Controls and Motivation", Human Resource Management, Vol.12, No.4, Winter 1973, pp.18-23.

March, J.G. and Simon, H.A., Organizations, New York, Wiley, 1958.

March, J.G., (ed.), Handbook of Organizations, Chicago, Rand McNally & Co., 1965.

Maslow, A.H., "A Theory of Human Motivation", Psychological Review, Vol. 50, 1943, pp.370-396. Also, Motivation and Personality, New York, Harper & Row, 1954.

Maslow, A.H., "A Theory of Human Motivation", reprinted in Lowry, R.J. (ed.), Dominance, Self-Esteem, Self-Actualization: Germinal Papers of A.H. Maslow, Monterey, California, Brooks/Cole Publishing Co., 1973. (Originally published in Psychological Review, Vol.50, 1943, pp.370-396.)

Massie, J.L., "Management Theory" in March, J.G. (ed.), Handbook of Organizations, Chicago, Rand McNally and Co., 1965, pp.387-421.

Massie, J.L., Essentials of Management, 2nd Edition, Englewood Cliffs, New Jersey, Prentice-Hall Inc., 1971.

- 310 -

Matheson, D., "Control", The Accountant's Magazine, Vol.LXXIV, No.773, November 1970, pp.549-552.

Matthews, L.M., Practical Operating Budgeting, New York, McGraw-Hill Book Co., 1977.

Matz, A., "After Cost Determination - Cost Control", The Journal of Accountancy, Vol.80, No.2, August 1945, pp.118-124.

Matz, A. and Usry, M.S., Cost Accounting: Planning and Control, 6th ed., Cincinnati, South-Western Publishing Co., 1976.

Mayo, E., The Human Problems of an Industrial Civilization, 2nd Edition, Cambridge, Massachusetts, The President and Fellows of Harvard College, 1946. Copyright Macmillan, 1933.

Merrill, F.H. (ed.), Classics in Management, New York, American Management Association, 1960.

Metcalf, H.C. and Urwick, L. (eds.), Dynamic Administration: The Collected Papers of Mary Parker Follett, London, Sir Isaac Pitman & Sons Ltd., 1941.

Miller, E.J. and Rice, A.K., Systems of Organisation: The Control of Task and Sentient Boundaries, London, Tavistock Publications, 1967.

Mintzberg, H., The Structuring of Organisations: A Synthesis of the Research, Englewood Cliffs, New Jersey, Prentice Hall, 1979.

Mixter, C.W., "The General Question of Extent and Method of Control Under Scientific Management", Harvard Business Review, Vol.II, No.1, October 1923, pp.13-22.

Mockler, R.J., The Management Control Process, New York, Appleton-Century-Crofts, Educational Division, Meredith Corporation, 1972.

Mooney, J.D., "The Principles of Organization", (presented 1937) in Gulick, L. and Urwick, L. (eds.), Papers on the Science of Administration, New York, Institute of Public Administration, 1937, pp.91-98.

Mooney, J.D., The Principles of Organization, New York, Harper and Row, 1947. (Originally published by J.D. Mooney and A.C. Reiley, 1939.)

Moore, C.L. and Jaedicke, R.K., Managerial Accounting, 5th ed., Cincinnati, South-Western Publishing Co., 1980.

Morris, D. (a), "Budgetary Control - II", The Accountant, Vol.XCIV, No.3212, June 27th, 1936, pp.965-969.

- 311 -

Morris, D. (b), *"Budgetary Control - I"*, The Accountant, Vol.XCIV, No.3211, June 20th, 1936, pp.925-928.

Morris, R.D.F., *"Budgetary Control is Obsolete"* in DeCoster, D.T., Ramanathan, K.V. and Sundem, G.L. (eds.), Accounting for Managerial Decision Making, New York, Melville Publishing Company, John Wiley & Sons, 1974, pp.381-388. (Reprinted from The Accountant, Vol.158, No.4874, May 18, 1968, pp.654-656.)

Morrow, I.T., *"Budgetary Control as an Aid to Management"*, The Accountant, Vol.CXIX, No.3839, July 17th, 1948, pp.44-46.

Morrow, I.T., *"Standard System of Accounting Control Embracing Financial and Cost Accounts: Is This Needed for Management Purposes?"*, The Accountant, Vol.CXX, No.3887, June 18th, 1949, pp.507-511.

Murdick, R.G., *"Managerial Control: Concepts and Practice"*, S.A.M. Advanced Management Journal, Vol.35, No.1, January 1970, pp.48-52.

Murphy, B., A History of the British Economy 1740-1970, London, Longman, 1973.

Muth, F.J., *"Selling Budgetary Control to the Supervisor"*, N.A.C.A. Bulletin, Vol.28, No.24, August 15th, 1947, pp.1501-1511.

MacDonald, J.H., *"Enforcing the Budget: With Particular Reference to the Use of Incentives"*, Industrial Management, Vol.LXXIII, No.1, January 1927, pp.49-52.

McClelland, D.C., The Achieving Society, Princeton, New Jersey, Van Nostrand, 1961.

McClelland, P.D., Causal Explanation and Model Building in History, Economics, and the New Economic History, Ithaca, Cornell University Press, 1975.

McDonough, J.J., *"The Accountant, Data Collection and Social Exchange"*, The Accounting Review, Vol.XLVI, No.4, October 1971, pp.676-685.

McGladrey, I.B., *"Budgetary Control"*, The Certified Public Accountant, Vol.XIV, No.8, August 1934, pp.483-488.

McGregor, D., The Human Side of Enterprise, New York, McGraw-Hill, 1960.

McGregor, D., The Professional Manager, London, McGraw-Hill, 1967.

McKenna, E.F., <u>The Management Style of the Chief Accountant: A Situational Perspective</u>, London, Saxon House, Teakfield Ltd., 1978.

McKinsey, J.O., *"Accounting as an Administrative Aid"*, <u>Journal of Political Economy</u>, Vol.27, No.9, November 1919, pp.759-781.

McKinsey, J.O., *"Budgetary Control and Administration"*, <u>Administration: The Journal of Business Analysis and Control</u>, Vol.1, No.1, January 1921, pp.73-82.

McMahon, J.T. and Perritt, G.W., *"Toward a Contingency Theory of Organizational Control"*, <u>Academy of Management Journal</u>, Vol.16, No.4, December 1973, pp.624-635.

National Association of Cost Accountants, Publication Department, *"Relation of Budgetary Control to Cost Accounting"*, <u>N.A.C.A. Bulletin</u>, Vol.III, No.8, January 15th, 1922, pp.3-14.

Onsi, M., *"Factor Analysis of Behavioral Variables Affecting Budgetary Slack"*, <u>The Accounting Review</u>, Vol.XLVIII, No.2, July 1973, pp.535-548.

O'Shaughnessy, J., <u>Business Organization</u>, London, George Allen and Unwin, 1966.

Otley, D.T., *"Budget Use and Managerial Performance"*, <u>Journal of Accounting Research</u>, Vol.16, No.1, Spring 1978, pp.122-149.

Otley, D.T., *"The Contingency Theory of Management Accounting: Achievement and Prognosis"*, <u>Accounting, Organizations and Society</u>, Vol.5, No.4, 1980, pp.413-428.

Otley, D.T. and Berry, A.J., *"Control, Organisation and Accounting"*, <u>Accounting, Organizations and Society</u>, Vol.5, No.2, 1980, pp.231-244.

Ouchi, W.G. and Johnson, J.B., *"Types of Organizational Control and Their Relationship to Emotional Well Being"*, <u>Administrative Science Quarterly</u>, Vol.23, June 1978, pp.293-317.

Ouchi, W.G. and Maguire, M.A., *"Organizational Control: Two Functions"*, <u>Administrative Science Quarterly</u>, Vol.20, December 1975, pp.559-569.

Palmade, G.P., <u>French Capitalism in the Nineteenth Century (1961)</u>, translated by Holmes, G.M., Newton Abbot, Devon, David & Charles, 1972.

- 313 -

Parker, L.D. (a), "Participation in Budget Planning: the Prospects Surveyed", Accounting and Business Research, Vol.9, No.34, Spring 1979, pp.123-137.

Parker, L.D. (b), "Divisional Performance Measurement: Beyond an Exclusive Profit Test", Accounting and Business Research, Vol.9, No.36, Autumn 1979, pp.309-319.

Parker, L.D., "The Bureaucratic Model of Corporate Activity: A Review" in Ashton, D. (ed.), Management Bibliographies & Reviews, Vol.4, Bradford, MCB Publications Ltd., 1978, pp.159-170.

Parker, L.D, "Systems Theory Approaches to Organisation and Management", Management Forum, Vol.6, No.4, December 1980, pp.232-243.

Parker, L.D., "Goal Congruence: A Misguided Accounting Concept", Abacus, Vol.12, No.1, June 1976, pp.3-13.

Parker, R.H., "Memorial: Frank Sewell Bray 1906-1979", The Accounting Review, Vol.LV, No.2, April 1980, pp.307-316.

Parker, R.H., "Room at the Top for More Academic Accountants", The Times Higher Education Supplement, 17th January, 1975.

Parsons, T., The Social System, New York, The Free Press of Glencoe, 1951.

Parsons, V.A. and MacDonald, G.A., "Standard Cost and Control System", Management Accounting, Vol.LII, No.5, November 1970, pp.19-24.

Peaker, A., Economic Growth in Modern Britain, London, Macmillan, 1974.

Pearson, N.M., "Public Administration: Fayolism as the Necessary Complement of Taylorism", The American Political Science Review, Vol.39, No.1, February 1945, pp.68-85.

Peck, S.A., "The Managerial Aspect of Controls", N.A.C.A. Bulletin, Section 1, Vol.20, No.8, December 15th, 1938, pp.471-490.

Peck, S.A., "Further Thoughts on the Management Aspect of Accounting Control", N.A.C.A. Bulletin, Section 1, Vol.21, No.9, January 1st, 1940, pp.549-568.

Peden, R.W., "Technique of Industrial Control", Management Accounting, (New York), Vol.18, Section 1, April 1st, 1937, pp.851-873.

Peery, N.S. Jr., *"General Systems Theory: An Inquiry into its Social Philosophy"*, <u>Academy of Management Journal</u>, Vol.15, No.4, December 1972, pp.495-510.

Peirce, J.L., *"The Budget Comes of Age"*, <u>Harvard Business Review</u>, Vol.32, No.3, May-June 1954, pp.58-66.

Perry, H.C., *"Control of Business Through an Integrated Corporate Budget"*, <u>7th International Management Congress (Proceedings)</u>, 1938, pp.26-28.

Peterson, J.M. and Gray, R., <u>Economic Development of the United States</u>, Homewood, Illinois, Richard D. Irwin, 1969.

Phillips, D.C., *"The Methodological Basis of Systems Theory"*, <u>Academy of Management Journal</u>, Vol.15, No.4, December 1972, pp.469-477.

Pollard, H.R., <u>Further Developments in Management Thought</u>, London, Heinemann, 1978.

Porter, L.W. and Lawler, E.E. III, <u>Managerial Attitudes and Performance</u>, Homewood, Illinois, Richard D. Irwin, 1968.

Potts, J.H., *"The Evolution of Budgetary Accounting Theory and Practice in Municipal Accounting from 1870"*, <u>The Accounting Historians Journal</u>, Vol.4, No.1, Spring 1977, pp.89-100.

Powell, R.M., *"Principles of Modern Managerial Control"*, <u>Financial Executive</u>, Vol.34, No.4, April 1966, pp.54, 56, 58, 60.

Probst, F.R., *"Probabilistic Cost Controls: A Behavioral Dimension"*, <u>The Accounting Review</u>, Vol.XLVI, No.1, January 1971, pp.113-118.

Puckey, W.C., *"Some Principles of Organisation"*, <u>British Management Review</u>, Vol.VII, No.3, 1948, pp.77-86.

Pugh, D.S., Hickson, D.J., Hinings, C.R. and Turner, C., *"Dimensions of Organization Structure"*, <u>Administrative Science Quarterly</u>, Vol.13, June 1968, pp.65-105.

Pugh, D.S., Mansfield, R. and Warner, M., <u>Research in Organizational Behaviour: A British Survey</u>, London, Heinemann, 1975.

Rathe, A.W., *"Management Control"*, <u>Advanced Management</u>, Vol.15, March 1950, pp.9-11.

Rautenstrauch, W. and Villers, R., <u>Budgetary Control</u>, Revised Edition, New York, Funk and Wagnalls, 1968.

Reeves, T.K. and Woodward, J., *"The Study of Managerial Control"* in Woodward, J. (ed.), Industrial Organization: Behaviour and Control, London, Oxford University Press, 1970, pp.37-55.

Revsine, L., *"Change in Budget Pressure and Its Impact on Supervisor Behavior"*, Journal of Accounting Research, Vol.8, No.2, Autumn 1970, pp.290-292.

Rhenman, E., Industrial Democracy and Industrial Management: A Critical Essay on the Possible Meanings and Implications of Industrial Democracy, London, Tavistock, 1968.

Rightor, C.E., *"Recent Progress in Budget Making and Accounting"*, National Municipal Review, Vol.VI, November 1917, pp.707-719.

Roberts, E.B., *"Industrial Dynamics and the Design of Management Control Systems"* in Litterer, J.A. (ed.), Organizations: Systems, Control and Adaptation, Vol.2, Second Edition, New York, John Wiley and Sons, 1969, pp.287-303. (Reprinted from Bonini, C.P., Jaedicke, R.K. and Wagner, H.M. (eds.), Management Controls: New Directions in Basic Research, New York, McGraw Hill, 1964, pp.102-126.)

Robertson, R.M.., History of the American Economy, 2nd Edition, New York, Harcourt Brace and World Inc., 1964.

Robertson, R.M., History of the American Economy, 3rd Edition, New York, Harcourt Brace Jovanovich, 1973.

Robson, L.W., *"Standard Costs as an Aid to Control - I"*, The Accountant, Vol.CXX, No.3873, March 12th, 1949, pp.199-202.

Rockness, H.O., *"Expectancy Theory in a Budgetary Setting: An Experimental Examination"*, The Accounting Review, Vol.LII, No.4, October 1977, pp.893-903.

Roebuck, J., The Making of Modern English Society from 1850, London, Routledge and Kegan Paul, 1973.

Roethlisberger, F.J. and Dickson, W.J., Management and the Worker, Cambridge, Massachusetts, Harvard University Press, 1939. (Fifteenth printing 1970.)

Ronen, J. and Livingstone, J.L., *"An Expectancy Theory Approach to the Motivational Impacts of Budgets"*, The Accounting Review, Vol.L, No.4, October 1975, pp.671-685.

Rose, T.G., *"Higher Business Control"*, The Journal of the British Institute of Management, October 1941, pp.129-141.

Rose, T.G., *"Higher Business Control: Training the General Manager"*, Industry, November 1948, pp.21-24.

Rose, T.G., *"Higher Control"*, The Accountant, Vol.CXXVI, No.4033, April 5th, 1952, pp.349-350.

Rushing, W.A., *"Organisational Size, Rules and Surveillance"* in Litterer, J.A. (ed.), Organizations: Structure and Behavior, Vol.1, Second Edition, New York, John Wiley and Sons, 1969, pp.432-440.

Russel, R.R., A History of the American Economic System, New York, Appleton-Century-Crofts, 1964.

Salaman, G., Work Organisations: Resistance and Control, London, Longman, 1979.

San Miguel, J.G., *"The Behavioral Sciences and Concepts and Standards for Management Planning and Control"*, Accounting, Organizations and Society, Vol.2, No.2, 1977, pp.177-186.

Sathe, V., *"The Relevance of Modern Organization Theory for Managerial Accounting"*, Accounting, Organizations and Society, Vol.3, No.1, 1978, pp.89-92.

Savitt, M.A., *"Limitations of Managerial Control"*, Advanced Management - Office Executive, Vol.1, April 1962, pp.20-23.

Scanlan, B. and Keys, J.B., Management and Organisational Behaviour, New York, John Wiley and Sons, 1979.

Schofield, J.J., *"The 'Anti-Chance Factor' in Business"*, The Controller, Vol.24, No.6, June 1956, pp.259-262, 290-291.

Schroeder, G.G., The Growth of Major Steel Companies 1900-1950, Baltimore, the Johns Hopkins Press, 1953.

Scott, D.R., The Cultural Significance of Accounts, Reprint, Lawrence, Kansas, Scholars Book Co., 1973. (Original published in New York, by Henry Holt, 1931.)

Scott, W.G., Organization Theory: A Behavioral Analysis for Management, Homewood, Illinois, Richard D. Irwin, 1967.

Scovell, C.H., *"Cost Accounting Practice, With Special Reference to Machine Hour Rate"*, The Journal of Accountancy, Vol.XVII, No.1, January 1914, pp.13-27.

Searfoss, D.G., *"Some Behavioral Aspects of Budgeting for Control: An Empirical Study"*, Accounting, Organizations and Society, Vol.1, No.4, 1976, pp.375-385.

Selznick, P., *"Foundations of the Theory of Organization"*, American Sociological Review, February, 1948, pp.25-35.

Sherwin, D.S., *"The Meaning of Control"* in Koontz, H. and O'Donnell, C. (eds.), Management: A Book of Readings, New York, McGraw-Hill, 1964, pp.426-430. (Reprinted from Dun's Review and Modern Industry, January 1956.)

Shields, B.F., The Evolution of Industrial Organisation, London, Sir Isaac Pitman, 1928.

Shillinglaw, G., *"Divisional Performance Review: An Extension of Budgetary Control"* in Benston, G.J. (ed.), Contemporary Cost Accounting and Control, Belmont, California, Dickenson Publishing Company, 1970, pp.304-319.

Shillinglaw, G., Managerial Cost Accounting, 4th ed., Homewood, Illinois, Richard D. Irwin, 1977.

Silverman, D., The Theory of Organisations: A Sociological Framework, London, Heinemann, 1970.

Simon, H.A., Administrative Behaviour, New York, Macmillan, 1957.

Simon, H.A., *"Approaching the Theory of Management"* in Koontz, H., (ed), Toward a Unified Theory of Management, New York, McGraw-Hill Book Co., 1964, pp.82-83.

Sisson, H.A., *"Business Control and Management"*, The Accountant, Vol.XCVI, No.3264, June 26th, 1937, pp.912-915.

Sizer, J., *"Budget Planning and Control"*, Accountancy, Vol.86, No.978, February 1975, pp.78-81.

Sizer J., An Insight into Management Accounting, 2nd ed., London, Pitman, 1979.

Slocum, E.L. and Roberts, A.R., *"The New York School of Accounts - A Beginning"*, The Accounting Historians Journal, Vol.7, No.2, Fall 1980, pp.63-70.

Smith, C.G. and Tannenbaum, A.S., *"Organizational Control Structure: A Comparative Analysis"* in Graham, W.K. and Roberts, K.H., Comparative Studies in Organizational Behavior, New York, Holt, Rinehart and Winston, Inc., 1972, pp.291-309. (Reprinted from Human Relations, Vol.16, 1963, pp.299-316.)

Smith, D., *"Control and Orientations to Work in a Business Organization"*, Journal of Management Studies, Vol.XV, May 1978, pp.211-222.

Solomons, D. and Berridge, T.M., Prospectus for a Profession: The Report of the Long Range Enquiry into Education and Training for the Accounting Profession, London, Gee and Co., 1974.

Soule, G., Prosperity Decade from War to Depression: 1917-1929, Vol.8, The Economic History of the United States, New York, Holt, Rinehart & Winston, July 1964.

Stacey, N.A.H., English Accountancy: A Study in Social and Economic History 1800-1954, London, Gee and Co., 1954.

Stedry, A.C., Budget Control and Cost Behavior, Englewood Cliffs, New Jersey, Prentice-Hall, 1960.

Stedry, A.C. and Kay, E., The Effects of Goal Difficulty on Performance: A Field Experiment, Cambridge, Massachusetts, Sloan School of Management, Massachusetts Institute of Technology, 1964.

Stephenson, T.E., *"The Longevity of Classical Theory"*, Management International Review, Vol.8, No.6, 1968, pp.77-83.

Stephenson, T.E., *"Why the So-Called Classicists Endure - A Reply"*, Management International Review, Vol.13, No.2-3, 1973, pp.135-144.

Stokes, P.M., A Total Systems Approach to Management Control, New York, American Management Association, 1968.

Stone, G.C., *"Budgetary Control"*, The Accountant, Vol.CXXVI, No.4021, January 12th, 1952, pp.31-34.

Stoner, J.A.F., Management, Englewood-Cliffs, New Jersey, Prentice-Hall, 1978.

Strong, E.P. and Smith, R.D., Management Control Models, New York, Holt, Rinehart and Winston, 1968.

Surana, H.M., *"Management Control Through Accounting"*, The Chartered Accountant, (India), Vol.XVIII, Part III, September 1969, pp.2, 140-141.

Sutcliffe, P., An Examination of the Historical Development of Accounting for Employee Performance Evaluation, Unpublished Minor Thesis, Monash University, Melbourne, October 1976.

Sweeny, A. and Wisner, J.N. Jr., Budgeting Fundamentals for Non-Financial Executives, New York, AMACOM, 1975.

Swieringa, R.J. and Moncur, R.H., *"The Relationship Between Managers' Budget-Oriented Behavior and Selected Attitude, Position, Size and Performance Measures"*, Journal of Accounting Research, Empirical Research in Accounting: Selected Studies, 1972, pp.194-205.

Szilagyi, A.D. Jr., Sims, H.P. Jr., Keller, R.T., *"Role Dynamics, Locus of Control, and Employee Attitudes and Behavior"*, Academy of Management Journal, Vol.19, No.2, June 1976, pp.259-275.

Tannenbaum, A.S., *"Control in Organizations: Individual Adjustment and Organizational Performance"* in Bonini, C.P., Jaedicke, R.K. and Wagner, H.M. (eds.), Management Controls: New Directions in Basic Research, New York, McGraw-Hill, 1964, pp.297-316.

Tannenbaum, A.S., Control in Organizations, New York, McGraw-Hill, 1968.

Tannenbaum, R., *"The Manager Concept: A Rational Synthesis"*, The Journal of Business, Vol.22, No.4, October 1949, pp.225-241.

Taylor, A.H. and Palmer, R.E., Financial Planning and Control, London, Pan Books, 1969.

Taylor, F.W., The Principles of Scientific Management, New York, Harper and Brothers, 1916, (copyright 1911).

Taylor, F.W. (a), *"Shop Management"*, published in his book Scientific Management, New York, Harper and Brothers, 1947, pp.17-207. (First published by the American Society of Mechanical Engineers, 1903.)

Taylor, F.W. (b), *"Taylor's Testimony Before the Special House Committee"*, Hearings before Special Committee of the House of Representatives to Investigate the Taylor and Other Systems of Shop Management under Authority of House Resolution, 90, Vol.3, 1912, pp.1377-1508, published in his book, Scientific Management, New York, Harper and Brothers, 1947, pp.5-287.

Taylor, R., *"Budgetary Control and Standard Costs"*, The Accountants' Magazine, Vol.L, No.500, December 1946, pp.417-425.

Temin, P., Iron and Steel in Nineteenth-Century America: An Economic Enquiry, Cambridge, Massachusetts, The M.I.T. Press, 1964.

Terry, G.R., Principles of Management, 4th Edition, Homewood, Illinois, Richard D. Irwin, 1964.

Thayer, F., *"General System(s) Theory: The Promise That Could Not Be Kept"*, Academy of Management Journal, Vol.15, No.4, December 1972, pp.481-493.

Theiss, E.L., *"Budgetary Procedure as a Means of Administrative Control"*, The Accounting Review, Vol.7, No.1, March 1932, pp.11-21.

Theiss, E.L., *"Accounting and Budgeting"*, The Accounting Review, Vol.10, No.2, June 1935, pp.157-161.

Theiss, E.L., *"The Beginnings of Business Budgeting"*, The Accounting Review, Vol.12, No.1, March 1937, pp.43-55.

Thierauf, R.J., Klekamp, R.C. and Geeding, D.W., Management Principles and Practices: A Contingency and Questionnaire Approach, Santa Barbara, John Wiley & Sons, 1977.

Thole, H., *"Looking Around: Management Control"*, Harvard Business Review, Vol.32, No.6, November-December 1954, pp.141-150.

Thornton, N., Management Accounting, London, Heinemann, 1978.

Tobey, J.R., *"The Preparation and Control of a Budget"*, N.A.C.A. Bulletin, Vol.VII, No.2, September 15th, 1925, pp.36-48.

Todd, J., *"Management Control Systems: A Key Link Between Strategy, Structure and Employee Performance"* in Organizational Dynamics, New York, AMACOM, Spring 1977, pp.65-78.

Todd, J., *"Management Control: A Zero-Sum Game?"*, Management International Review, Vol.18, No.4, 1978, pp.73-78.

Toffler, A., Future Shock, London, Pan Books, 1971.

Tosi, H.L. and Carroll, S.J., Management: Contingencies, Structure and Process, Chicago, Illinois, St. Clair Press, 1976.

Trist, E.L. and Bamforth, K.W., *"Some Social and Psychological Consequence of the Longwall Method of Coal-getting"*, <u>Human Relations</u>, February 1951, pp.3-38.

Trist, E.L. and Bamforth, K.W., *"Selections from Social and Psychological Consequences of the Longwall Method of Coal-Getting"* in Litterer, J.A. (ed.), <u>Organisations: Structure and Behavior</u>, Vol.1, Second Edition, New York, John Wiley and Sons, 1969, pp.263-275, (reprinted from <u>Human Relations</u>, Vol.4, No.1, 1951, pp.6-38).

Tsuji, A., *"Shades of the Past: Budgeting in the Early 1900s"*, <u>Managerial Planning</u>, Vol.23, March-April 1975, pp.23-29.

Turcotte, W.E., *"Control Systems, Performance and Satisfaction in Two State Agencies"*, <u>Administrative Science Quarterly</u>, Vol.19, March 1974, pp.60-73.

Tuttle, F.W. and Perry, J.M., <u>An Economic History of the United States</u>, Cincinnati, South-Western Publishing Co., 1970.

Urwick, L. (a), *"Scientific Principles and Organisation"*, <u>Industry Illustrated</u>, August 1942, pp.8-9.

Urwick, L. (b), *"Scientific Principles and Organisation"*, <u>Industry Illustrated</u>, October 1942, pp.8-10.

Urwick, L. (a), *"Organization as a Technical Problem"*, (presented 1933) in Gulick, L. and Urwick, L. (eds.), <u>Papers on the Science of Administration</u>, New York, Institute of Public Administration, 1937, pp.49-88.

Urwick, L. (b), *"The Function of Administration"*, (presented 1934) in Gulick, L. and Urwick, L. (eds.), <u>Papers on the Science of Administration</u>, New York, Institute of Public Administration, 1937, pp.117-130.

Urwick, L., *"Administration in Theory and Practice"*, <u>British Management Review</u>, Vol.5, No.1, January 1944, pp.37-59.

Urwick, L.F. (ed.) (a), <u>The Golden Book of Management: A Historical Period of the Life and Work of Seventy Pioneers</u>, London, Newman Neame Ltd., 1956.

Urwick, L.F. (b), <u>The Pattern of Management</u>, Minneapolis, University of Minnesota Press, 1956.

Urwick, L.F., *"The Span of Control"*, <u>The Scottish Journal of Political Economy</u>, Vol.4, June 1957, pp.101-113.

Urwick, L.F., *"Why the So-Called 'Classicists' Endure"*, Management International Review, Vol.11, No.1, 1971, pp.3-14.

Urwick, L. and Brech, E.F.L., The Making of Scientific Management, Volume I, Thirteen Pioneers, London, Sir Isaac Pitman and Sons Ltd., reprinted 1951, 1955.

Urwick, L. and Brech, E.F.L., The Making of Scientific Management, Volume II, Management in British Industry, London, Sir Isaac Pitman and Sons Ltd., reprinted 1957.

Vancil, R.F., *"What Kind of Management Control Do You Need?"*, Harvard Business Review, Vol.51, No.2, March-April 1973, pp.75-86.

Vatter, W.J., Operating Budgets, Belmont, California, Wadsworth Publishing Co., 1969.

Vickers, Sir G., *"Positive and Negative Controls in Business"*, Journal of Industrial Economics, Vol.6, No.3, June 1958, pp.173-179.

Vieh, W.F., *"Why the Budget?"*, The Journal of Accountancy, Vol.40, No.3, September 1925, pp.173-179.

Villers, R., *"Associating Operating Control with Financial Control"*, Financial Executive, Vol.37, No.10, October 1969, pp.65-75.

Vroom, V.H., Work and Motivation, New York, John Wiley and Sons, 1964.

Vroom, V.H., *"Some Psychological Aspects of Organizational Control"* in Cooper, W.W., Leavitt, H.J. and Shelly, M.W. III, (eds.), New Perspectives in Organization Research, New York, John Wiley and Sons, 1964, pp.72-86.

Wallace, M.B., *"Behavioral Considerations in Budgeting"*, Management Accounting (N.A.A.), Vol.47, August 1966, pp.3-8.

Warmington, A., *"Design, Control, Behaviour and Performance"*, Personnel Review, Vol.3, No.1, Winter 1974, pp.32-42.

Warren, K., The American Steel Industry 1850-1970: A Geographical Interpretation, Oxford, Clarendon Press, 1973.

Waterhouse, J.H. and Tiessen, P., *"A Contingency Framework for Management Accounting Systems Research"*, Accounting, Organizations and Society, Vol.3, No.1, 1978, pp.65-76.

Watson, D.J.H., *"The Structure of Project Teams Facing Differentiated Environments: An Exploratory Study in Public Accounting Firms"*, The Accounting Review, Vol.L, No.2, April 1975, pp.259-273.

Watson, D.J.H. and Baumler, J.V., *"Transfer Pricing: A Behavioural Context"*, The Accounting Review, Vol.L, No.3, July 1975, pp.466-474.

Weber, R.P. and Stevenson, W.C., *"Evaluations of Accounting Journal and Department Quality"*, The Accounting Review, Vol.LVI, No.3, July 1981, pp.596-612.

Weeks, D.R., *"Organisation Theory - Some Themes and Distinctions"* in Salaman, G. and Thompson, K. (eds.), People and Organisations, London, Longman, Open University Press, 1973, pp.375-395.

Weger, C.E., *"The Preparation and Administration of Budgets"*, National Association of Cost Accountants Bulletin, Vol.7, No.9, Section 1, January 1st, 1926, pp.327-340.

Weiser, H.J., *"The Impact of Accounting Controls on Performance Motivation"*, The New York Certified Public Accountant, Vol.38, No.3, March 1968, pp.191-201.

Weiss, R.S., *"A Structure-Function Approach to Organisation"* in Litterer J.A. (ed.), Organizations: Structure and Behavior, Vol.1, Second Edition, John Wiley and Sons, New York, 1969, pp.58-62.

Welsch, G.A., *"Some Behavioral Implications in Profit Planning and Control"*, Management Adviser, Vol.8, No.4, July-August 1971, pp.21-27.

Welsch, G.A., Budgeting: Profit Planning and Control, 4th Edition, Englewood Cliffs, New Jersey, Prentice-Hall, 1976.

Werolin, A.E., *"Effective Controls for Top Management"*, Advanced Management, Vol.XII, No.3, September 1947, pp.120-128.

Wharton, K.J., *"Administrative Organisation and Control - II"*, The Accountant, Vol.CXVII, No3792, August 23rd, 1947, pp.117-119.

Wheatcroft, M., The Revolution in British Management Education, London, Pitman Publishing, 1970.

Whisler, T.L., Meyer, H., Baum, B.H. and Sorenson, P.F. Jr., *"Centralization of Organizational Control: An Empirical Study of its Meaning and Measurement"*, Journal of Business, Vol.40, No.1, January 1967, pp.10-26.

Whitehead, T.N., <u>The Industrial Worker</u>, Cambridge, Mass., Harvard University Press, Vol.II, 1983.

Wight, L.A., *"Budgetary Control and Application of Overheads"*, <u>The Accountants' Magazine</u>, Vol.38, No.376, June 1934, pp.359-366.

Wilks, P.A., *"Budgets and Budgetary Control"*, <u>N.A.C.A. Bulletin</u>, Section 1, Vol.28, No.18, May 15th, 1947, pp.1138-1148.

Wilson, R.M.S., *"Perspectives in Accounting for Control"*, <u>Management Accounting</u> (U.K.), Vol.48, No.8, August 1970, pp.285-294.

Woodward, J., <u>Management and Technology</u>, London, H.M.S.O., Department of Scientific and Industrial Research, 1958.

Woodward, J., <u>Industrial Organisation: Theory and Practice</u>, London, Oxford University Press, 1965.

Wren, D.A., <u>The Evolution of Management Thought</u>, Second Edition, New York, John Wiley and Sons, 1979.

Wright, J.O., *"The Use of Management Controls"*, <u>Financial Executive</u>, Vol.33, No.11, November 1965, pp.54-57.

Wright, R.E., *"Why Budgets?"*, <u>Special Libraries</u>, Vol.18, No.1, January 1927, pp.5-8.

Youngson, A.J., *"Great Britain 1920-1970"* in Cipolla, C.M. (ed.), <u>Fontana Economic History of Europe: Contemporary Economies Part 1</u>, Glasgow, Collins/Fontana Books, 1976, pp.128-179.

Zur-Muchlen, M.V., <u>Business Education and Faculty at Canadian Universities</u>, Halifax, Economic Council of Canada, 1971.